In the Sun's House

Kurt Caswell

In the Sun's House

*My Year Teaching
on the Navajo Reservation*

Afterword by Rex Lee Jim

Trinity University Press
San Antonio

Published by Trinity University Press
San Antonio, Texas 78212

Cover design by Nicole Hayward   Book design by BookMatters, Berkeley

This book was made using recycled components:

text stock: Enviro 100
[100% recycled paper made entirely from post-consumer waste (PCW)]
cover stock: Kallima FSC-certified [10% PCW recycled content]
binders boards: 100% recycled, FSC-certified

♻ The paper used in this publication meets the minimum requirements of
the American National Standard for Information Sciences—Permanence
of Paper for Printed Library Materials, ANSI Z39.48-1992.

Library of Congress Cataloging-in-Publication Data

Caswell, Kurt, 1969–
   In the sun's house : my year teaching on the Navajo reservation
/ Kurt Caswell ; afterword by Rex Lee Jim.
      p. cm.
   Includes bibliographical references.
   SUMMARY: "With an afterword by Rex Lee Jim, this book describes Caswell's
year teaching at Borrego Pass, a remote Navajo community in northwest
New Mexico, detailing his failings and successes as he struggles to bridge
the gap between himself and the community"—*Provided by publisher.*
   ISBN 978-1-59534-060-3 (hardcover : alk. paper)
   ISBN 978-1-59534-056-6 (pbk. : alk. paper)
   1. Caswell, Kurt, 1969– 2. Teachers—New Mexico—Biography.
3. Navajo teenagers—New Mexico—Education.   4. Navajo teenagers—New Mexico—
Attitudes.   5. Teacher-student relationships—Navajo Indian Reservation.   6. Navajo
Indian Reservation—Social life and customs.   I. Title.

LA2317.C37C37   2009
371.829'97260789—dc22   2009020128

13   12   11   10   09   —   5   4   3   2   1

This book is for my family

*especially for my father and mother
for Rebecca, Wally, Tyler, and Troy
for Cari, Chadd, Drew, and Leah
for David, and for Maxine*

Contents

Acknowledgments

The names of most of the people who appear in this book have been changed to protect them from further scrutiny or criticism, hopefully not from praise.

The first chapter of this book, "This Is Borrego," was first published in a slightly different form in the inaugural issue of *Unbound Press*, 2006.

I wish to express my deepest gratitude to the following people who gave generously of their time in reading early drafts of this manuscript and offered exceptional advice and suggestions toward revision: Margo Aragon, Spike Bighorn, Sven Birkerts, Matthew Bokovoy, Tracy Ane Brooks, Steve Cassells, Scott Dewing, Jerry Gidner, Donna Glode, Debra Gwartney, Brett A. Houk, Phillip Lopate, Barry Lopez, Bob Shacochis, Lynne Sharon Schwartz, Susan Tomlinson, and Jeff Williams. To Mary Juzwik, whom I depended on so ardently during my time at Borrego. To Phil Sittnick, and especially to Lauren Sittnick, who made numerous essential suggestions, corrections, and additions.

I am grateful to Barbara Ras, my editor at Trinity University Press, for believing in me and in this book. And to Sarah Nawrocki, also at Trinity, whom I worked with on a final, deep revision.

I owe the greatest debt to the people of Borrego Pass, New Mexico, whose stories commingle here with mine.

Preface

When I sat down to begin work on *In the Sun's House*, I did so with an impassioned host of feelings that aligned in complement as often as they came into conflict. I felt a deep desire to again walk the dry, desert country around Borrego, where I had wandered day after day, up and down the arroyos and through the tall pines, scrambling over rocky ledges and up through cracks in the mesa top, roaming with my dog, Kuma, under the open New Mexico sky. I wanted to engage again with the students there who so challenged me, to hear their playful joking and innocent questions, their sometimes cruel antics. I wanted to be immersed again in a foreign land, in a culture I did not wholly understand, in a mystery. I wanted to see coyote slipping out of my sight, the brush of his tail disappearing in the young pines. Though these were lonely times, they were vivid too, and clear and pure in a way that only comes in your youth, and perhaps later in fleeting catches when you wake to a new sun after restful sleep, or the scent of baking bread from the oven allows you to believe in eternity, or you crystallize your love for someone into an embrace, a look in the eyes, a word.

When I sat down to write, I felt an urgency to bring alive the stories of the people I had lived and worked with at Borrego, to honor them by bringing to light the way their struggles and triumphs inform us all about friendship and community, about self-definition and individuation, about beauty, about endurance. I felt that my year at Borrego had transformed me, and to understand how, I needed to write about it. The story of that year had taken up a place at the edge of my imagination and would not be dislodged. To move beyond it as a writer and as a person, I had to move through it. So I began to tell the stories I knew best.

I don't presume to be an expert in Navajo or American Indian culture, history, mythology, or cosmology, and I claim no American Indian heritage. As far as I know I'm a white boy from Oregon, a concoction of Danish, English, and German peoples, maybe other heritages as well. I admire, but do not idealize, American Indian spirituality, and several years after I lived at Borrego I participated in regular sweat lodge ceremonies with my neighbor in Northern California, Charlie Duncan, a man of Cherokee and Scots descent. You don't have to be an Indian to appreciate a good sweat lodge run by someone properly trained in that tradition. I hardly believe in miracles or life events that are "meant to be"; in general, I'm a skeptic. I enjoyed a rural and wild boyhood, mostly in Oregon, and if I have a god at all, it's a god of nature, a god of the earth.

So I began to write the stories down. As I did so, I was aware that I was writing about a younger person, a younger me, who had grown and changed over the decade from that time to this. I was writing about me, but I was also writing about someone else. Surely you know what I mean. I didn't want to write about how I might have done things differently, about my year at Borrego as a series of errors I might have corrected, to fabricate a regret I didn't feel. I can't imagine how I could have done things differently. I was the person I was in that time and place. Besides, holding on to a world that might have been is the best way I know to live inside an illusion. No one lives very well for very long in an illusion, and after a while regret becomes a bore for you and everyone around you, especially the people you love best.

It is true, however, that as a teacher I have learned a great deal since then. I've worked in two private high schools and a community college in Wyoming, and I'm now an assistant professor at a major research university in Texas. I've come to believe, and I have testimony from former students, that education, that the classroom combined with life experience, can and does change people's lives for the better. Though I don't regard teaching as easier, except that it is more familiar, I know that if I were to take a position at Borrego Pass School now, it would be a very different kind of year.

As I was writing, one story led to another, and the book began to take shape. I wrote the stories that persisted most ardently in my memory first, helped along by the notes I kept in my journal, by talking with some of the people I shared that year with, by files I retained from the classroom, by school work my students had given me, by maps, and by books I read then and later. Many of the stories centered on struggle and violence and sorrow, and some on joy and light. I don't see them as reports of gossip or tales of how bad things were. I put them down, page after page, as I experienced them, working hard to honor the events of that time and the people and the place by getting it right.

At some point I began to ask how I might regard the book if I were one of its subjects—well, indeed I am, but I am so voluntarily. I began to ask, How would I respond to these stories if I was from Borrego Pass, a parent of one of these children, say, or one of the students in my classes? How would I respond if I were a Navajo from another part of the reservation, or another part of the country? How would I respond if I were a teacher at Borrego now or then, or at another school nearby? For several months I was convinced that I could not finish the book, that the stories were too personal, too sensitive, too raw. No matter how I strived to get it right, it was getting it right that was the problem. Was I violating people's privacy by writing about them? Perhaps every writer faces this question. I changed the names of people to protect them, which seemed to help, but in a small community like Borrego I was sure people would recognize themselves and each other. They would recognize their stories. I wondered if it was ethical to continue.

I kept writing anyway, unable to leave the work unfinished, bound for the reckoning. And as I did so, I began to regard the story as my own. Certainly there were a number of other people involved, but I was trying to tell the story of my year teaching on the Navajo Reservation, not the story of people who live on the Navajo Reservation, and certainly not the story of the Navajo people. I think it is a mistake to think of *In the Sun's House* as a book about Navajo people. That story belongs to them, and it is, for someone like me who is not Navajo, nearly unknowable. In writing this book, I had only my limited point of view, informed by my personal experiences and the experiences of the people who lived it with me. I had the accounts of writers and scholars who lived and worked with Navajo people in former times and in this one. And I had some of the published stories of the Navajo people. In this spirit, then, I finished.

For my part, any errors or misconceptions in this book, any flaws or gaps in understanding, are my own. I have worked hard to be true to the story, and I feel good about saying that, for me, during this time, this is the way it was.

Kurt Caswell

Psychiatrists, politicians, tyrants are forever assuring us that
the wandering life is an aberrant form of behaviour; a neurosis;
a form of unfulfilled sexual longing; a sickness which, in
the interests of civilization, must be suppressed. . . .

Yet, in the East, they still preserve the once universal
concept: that wandering re-establishes the original harmony
which once existed between man and the universe.

—Bruce Chatwin

And so it now is that the Navajo people never abide in one dwelling. . . .
Instead they migrate constantly from place to place, from place to place.

—from *Diné Bahane': The Navajo Creation Story*

ONE

THIS IS BORREGO

"You wanna be an Indian?" Charlie Hunter asked.

"No," I said. "I don't want to be an Indian."

"You wanna be a cowboy?"

"No," I said.

"You wanna be a bronc rider!?" Charlie asked.

All the boys laughed.

"No," I said. "You wanna be a bronc rider?"

"Yeah," Charlie said. "We all wanna be bronc riders."

And then they all laughed again.

Charlie wore jeans with a big shiny buckle on his belt, cowboy boots, and a western-style shirt, red with a white yoke. He was rail thin, and his eyes were focused and lean, his face dark and pure. He and the other boys who had gathered with him there in the cafeteria my first morning at Borrego Pass School would all be students in my sixth-grade language arts class, and later I would come to know their names: Shane Yazzie, Joseph Jones, Kyle Bigfoot, and John George.

They all wore their hair cut short, and Shane wore his in a military buzz with a little rooster tail in the back. I had worn my hair long for several years now, and today I wore it down and loose, defying advice given me by a friend: Navajos equate loose hair with loose thoughts. I wondered if this was the reason for Charlie's first question. Did he think I was a New Age Indian wannabe?

"You gotta horse?" Charlie asked me.

"No," I said.

"You gotta truck? A real big one, like a big Ford truck?"

"No," I said. "A little one, like a little Dodge truck." I tried to talk like him a little, to make a joke on him, but he didn't notice, and kept right on talking.

"Oh yeah," he said. "I seen you wash it."

"Yeah," Joseph Jones said. "You always like to wash it."

"Hey Mr. Caswell," Shane Yazzie said. "That's your name right? Mr. Caz-well. You ever go over there to Gallup?"

"Yeah," I said. "Sometimes I go to Gallup."

"Yeah, I seen you over there," he said. "They got a real big Wal-Mart over there. And I seen you over there in a sheepskin runnin' a hun-dret miles an hour!" and they all laughed again.

Then Charlie said, "Hey. You ever seen a skinwalker?"

"No," I said.

That's what Shane meant by my wearing a sheepskin—that *I* was a skinwalker, a Navajo witch.

Then Kyle Bigfoot spoke up. He said he had. He'd seen a skinwalker just last night. Then the little circle at the breakfast table got real quiet and serious. And we all leaned in as Kyle told his story.

He was home alone, he said, because his parents were out somewhere, he didn't know where, and it got cold and dark real fast because it was fall and winter was coming. Kyle heard something outside. And then he heard the dogs barking, a sure sign that skinwalkers are about. So he looked out the window of the little hogan. He didn't see anything at first, he said. But he kept looking. He stood on a chair and crouched down so that his eyes were just above the bottom edge of the window; he could just see out over the bottom of the window. He didn't want anything to see him. And then he saw it, a skinwalker moving from behind the woodpile to the little shack out there, just a dark shade floating above the ground. And when it came into the clearing there between the two hiding places, it stopped. And Kyle froze, he said. He held his breath. He didn't breathe at all. And the dark thing turned toward him and looked at him. Their eyes met for a moment, and then Kyle sucked in his breath and made a sound, and the skinwalker opened its mouth and Kyle gasped and ducked down below the window, shaking and scared and mewling like a kitten. And the dogs barked outside and one of them yelped a little. And Kyle closed his eyes and hugged himself with his arms and shook like a leaf in the wind.

And after awhile he peered up over the edge of the window again. And there was nothing there.

Then Louise Fairchild, the fifth-grade teacher and vice principal at Borrego, yelled from the doorway that it was time to go to class. "It's time to go to class!" And all the boys jumped, and then they all moved back in their chairs like they hadn't.

And John George said, "Ah. That ain't nothin'."

And then all the boys scrambled for the door to line up behind Mrs. Sittnick, their reading teacher, so she could lead them to class. And I heard Charlie Hunter say, "Hey Mrs. Sittnick. You wanna be a bronc rider?"

I was twenty-six when I taught sixth-, seventh-, and eighth-grade language arts at Borrego Pass School in northwest New Mexico. I never intended to be a teacher. I didn't have any real devotion to or belief in education. I had finished my undergraduate degree in English and taken a teaching job in Hokkaido, Japan, because, like a lot of young men my age with literary aspirations, I wanted to travel and see the world. After two and a half years in Hokkaido, journeys in Korea and China, a few days in Morocco, a few months in Europe, my romantic adventure began to feel like everyday life again. I was just going to work and paying my bills. Maybe it was time to choose. Not to stop traveling altogether, but to at least decide where I was going to make my home. I could make a go of it in Hokkaido, and I considered that, but I felt drawn to my boyhood landscape in the Cascade mountains of Oregon, and of course to family and old friends. I left my teaching job in Japan, left Sakura, my Japanese girlfriend, too, and headed back to the American West.

Following that, my path to Borrego was part accident, part necessity. I needed a job, and this one presented itself. I might well have chosen some other profession upon my return, but with my teaching experience in Japan, I found that schools were receptive to me. Beyond that, taking a job at Borrego Pass was attractive because I would have friends nearby whom I knew from graduate school. Mary Juzwik was teaching in a Navajo middle school in Ganado, Arizona, about a hundred miles west of Borrego, and Lauren Sittnick would be my colleague at Borrego. She and her fiancé, Phil, who taught at Laguna Pueblo just east of Grants, had alerted me to the job in the first place.

But those are practical considerations. I cannot deny that the thought of living with Navajo people in the New Mexican desert sounded like another great adventure to me, another thing to do that later I would be proud to say I had done. I wasn't ready, or perhaps I wasn't able, to give up the thirst for discovery that had taken me to Hokkaido. I wasn't ready to live a settled life in suburbia. Those two words—*settled* and *suburbia*—frightened me. Yes, I did want to make my home in America, but at the same time the last thing I wanted was a home in America. It was with this kind of youthful ambivalence that I arrived at Borrego.

Borrego Pass, New Mexico, is on the Continental Divide, sixteen miles up a dirt road, north off Interstate 40 at the Prewitt exit, which is about halfway between Grants and Gallup. The surrounding landscape is a vast desert of high sandstone mesas and low escarpments covered over in cactus and spiky shrubbery. As you drive that lonely road, a coyote might cross in front of you—ragged and thirsty, scrawny and hungry—or become visible for a moment in the distance moving fast over the dry earth. A red-tailed hawk might appear gliding low on the hunt, or high and away, a black spot against the still, vast blue. It's possible that another vehicle will come up behind you, hug your bumper until the blind corner straightens into forever, and then speed by in a twisting tornado of dust and kick stones into your grille and windshield. It's possible that a vehicle will pass by headed in the opposite direction, the driver lifting one finger off the wheel to wave hello, to let you know that you're not alone. But you are alone, mostly, because not many people live out this way. Because you're a stranger and no one knows you here. Because you're a white person, a *bilagaána*, in an Indian land. You may find some comfort in passing the few hogans and houses scattered about near the school and the community of Casamero Lake, which sounds like a nice place, a green place, as the Navajo name means "water waves among the rocks," but that water, the lake, dried up years ago.

Borrego is the Spanish word for "lamb," and the Navajo name for this place is Dibé Yázhí Habitiin, which means "little sheep's path." The Navajo people, and likely others, used this pass to move their sheep herds over the Continental Divide to Crownpoint for at least as long as people have lived in that town, about a hundred years, and perhaps as long as Navajos have kept sheep, about three hundred years. Before that, long before that, the Anasazi came this way traveling the great roads in and out of Chaco Canyon. The elevation at Borrego is about 7,000 feet above the sea. The top of the mesa behind the school is just about 8,000 feet. It doesn't rain much here. Like most of the desert Southwest, it gets less than ten inches each year, but that's enough to support juniper, pinyon pine, and a few ponderosa.

Coming up the dirt road from the interstate, after passing the

Pink Tomahawk bar at the Prewitt junction, where a collection of lost and broken-down men, always men, congregate beneath the little junipers in the shade to sleep off their drunken melancholia, and after passing the great coal-fired power plant and its dirty smokestack beshitting the air but keeping the lights on, the only mark of habitation distinguishing Borrego from the surrounding desert is the water tower, a great white bulb on top of great white pillars that looms over the little school like a huge spider. For a lot of people living out here, running water at home is not an option, and this tower is the closest clean water source. The school officials keep an open-door policy, mostly, for most people who need it, as long as it isn't abused, and so people routinely pull up and fill up, and motor on home. The school itself is almost invisible against the great mesa that backs it. A fairly modern, stucco building in the shape of an L, it's the color of desert sand, with a black and red angular pattern painted on the outside of the high wall that is the gymnasium. A few small deciduous trees planted in front of the school are the only shade, except for the building itself. Inside the angle of this L is a paved parking lot where the buses pull up to load and unload the kids, and beyond that a wide and level dirt playground with some swings and monkey bars, and a few portable buildings that masquerade as classrooms.

In contrast to many reservation schools in the U.S., the Navajo Nation runs things at Borrego Pass. The school has a two-part life story, the first half under the direction of the Bureau of Indian Affairs (BIA), the second as a federally funded grant school managed by a local Navajo school board. The BIA targeted Borrego Pass School for closure in 1965, which would have been a great loss for the surrounding communities. The people of Casamero Lake, Littlewater, and Borrego Pass rallied in support of it. They held a meeting to decide what to do. Perhaps they could establish a grant school under the Indian Self-Determination Act. They set to it. In 1972, the school was incorporated by the state of New Mexico. Construction of the current school facilities was completed in 1985. Full conversion to an elementary and secondary education grant school was finalized in the latter part of 1990. Funding is determined by the number of students who enroll and the number of students who qualify for special help under programs like Chapter One, Gifted and Talented Education (GATE), and Special Education.

The surrounding campus of employee homes carries the feeling of a decommissioned army base, solemn, alone, and all one color. From Borrego Pass Road marching back toward the mesa is a row of cinder block duplexes, backed by a row of dilapidated trailers, and up on the rise a cul-de-sac of modern stucco houses, most of the windows closed off by drab curtains. When I moved in, the whole place looked deserted, as if everyone had packed up and gone away. No trucks or cars in the parking lot in front of the school. No laundry hanging out to dry. No light music from an open window. Even the school, which had been so full of life when I interviewed, stood empty and silent like the great sandstone mesa behind it, the front doors locked tight. There seemed to be nothing growing, nothing green, nothing alive.

A mile north of the school, the Borrego Pass Trading Post offers a modest selection of groceries, basic hardware, and the work of local Navajo artists. Gas is available too, but who wants to pay those prices? The Navajo community of Crownpoint is ten miles beyond that, out a roughshod dirt road headed north and west. The town offers a full-sized grocery store, a laundry or two, a couple gas stations, and maybe a restaurant depending on whether or not you get to town before someone's dream goes out of business, again. For any other needs, you have to go east to Grants or west to Gallup, about a one-hour drive on I-40 in either direction. But it isn't these distances that isolate Borrego, it's that all roads leading in and out are dirt.

When it rains or snows in this high desert, the roads become nearly impassable.

My first mistake as a teacher at Borrego was the hard eye I fired at Caleb Benally, who sat in the back of the classroom tipped back on his chair. I had not started teaching yet. I was still a guest, sitting in on classes to get a good look at things, but Caleb stirred something inside me, something aggressive, something possibly violent that I hadn't felt in a long time. Maybe not ever.

After breakfast, Linda Bitsy, the Navajo language and culture teacher, led me to the science room and my seventh-grade class. I learned then that the school didn't have enough classrooms to go around. I would be sharing space with the science teacher. I also learned that first morning that I would be the seventh-grade home-room teacher and class sponsor. My primary duty in this role would be to help the class earn money throughout the year and then organize and lead a field trip. I had missed the first week of school because I was hired at the last minute, and Linda had been teaching my classes as well as her own. When I arrived that Monday morning, she was very happy to see me. I would have a two-day grace period while she introduced me to my students and showed me what they had been doing. Then I was on my own.

Linda was a heavy, jovial woman. She wore glasses, and her hair was cut shoulder-length and curled under. She wore a short orange dress that settled softly over her wide, powerful shoulders and substantial hips. She smiled warmly at me and shook my hand, not the tight-gripped, competitive handshake I was used to, but a soft, welcoming handshake. In fact it didn't feel like a handshake at all, but as if she were holding my hand to comfort me, her thumb and index finger wrapped loosely but confidently around mine. I liked her right away.

Linda sat at the head of the room behind the teacher's desk while the seventh-grade class worked busily in their notebooks. A few of the students stopped writing to get a look at me. I heard them whispering in Navajo.

"Keep writing in your journals," Linda barked at them.

I surveyed the room, noticing some of the students happily following Linda's order, some not doing anything at all. That's when I caught Caleb Benally's eye. He looked straight at me, and I looked straight back at him. His eyes were of the darkest black. He had a handsome, strong jaw and smooth, perfect skin. His shoulders were wide and muscled, not bulky, but sinewy, flexible. Even sitting down I could see that he was a natural at something with a ball, or at running, or possibly fighting. Probably fighting. He didn't look away from me like the other kids in the room, and so I surmised that he was in charge of the seventh grade. I thought that his physical beauty was also his power over the other boys, with adults too, probably with women. He was just a boy, but I sensed he was capable of a man's actions. Caleb looked filled with promise too, but promise for what, I didn't know.

Part of a teacher's job is to evoke such promise in students and channel it toward the goals of the course in the short term, and the goals of each individual's life in the long term. I didn't know it then, but in this charge, I was already remiss. Instead of redirecting Caleb's powerful energy, his gaze, in a constructive way, I tried to seize it and throw it back at him. I didn't just make eye contact with him that first morning; I returned his gaze, pushed hard at him with my eyes, tested him, challenged him. The more I did, the more penetrating and aggressive his eyes became, until we seemed to acknowledge a stalemate.

I knew very little about Navajo culture. At first this may have worked to my advantage. When the school board questioned me on this point during my interview, they learned that I was no junior anthropologist looking for a research topic and no white shaman looking for a religious experience. I was simply an English teacher. A foreigner, yes, an outsider, but also a guest. On this morning what I didn't know worked against me. I did not know, for example, that Navajos have an intractable fear of strangers. Many of them fear almost everyone who is not related to them and believe that whenever they venture into a crowd it is best to carry protection against witchcraft. I did not know the most basic social etiquette. I did not know that looking someone directly in the eye can be an insult, even an act of aggression. Upon meeting someone for the first time, Navajo people generally look slightly down or just beyond the person, rarely directly at them, at least not for more than a moment. What appears to be shyness or submission is really a gesture of respect. But I heard later, too, that many Navajos reject these ideas—that their culture is no more wary of strangers than any other culture, and they do not avoid looking people in the eye. I didn't know what to believe, but I was certain Caleb's aggressive stare was not a friendly hello.

Later I happened across the Navajo story of the eye killers, monsters from Navajo mythology that can paralyze and kill by simply staring at their victims. They were born of a chief's daughter who masturbated with a sour cactus. They had no limbs or heads, but were roundish creatures with one end that came to a point. At the topmost part of them were two depressions, great eyes from which lightning flashed into their victims. They lived at the base of Mount Taylor near Grants, one of the four sacred Navajo mountains, and the one closest to Borrego. The Hero Twins, who in the myth-time rid the world of most of its monsters, slew all but two of the eye killers by throwing salt into them and then destroying them with flint clubs. The two that survived became owls: elf owl, who warns listeners of approaching enemies; and screech owl, who helps make the earth beautiful. Another account has the two eye killers becoming poorwills or nighthawks that sleep during the day and come out at night to beautify the world. Both accounts sounded like happy endings to me, but Navajos regard owls as couriers of bad luck and death.

Caleb probably did not have these stories in mind when he stared me down, but this business with the eyes, the gravity of aggressive staring, seemed to run deep in the Navajo culture. Caleb knew what he was doing anyway, sizing me up, challenging me. His gaze was hostile from the start, but it was only later that I understood how hostile my response had been. And it was only later that I realized my response would not be readily forgotten. In this initial meeting, I had helped determine the terms of our relationship: we would be enemies. And because many of the other students, boys especially, took their cues from Caleb, in the first minutes of meeting them, I had set myself against my entire seventh-grade homeroom. I didn't know it then, but I would spend the entire year trying to sort this out.

"Who is he?" Caleb said out loud. He didn't address his question to anyone, but sent the words out into the room as if he and Linda were the only two people in it.

She looked up at him. For a moment it seemed that she planned not to answer. Then she said, "This is Mr. Caswell. He's your new language arts teacher."

"New teacher," Caleb said. "We don't need no new teacher. You can teach us." He wasn't offering Linda a compliment, but rather issuing her a command.

"Well, you got one," Linda said. "I got my own classes. Mr. Caswell will be taking over this class tomorrow."

Everyone groaned.

Tomorrow? I thought I was to enjoy a few more days of observation.

"We don't need no new teacher," Caleb said again. "Especially him. You can teach us."

"Yeah," said Clemson, who I would later learn was Caleb's cousin. "You can teach us."

A few other boys nodded their heads in agreement. The girls did not seem to be interested in taking a side, or even acknowledging the conversation. A few looked up briefly to see what was happening, or to see what was going to happen, but most of them kept on writing.

"Well, Linda," Caleb said. "You gonna teach us or what?"

A long silence settled over the room. We were all waiting for Linda to respond. I was waiting for her to defend me somehow. To reintroduce me in some way that would reassure the class. She didn't. She reached into her bag and pulled out her needlepoint. She went to work on it. Some pattern of reds and browns and a little yellow, but I couldn't make it out. "Get back to work in your journals!" she said, without looking up.

I felt Caleb's eyes on me, but I didn't look at him again. I just sat there stupidly in front of the class until the clock ticked down the hour. Caleb got up and started toward the door as Linda said, "Okay. Time's up. Go to your next class." Then everyone did.

By the end of my first day, I already felt like a failure. Not a feeling of dark, self-loathing brought about by too little confidence. Rather, sitting in on classes with Linda had confirmed my greatest fear: I had no idea what these kids needed, or how to offer it to them. I had no idea what I was going to do when the classes were turned over to me in the morning. It was different when I considered this point before I arrived at Borrego, because teaching middle school on the Navajo Reservation was still merely an idea of adventure, a thought that passed in and out of my mind. Now I had real people in front of me, real students, real human beings with aspirations and dreams, talents and weaknesses, needs and fears. They each had a name. I would have to get to know those names and get to know them. For the rest of the year, I was charged with caring for these kids, for the improvement of their reading and writing skills, for influencing the way they came to regard the world around them. I needed to care about them and their lives. I needed to care about their future. And upon meeting them for the first time, I didn't. I didn't feel anything for them except an uncomfortable antagonism. What was I thinking when I accepted this charge? I was not prepared or qualified to take on this kind of responsibility.

I had a few free hours at the end of the day before the buses loaded up the children. I didn't have a classroom, so I took a seat in the library to work on lesson plans. If I was going to be on my own in the morning, I had to be ready. I wrote out all my ideas, several pages of notes, most of which I then threw out (they all seemed either too complex or too simple). Remembering how I structured my lesson plans in Japan, I decided to break the seventy-five-minute class period into five- and ten-minute mini-lectures accompanied by exercises. Shorter is usually better. I would only be able to keep their attention for short bursts of time, so the lesson had to push this cadence, not be pushed by it. Before they got bored, we'd move on to something else.

"So sorry not to have been here to welcome you," Principal Bob King said as he walked into the library and shook my hand. "I was away at a board meeting all day."

"Hello," I said. "I was wondering when I'd see you." He asked if I had a few free minutes, and together we walked down to his office.

Bob King's belly was round and firm and pushed out over his wide leather belt. He stood at least six foot two and was handsome in a cowboy way, clean-faced and well groomed. His eyes were startlingly blue. He kept his brown curly hair cut short, and he wore crisp jeans and polished cowboy boots. His face was always ruddy, as if bitten by the desert wind. Everyone always referred to him as "Bob King," never simply "Bob" or "King." He loved to hunt, he told me, and this was one of the two reasons he lived at Borrego, to be at the center of so much open space. The other was that he had married a young Navajo woman. Like me, Bob King had landed a teaching job at Borrego early in his career. He taught science, and during his interview, he told me, one of the members of the all-Navajo school board asked him what his goals were. He looked the man in the eye and said, "I want your job." He must have said it so that it sounded like youthful ambition instead of a threat, because he got the teaching job, and a few years later the board made him principal. Still, as a white principal in a Navajo school, his command stretched only as far as his service to the board. He was temporary; they were forever.

The story of Bob King's courtship and marriage I heard around campus and accepted as a collage of rumor and truth, depending on who was doing the talking. This is the story, as I pieced it together: Bob King fell in love with one of his eighth-grade students. She could have been as old as seventeen when they met, as Borrego students were notorious for skipping a semester here and there, even skipping a year or two, then returning without warning. Or they might not begin going to school until very late. She could also have been as young as thirteen, the age of most eighth graders in the U.S. Some people said one thing, others said another. Everyone who told me the story affirmed that the young woman Bob King married was the daughter of one of the school board members. Wouldn't it be interesting if she was the daughter of that same school board member who asked Bob King about his goals? I heard that she was. I also heard that she was not. When she went on to the ninth grade at another school, Bob King invited her to live with him. She moved in. At first, the community was outraged. Perhaps it was the difference in their ages, or that Bob King had been her teacher, or that Bob King was white. Whatever, things eventually settled out, and Bob King married her. Shortly after that, he was made principal. With his new bride, he moved into the best house on campus.

During my time at Borrego, Bob King's wife was mostly invisible, hidden up there in the house behind drawn curtains. She rarely came down to the school, at least not when I was working, and I never saw her at a school event. It wasn't something to ask about, I guessed, and Bob King didn't volunteer anything. For me, she was formless

and faceless, a wraith that floated just outside our lives at Borrego. Yet
there is this one detail: she drove a white sports car, of what make and
model I don't know, with a blue stripe down the center and impossibly low clearance. It must have been precious to her because she took
it out only on the finest days and only after the road had been newly
graded. I caught sight of her one afternoon getting into her white car,
and her hair, black as jet, fell all the way to her knees. As she opened
the car door, her hair spread over her shoulder like a cloak, reflecting light like lightning directly into my eyes. Not so many years from
now, after she and Bob King eventually split up, she would be dead,
murdered in her home in Santa Fe by her new boyfriend.

Bob King showed me into his office, and we sat down, him behind
the desk and me in front of it. I could see a long way south from the
office window, the desert golden and empty, stretching far and away.

"This is Borrego," he said enthusiastically. "I hope you're settling in. If you like the outdoors, this is a great place to be."

He sounded like he was trying to sell me the job, to convince me
to say yes, but I already had.

"You see that out there?" he said, standing up.

I stood with him and we looked off through the window. I could
see even farther now, down into the valley and across, up into a high
plateau of trees and shrubs and cactus visible where the sun went
down.

"That's the Cibola country," he said. "The Continental Divide
runs through it, and another piece lies farther east surrounding
Mount Taylor. There's all kinds of mines and old homesteads and
wild places down there. And beyond that is Zuni. A whole different
world. That's why I live here," he said. "I love that country down
there."

We stared out for a few moments more and then returned to our
seats.

"I'll have to explore all that," I said. "I love getting outside."

He nodded. "How was your first day?"

"It was okay," I said. "It's a lot to take in all at once."

"That's right," he said. "I remember when I first arrived here. I was completely overwhelmed. You know the teacher you replaced was here for seven years."

Was this the term he was asking me to fill?

"Seven years," he said again. "She called me just recently," he went on, "said she really missed the kids at Borrego. That's the part she really missed. These kids."

"And why did she leave?"

"She loved it here. She really did. Really got involved with the community. She was attending ceremonies and getting invitations to people's homes. That's a big deal around here. If you get invited to a Navajo's home, that's really something. It means they trust you. It means you're like one of the family."

But my predecessor's story was not so rosy as Bob King made it out to be. Later I learned that the school administration had strongly encouraged her to leave. She was mentally ill, people said, and likely using something with a needle. Some days she showed up at school barely able to speak. She was a complete tragedy, a liability, a lost opportunity for the students at Borrego, who would attend her class and come away with nothing at all. I did not know it at the time, but Bob King was lying to me, padding the truth anyway. He offered me a Borrego of great beauty and natural power, of community solidarity and family values. He was telling me I had made the right choice by coming to Borrego, and that here I would find a life worth living. Was this the life he imagined for himself, but didn't have? Was he exhausted by trying to fill so many vacant posts at the school, and hoping I'd stay on a couple years? Was he, like any parent, protecting me from a harder truth?

I noticed the cell phone on Bob King's desk, a three-watt bag phone.

"Does that thing work from here?" I asked.

"Sure. Mostly," he said. "There's a repeater tower just south of here. It works on a clear day anyway. Those little cell phones don't work up here at all." He paused. "A teacher like you," he said, changing the subject, "doesn't stay in a place like this. You'll have other options next year, you know. Other schools will want you. But you are welcome here for as long as you want. I want you to stay."

He said it longingly, like he was talking about himself. Of course he hadn't seen me teach yet. We'd only spent a few hours together, and that included the interview.

"Thank you," I said. "That's nice of you to say." Then I added, "The phone at my place doesn't work. Who can I ask about that?"

"I mean that," he said. "You're welcome here as long as you want to stay. Whatever you need, just ask. I'll try to get it for you. I just want you to have a good first week. A good first year."

"Thank you," I said again.

I did feel welcome, at least now, and the stress and failure of my first day seemed to be falling away. I would be ready in the morning for the second day. And I felt charged up about exploring the country around Borrego and the rest of Navajoland. I had that to look forward to, but I wanted to resolve this issue with the telephone.

"What about the phone?" I said. "How can I get it working?"

"Oh, that," he said. "Maybe you can't. I'm not sure. Not so many lines coming in here."

"Really?" I said. "How do I find out? I didn't know I might not have a phone."

My ties to the outside world were being stripped away, one by one. I had no TV, and my radio seemed attracted to stations broadcasting only in Navajo. And now the news that I might have no telephone? If I looked at the bright side, perhaps I'd get lots of reading done. If I looked at the dark side, perhaps I'd be undone.

"Try calling Navajo Communications," Bob King said. "They

take care of things up here. They can tell you. Don't count on it, though. Took me years to get a phone at my house." Then he said, "Well, I have to get home to supper. Try calling from Deena's phone tomorrow in the office. I'm sure there's a solution. And stop in to say hello anytime, or if you need anything."

"Okay," I said. "I will. See you tomorrow."

We shook hands and said good night.

Like most new teachers, I wanted my students to like and respect me, which are not necessarily the same thing, especially with middle schoolers. The boundary between the two is delicate, and different with every class, with every group. Earning admiration and respect is a skill most teachers cannot learn in an education program and the skill all teachers need most. Perhaps apprenticing with a master teacher might help one make long strides in this direction. Not student teaching (which I never had to endure), but apprenticing. The other way to learn the balance between being liked and respected is by teaching, by trial and error, or rather, as it turned out for me, trial by fire.

By the next morning, I had thrown out all the lesson plans I wrote in the library, thinking I needed to start at the beginning. I would begin the first day with a lecture expounding the value of reading and writing the English language. All instruction at Borrego was in English, with the exception of Linda Bitsy's Navajo language and culture class. All the students spoke English, but for many of them, it was their second language. They grew up speaking Navajo, especially in the home, where grandparents and sometimes parents did not speak English at all. So speaking Navajo was essential to home and community life, and speaking English was essential in the classroom and most everywhere else.

I hadn't begun to get mixed up in taking a position on how an increasing reliance on English could result in the loss of the Navajo language, as is the story with so many other American Indian languages. I suppose it is possible with Navajo, but there are some 300,000 Navajo people living on and off their 27,000-square-mile reservation and, among them, plenty of Navajo speakers to keep the language alive. Besides that, I had been hired to teach English by Navajos, not the Bureau of Indian Affairs or a white school board deciding what was best for Navajo people. That is, however, the way it used to be, following the Navajo's "defeat" by Colonel Kit Carson, and their subsequent imprisonment at Bosque Redondo. It was part of the U.S. government's assimilation policy, their attempt to transform Navajo people into little white farmers, pressuring schools to teach English and forbid the use of Navajo. Now the Navajo Nation was regaining control of its own education system, deciding for itself that English was a powerful tool and should be a central part of the school curriculum. I was in the service of the Navajo Nation, not the U.S. government, and I would do what it asked of me.

I decided that following my lecture, I would ask my classes to consider what I had said, then respond in the journals they had begun writing in with Linda. I wanted them to write vigorously, without stopping, for fifteen minutes or so. Then students would volunteer to read aloud, which would fuel a vibrant discussion about learning, reading and writing, the value of mastering English, and their individual life goals.

For homework I would ask my students to read the next lesson in their textbook, picking up where Linda left off. I had not seen their textbook yet. I had asked Bob King for copies of the books for each of my classes after he made the job offer, but he told me not to worry about those details. We'd figure it all out when I arrived, he said. This was fine by me, as I knew I would not have much time to look the books over before I arrived. If Linda had not used the book during that first week, that was fine too. We'd begin at the beginning. I just needed to dive in, to get going. Whatever I assigned as homework would be homework for me, too.

My longer vision was that I would open my students to an entirely new world of thinking and feeling and responding to the world around them. They would use the lens of literature to access this new world, and they would use their own writing to explore this new world, which would then prompt them to not only continue on in their education but also travel and explore and experience. They would recognize me as the source of all this goodness, and they would love me for it.

My seventh-grade class filed in looking stern and united, as if they had determined already that they didn't like me. In fact, I was certain they had. Yesterday's class visit proved it. Caleb Benally rejected me outright, demanding that Linda Bitsy remain their teacher. And the rest of the class, in their silence, acknowledged that Caleb was speaking for them too. How was I to overcome this? In Japan, I was received with such openness and generosity, respect and attention in the classroom that I had had no need or opportunity to develop classroom management skills. I floated along on a little jet stream of good feelings—this teaching thing is easy, I told myself, and I must be a natural at it. But here, faced with my first class on my first day, I wondered if I wasn't doomed before I started. I checked myself, however. I did not know anything about these young people. I had no idea who they were, where they were headed, and what they needed to get there. Once I learned these things, I told myself, I would be able to develop course goals that would make sense to their everyday lives. The first day with a new teacher, I counseled, they were bound to be a bit reserved, a bit wary. I was an outsider, after all. The worst thing I could do was take up a defensive posture. If I did, so would they. Despite my first-day jitters, I had to open myself to them. Only then would they open themselves to me.

The students sat down at their desks. No one said a word. I surveyed the room. They looked attentive anyway, even studious in their silence, ready to get going. The long row of windows on the north side brightened the classroom, and we were surrounded by images of the natural world: whales and animals of the Serengeti, a wall calendar with pictures of wolves, a periodic table of elements, a poster of dinosaurs. Cabinets filled with beakers and test tubes and things for measuring and cutting lined the back of the room. I had always loved science, especially as a way to explore and understand the natural world, but the science classroom seemed a strange atmosphere for reading and writing. Or maybe it was the perfect classroom. Be flexible. Be malleable. Adapt, I told myself.

I called roll, and everyone responded in turn by raising their hand. I marked the sheet and left it on the door for someone to pick up. So far, so good.

"Okay," I said. "Let's begin." I started in on my lecture. "Good morning. I'm Mr. Caswell, and—"

"Where's Linda?" someone said.

I stopped. "She's out in the hogan," I said. "She has a class out there this period. I'll be here from now on." Of course they knew this already, but perhaps they needed an official announcement. "I'm your new language arts teacher," I said.

I heard a few groans.

"I'm not staying with you, *bilagáana*. I'm goin' out there," said Maria Young. "I'm not stayin' in here."

I heard snickering from the back of the room.

Maria had thick curly hair cut at shoulder length, and wide, round eyes. Based on where she sat, in the front row, I had pegged her as an eager, compliant student, until she used that word. *Bilagáana*, the first Navajo word I learned, means "white person." Some white people who live in Navajoland use the word in reference to themselves. Because Navajos often include their clan names when introducing themselves, a white person might use the tag *bilagáana* because they have no clan. In context, though, there was nothing neutral or descriptive about Maria's use of the word. She seemed to be insulting me. Or was I just overly sensitive? The Japanese equivalent, *gaijin*, can have a negative connotation. It means "foreigner" or "outsider," which may be used simply to express: "This person is not Japanese." However, it may also be used in a derogatory fashion, as in: "Go home, *gaijin!*" I couldn't help but feel this was what Maria intended.

I tried to brush it off. I tried to ignore it. "You can't go out there," I said. "Linda has another class out there. You can't go out and interrupt her."

"I don't care," Maria said. "She likes us. She'll let us in. We can make stuff out there."

"Well, maybe so," I said. "But you're in language arts this period. You need this class."

"No, I don't," said Maria.

Then Jolanda Jones said, "Yeah, me neither. I don't need it."

Jolanda was tall and wore her hair long and straight down her back. Her face was round and lightly soft, pretty. She looked older than the other girls, and walked confidently, with her shoulders squared back, her chest thrust out. She looked angry.

"Yeah. Let's go out to the hogan with Linda," someone else said.

"Right," said Jolanda. She made a move as if to get up.

I hadn't expected this. A mutiny. This wasn't going at all the way I imagined it, and my little teaching fantasy vanished. Still, the best thing to do, I thought, was go ahead with my lesson plan. I had invested some effort in preparing for this day, and I wasn't ready to give up on it. Even if the students didn't respond to me the way I thought they should, at least they would receive the information I had prepared for them. They would still learn something, and I'd send them home with work to do for the next class.

"No one is going out to the hogan," I said. "This is language arts. So let's begin."

Jolanda sat back down. I continued on with my lecture.

"Why don't you cut your hair?" Maria burst out.

"Yeah," another girl said. "You should cut it. It looks stupit."

Then Clemson Benally, Caleb's cousin, said, "Yeah, hey, why do you have it like that?" and he grinned at Caleb, who thrust his lips out and made a clicking sound in his mouth. "You should cut it, or you should braid it," Clemson said.

Then Caleb said, "Or you should wear it tied up in back in a little tamale like Thomas," and then he clicked again in his mouth and everyone laughed.

Thomas, the librarian, was into his sixties maybe, and he wore his long graying hair tied in a traditional chongo knot, a little bun bound with cotton yarn. Most of the men and boys at Borrego wore their hair cut short, or even buzzed tight against their skulls like marines.

"Why did you come here, anyway?" Jolanda said.

"Yeah," everyone said. "Why did you come here? Why don't you go home?"

"Yeah. Why don't you go home?" Jolanda said.

That stung me. "Why don't you go home?" I had not expected this much resistance from the students. In all honesty, I hadn't expected anything. It all happened so fast. My departure from Hokkaido. The interview at Borrego. The packing up and moving in. I had been traveling from place to place with relative ease, and why should Borrego be any different? I would show up, and do good work. Meet good people, and learn from them. And maybe they would learn from me too. When the time came, I'd move on, a wave of good feelings following after me. It was the kind of simple and rewarding life I had always imagined. But this?

I heard the words again in my head: Why don't you go home?

Right, I thought, why don't I go home? As I asked myself this question, I felt hurt, insulted, rejected, and my anger grew.

"That's rude," I said. "You can't say that."

Jolanda smiled at me and said something in Navajo.

"What was that?" I said. "I don't speak Navajo."

She didn't answer.

Then George George, a skinny, wiry kid with freckles splashed across his cheeks and hair that looked like his grandmother had dropped a bowl on his head and cut around it, raised his hand. The classroom went still. George smiled, his hand in the air as if he wanted to say something important. Maybe his grandmother had used a bowl to cut his hair, but no matter, he was about to take my side. He was about to address his classmates about their rudeness. I called on him.

"George?" I said, unsure whether I was calling his first name or his last.

"Mr. Caswell," he said, and then he spoke a long string of Navajo, in which I heard again the word *bilagáana*. He rested a moment, switched to English, and said, "How come you got yellow teeth?"

The whole room burst into laughter.

I stood before them, anger and frustration welling inside me. They had me, and I knew it. What was worse, they knew it. I became suddenly self-conscious about my teeth, and I became suddenly aware of the door, as if I was about to make a run for it. The class laughed and laughed. I frowned and fumed.

Then I remembered the detention room. Earlier that morning I had met Dallas West, the detention monitor, and he showed me his office. If I needed help in the classroom, he told me, I could call on him. He'd come by and pick up any student who was causing trouble. Well, they were all causing trouble now, and I wanted them all to be punished. But I wasn't going to quit just yet.

It came to me just then, a bit oddly, that it was true what George said. Everyone in the room except me had beautiful white teeth, all the more white and clean against their darker skin. Few white people had teeth that white, and mine were straight and healthy, the dentist always said so, but they were dullish and discolored in comparison. Was George simply asking about an ethnic difference he'd observed? Or was he insulting me?

I tried to pull myself together. I tried to regain control of the class, to redirect the students to our subject.

"All right!" I said, raising my voice. "That's enough! Let's get back to our lesson."

I remembered the homework, the assignment I would give from their textbook. Perhaps they would settle down if they just had something to keep them busy. They could use the rest of the class time for quiet, individual work. At least that might take the heat off me.

"I want you to take out your textbooks," I said. "You'll have some homework tonight, so you might as well start on it now."

"We don't got no books," Jolanda said.

"Yeah, and we don't want none," said Maria.

"Sure you do," I said. "Every class has a textbook."

"No, we don't," Maria and Jolanda said at the same time. They looked at each other and grinned.

"Yes, you do. Take out your books," I ordered.

"There ain't none," said Clemson. "Really, Mr. Caswell. We don't got none."

I still didn't believe them, but we weren't getting anywhere. I would have to make up something for them to do, fast.

Then I had a moment of teacherly brilliance, or so I thought. If the class was not going my way, I would ask them what they wanted to do, and make it go their way. Then they would have nothing to complain about. This is a mistake many new teachers make, giving up control of the classroom to the class. It's especially true when teaching middle school, because middle schoolers have no idea what they want, and whatever they say they want changes the moment they say it. This is a generalization, of course, but it's true. In any case, I'd already lost control, so it didn't matter.

"Okay," I said. "Then your homework is to write two pages in your journal about what you think we should do this semester in language arts class. You have to start now."

I looked at the clock. Most of the class period had slipped away into chaos, and we'd accomplished practically nothing. What a failure, I thought. I couldn't let this happen again.

"We've got ten minutes left," I said. "The more you write now, the less you have to write at home."

"We can say anything?" Clemson asked.

"Anything," I said. "Write down what you think we should do in this class until December."

"All right!" Clemson said, and went straight to work on it.

Most of the class got out their journals and a pen, and some of them started writing. Others began drawing. Clemson wrote steadily, glancing up at me and then at Caleb, who sat back on his chair watching the clock.

A few minutes passed in silence. Good, I thought. I think I understand how this works now. Put them to work. Don't allow them to have any idle time. That's how to do it. Keep them busy.

Then Maria said, "What're we supposed to write about?"

"Yeah," said Jolanda. "What're we supposed to write about?"

"I just told you," I said. "Write about what you think we should do this semester. Do you think we should read a lot, write a lot, or both equally? Do you think we should practice spelling and grammar? Do you think we should study poetry or fiction? Do you think we should go outside often and write in the outdoors? Do you want to read stories aloud to each other, or silently to yourselves, or both? Do you want to watch movies too? Tell me what you want to do most."

The room was silent again, and almost everyone was writing.

Maria still hadn't written anything, but she seemed to be thinking, thinking hard, her pen in hand, poised to make the first words out on the page.

"Hey, can I use a pencil, Mr. Caswell, or do I gotta use a pen?" asked Samuel Smith.

"Sure, you can use a pencil. I don't care. Whatever you like best," I said.

"I don't got nothin' to write about," Maria said suddenly.

"Yeah, me too. And I don't wanna do it anyways," Jolanda said, and put her journal away in protest.

"Me too," said Maria. "I'm not doin' it."

"Hey, Mr. Caswell," Caleb said, sitting forward on his chair. "You got a woman?"

Everyone laughed.

I shook my head and looked down. I wasn't going to respond to that question. Caleb wasn't interested in my personal life. The question was just his way of trying to regain power, power I wasn't going to let him have.

"Get to work, Caleb," I said. "You've got only a few minutes left."

Then George raised his hand again. It had worked the first time, he probably thought, so he might as well try it again. Everyone looked at him, waiting for his question. He smiled big, his white teeth like porcelain.

"Yes, George?" I said, a bit wiser, a bit warier, but willing. "What do ya got?"

"Or," he said, employing a dramatic pause, "you got a man?"

The class roared with laughter.

"Goddamn it!" I said. "This room better be quiet until the end of class!"

I felt the heat of my frustration and anger surging into my face. Maybe I was turning red. I didn't know what to do. I hadn't meant to curse. It just came out. I was certain these kids had heard "Goddamn it" before, but it was likely they had never heard their teacher cuss at them in the classroom. Maybe. I didn't know. Caleb and George snickered, not because I had cursed, but because they knew I was at the edge of my temper. I didn't think I had much of a temper, but maybe it just hadn't been tested in awhile, because now I felt myself trying to hold it in. I wanted to take hold of that little shit, George, and bloody him real bad. I looked at the clock. Six more minutes. When was it going to end? I wanted it to end. At first, time had whizzed by, and now it seemed to drag on and on forever. I didn't care if they learned anything anymore. I just wanted it to end.

Miraculously, the last few minutes leaked away, and the kids got up, gathered their things, and went out the door. Was I supposed to dismiss them? Was I supposed to say goodbye to them? Was I supposed to wish them a fine day and happy studying, be careful and say I looked forward to our next class? I didn't. Good riddance, I thought.

I stalked around inside the empty room like a caged animal. I felt violent and defeated, cornered and desperate. I had to cool off. Another class would be coming in, a science class, and I had to walk out that door now and down the hallway through the kids crowding at their lockers, the entire middle school. I knew if my anger was visible, the word would get out that I could be easily defeated. Likely, the word would get out anyway.

I had not finished my lesson, of course. I had not really even started. All I had taught my class today was that they could tip me over the edge, that I had little defense against them. They had tested the boundaries of my anger, and now they knew right where to find it. I didn't think of myself as an angry person, but I was angry now. I was angry that I had allowed them to make me angry. No real teacher would allow that to happen. No real teacher would curse at his students. No real teacher would treat his students that way, no matter how they behaved. I wondered if news of my cussing at the kids would get back to Bob King. Maybe I'd lose my job over it. If that happened, maybe it would be for the best. I could transform my anger into action. I didn't have to stay here. I wouldn't stay here in this miserable place. I'd pack up and leave. I imagined the sequence of events that would lead me down the road and back north. My anger cooled. And cooled some more. I'd find something else to do. Maybe find my way back to Japan, or even try teaching in China. I knew I could handle that. More likely I'd quit teaching all together. I never wanted to be a teacher anyway.

I walked out of the classroom into the fray of kids in the hallway, confident that I would soon be moving on.

The school day ended. I assembled outside with the rest of the teachers to help monitor the kids as they got onto the buses. I stood next to Lauren Sittnick.

Lauren had not been living in Navajoland for very long either, just since last spring. She was from South Carolina, and fell in love with Phil Sittnick, who had been teaching at Laguna Middle School at Laguna Pueblo for some half dozen years. They met at the same place I met them and Mary Juzwik: the Bread Loaf School of English, a master's degree program designed for working teachers, at Middlebury College in Vermont. Lauren suffered through a winter deliriously in love and in the spring told her principal that he should start looking for someone else because she was moving to New Mexico. She found work at Borrego during the final months of the previous school year. Lauren's friends called her "Ren." When she moved to the desert, Phil was fond of saying that she had gone from being a Carolina wren to a cactus wren. I liked that, as cute as it was.

Lauren had kind, warm eyes and an innocent manner. Until I got to know her, I thought of Lauren as spacey, naive, a little childlike, but that lightness had more to do with her willingness to bend, her openness to new ideas, the generous way in which she withdrew her force of character to allow the people around her to be themselves. Good qualities for teaching. She wanted children with Phil, she once told me, but for now she channeled all her motherly energy into her classroom. She believed very deeply in the power of education, especially in mastering the art of reading. For her, the world was a closed book, and learning to read was the key to opening it. She didn't read very well as a child, she told me, but when she finally did learn, a world of information and opportunity came alive for her. She read as much as she could because the more she read, the more she discovered. Her world grew larger and more tragic and more beautiful. Naturally, she became a teacher to help children learn to read. And she was a masterful teacher.

"Are you all right?" she said. She let a little silence go between us. She could see it in my face. Then she said, by way of comfort, "How was your first day in the classroom?"

"It was okay," I said. "I don't know. I mean it wasn't okay. It didn't go very well."

"It will get easier," she said. "They're testing you."

"Well, I didn't pass," I said.

"Yeah," she said. "I've been teaching a long time, and I've never had to endure anything like this. Some of these kids are really angry. Really mean. It's not you. It's not your fault."

"I don't know if I'm cut out for this," I said.

"They're testing you," she said. "It gets better. A little, anyway. Ask Phil. He'll tell you. I cried every day after school last spring." She smiled warmly.

"Really?"

"Really. In fact, I'll probably cry half the time this semester, too." She laughed a little, and put her hand on my shoulder. "Just ask whenever you need something. We can help each other."

The buses pulled away and bounced over the cattle guard.

"One day at a time," Lauren said. "See you tomorrow."

I walked back to my duplex apartment on campus. I felt a strange panic in my chest. I had made a mistake in coming here, I thought. Now I needed to figure out how I was going to get out of it. Would Bob King understand if I told him I could not do it? If I quit? I recalled what Louise had told me during my interview: "Some of the teachers we've invited out to interview," she said, "when they get out here and see where Borrego is, they just keep right on going." Who could blame them? Who could blame me? If I left, I'd just be one more name on that list of people who kept right on going. Or maybe, and better yet, I could come up with a plausible excuse. Someone in my family was dying and I had to return home to Idaho. Or I had proposed to Sakura, and she said yes, but only if I would return to Japan and make my life there. Or, something terrifying and secret had happened, and no one could know about it, but please trust, I'd explain, that I would not do this without good reason. Whatever, in a few years none of it would matter.

Even though my things were unpacked and arranged nicely in the duplex, the space felt unusually cold and foreign to me when I walked in. It felt empty and dead. Something in the air smelled like a sewer. I thought it was just my temperament, but the smell grew stronger as I followed my nose to the bathroom. There, coming up out of the bathtub drain—three inches of water and piss and shit. I stared at it a moment, as if maybe it wasn't really there, just an illusion, a metaphor I'd constructed in my heated brain. But there it was, and it stank.

This was the end. I really had had enough.

I went out the front door and got into my truck. I drove south on Borrego Pass Road. I concocted a scheme as I drove, a purpose, a destination: I had to make a phone call in Prewitt; I had to buy a few necessaries in the store at the gas station; I had to put gas in my truck. I had to get out. But I drove past Prewitt and west onto Interstate 40.

Soon I was in Gallup. I didn't stop there either. I wanted to stop, but I couldn't. I pressed on and drove to Window Rock. I started to worry that I might not stop driving at all, that I might just drive north until I ran out of road, leaving all my effects in the duplex. Someone could have it all, I thought. I didn't need any of it. I couldn't even remember now what was in there, what stuff I owned, what stuff was so important I had humped it all the way south to New Mexico. I drove on through the cool trees on the Fort Defiance Plateau and into Ganado to Mary's place.

I knocked on the door. She wasn't home. I dropped the tailgate of my truck and sat on it awhile. Then I lay back and stared at the sky, my legs dangling.

Mary Juzwik taught the eighth grade at Ganado Middle School. This would be her third year teaching on the rez. Her first year, she taught the fifth grade, all subjects, at Kinlichee Boarding School, just a few miles east of Ganado. I admired Mary's energy and optimism. She could find such excitement and hope in the world as to become giddy, to shake a little in her hands, to laugh recklessly. Of all the people I knew, she had achieved a level of physical and mental toughness that I wanted for myself. I thought of her as impervious to loneliness and pain. Her students in Ganado called her "Miss Just-wicked." She wore her brown, curly hair cut just above her shoulders. Her face looked always brushed by the desert, her eyes gentle and open. Her ears were tiny little things. She had finished her undergraduate degree in English at Wheaton College, an interdenominational Christian school in Illinois with the motto "For Christ and his Kingdom." But Mary had not come to the reservation to proselytize; rather, she loved the desert and she loved being outside. She was a runner, a rock climber, a backpacker. She loved big sky and open spaces. In fact, I didn't know the side of her that would have prospered at a place like Wheaton. She mentioned her experiences there only cursorily, as if she had moved on from that life, moved on from that kind of thinking to a new cosmology founded on a love and respect for nature, perhaps not unlike that of traditional Navajos.

Mary walked up, saw my truck, and came over. She'd been working in her classroom. She seemed to know just what was going on. She invited me in and made me a cup of Navajo tea. I helped her prepare a light meal. We ate and talked and shared the closing hours of the evening. Mary consoled me, she patched me up. She said that her first year teaching Navajo kids went about the same.

"How did you survive it?" I asked, knowing she wouldn't really have an answer.

"They'll come around," she assured me. "It'll get better. They're just testing you."

"That's what Lauren said."

"It's true," Mary said. "I'll help you. Whatever you need."

I felt a little silly for feeling so weak, but better now that Mary offered her help. "All right," I said. "I don't like to ask for help, you know."

"I know. But you have to. Or you won't make it here."

In the morning, I got up before the sun. I had to drive the one hundred miles back to Borrego before my classes started. Mary got up with me, and made me a strong cup of coffee. Before I left she invited me to come back on Friday night and stay for the weekend, to meet some of her friends in Ganado and explore some places she knew. I said I would, gratefully. Now I had something to look forward to.

TWO

SCHOOL DAYS

I heard the big yellow school buses cross over the cattle guard on their way out. It was the double pulse of the tires over the steel grate that drew me, a rhythm I would become so accustomed to I could keep time by it. I looked out the kitchen window and watched as the red lights high on the back of the bus faded out into the milky dawn. Most mornings, I was up early, and I would hear the buses twice, first on their way out, empty and cold, and then on their way in carrying the children, who were the center of everyone's work and life here. And when I came to know the bus drivers, I also came to know who drove which bus over which route, the drivers making the longer routes departing first, as they came to a stop at the cattle guard, idled a moment, and then pressed out into the darkness.

These were no ordinary school buses. They sat high off the ground on huge knobby tires. They were tightly sprung, so as to negotiate the rough dirt roads. One of them had four-wheel drive, so it was dependable in every kind of weather. When it snowed or rained at Borrego, I listened for the buses, my indication that the weather was or was not going to stop us from holding school. Even on days of questionable weather, however, the children of Borrego had to eat, and there was likely nothing for them at home. Classes would be canceled, but the buses would be trotted out to bring the kids in to breakfast, and then hustle them back home. Such days were known locally as "consommé days." It was a rare and violent storm indeed that forced Bob King to cancel school completely. But it did happen, like the winter storm some years ago, Bob King told me, when the National Guard air-dropped supplies into Borrego because the snow was so deep no one could get in or out for days. When Navajos were sliding off the roads in the mud and snow, abandoning their vehicles in the ditches, the Borrego buses motored on, delivering the schoolchildren safely to their homes and sometimes collecting people along the way who found themselves unexpectedly on foot. This was an unspoken law of reservation life: never pass by someone on foot on a dirt road. You stopped and offered them a ride because it was not a matter of *if*, but of *when* that person on foot would be you.

I readied myself and went to school.

Deena Bell greeted me in the front office. She was a tall, graceful Navajo woman with light-colored skin and a round face. She paid a great deal of attention to making herself up, the colors worked into her cheeks and across her eyes, her nails long and manicured, her hair black as jet and sprayed up into a tent on top of her head. Her eyes were dark brown, maybe black, and warm and inviting. She was the most beautiful Navajo woman I had met. She sat eternally behind the front desk. I rarely saw her standing or walking, just there behind the desk, a bright face to greet me. Later I came to know her outside of school, and to know Kestrel, her son, and Frank, her husband.

"Good morning!" she said. "How are the kids treating you? I sure hope they're not giving you any trouble."

"It's okay," I said. "I think I'm doing all right."

"Please ask if you need anything," Deena said. "The first couple weeks are always the hardest for new teachers. We'll make sure you get what you need. Right, girls?"

"We sure will," said Arlene, who sat at the desk next to Deena. Betsy, who was busy digging in a file drawer, nodded her head.

"Please ask us," Deena said, and she winked at me.

"May I use your phone again?" I asked.

"Of course you can," Deena said.

"I need to try Navajo Communications again about getting my phone hooked up," I explained. "I can't seem to get an answer out of them. They just tell me to call back later."

She paused and looked at me. "Hmmm," she said. "Well, if they say that again, you should try going down there. You'll never get anything out of a Navajo over the telephone. You have to go talk with them face to face."

"All right," I said. "I'll go down there."

"Go soon," she said. "Do it real soon."

"All right."

I dialed the number. The receptionist at Navajo Communications told me to be patient, to wait, just for awhile, she said. The company planned to rebuild the entire system up to Borrego Pass, and then everyone living there would have a telephone in their home.

"That's great news!" I said. "How long will it take?"

"Well, I'm not sure," the receptionist said. "Not long, anyway. If you can just wait for awhile . . ."

"I can do that," I said. "Should I call back in a couple weeks?"

"Oh no, don't worry about that. It'll all be finished up soon," she assured me. "We'll take care of it. Thank you very much for calling. You have a nice day."

"I will. Thank you." I hung up the phone. "Deena! Really good news," I said, and then I told her all about it.

"Is it?" she said, singing the words out into a question. She glanced at Arlene. Then her eyes refocused on me like she had remembered something. "Well, yeah. That is good news. But how long do you plan on staying here? They've been saying that for the past five years."

My heart sank. "What?"

"Yeah," Deena said. "At least five years."

"Good morning, Mr. Caswell," said Louise, making her way through the door. She wore a big, loose dress, and she walked with a limp, a sort of jerking lean to one side. Her face was wrinkled and groggy, sun-worn, and her short white hair went in every direction. "Have you had your breakfast yet this morning? You can have breakfast with the kids if you want."

"Yeah, I know. I usually eat before, though."

"Not bad food," she said, a bit out of breath. "And the kids like you to have breakfast with them if you can."

I nodded. Then I said, "Thank you for your help, Deena."

I needed to let the telephone thing go for now. The workday was about to begin, and I would have plenty of time to be miserable about it later.

"You ready for the day?" Louise asked me, but she didn't wait for an answer. "Deena, what about that parent meeting today? Are they coming in or not?"

Then she turned back to me. "I've hardly gotten around today," she apologized. "But I just wanted to make sure everything is going okay for you. Do you need anything or can I help you somehow?" Then she looked back at Deena. "So what's the story?"

"I think I'm okay," I said. "Thank you."

"We told him the same thing," Deena said. "Anything he needs, he should come to us."

"Good girls," Louise said.

"And they're coming in, for sure," Deena said. "As sure as that can be."

"Oh, god," Louise said. "I was hoping they'd cancel. I can hardly face it today."

"Well," Deena said. "You know them. You probably won't have to."

I wondered about Louise, a big white woman in her later years, living alone in the desert, teaching Navajo kids. How long had she been here? Why was she here? She didn't seem to fit in on the reservation, but then maybe no white person did. Maybe no Navajo person did either. Navajo people belong to this landscape, to be sure—the reservation covers roughly that same country they lived in before the U.S. government took it by force—but I mean the reservation, the genesis of it, which was more akin to a prison than a sanctuary. Maybe the question came to me because during the brief time I had so far spent with Louise, I doubted that she was happy. I saw longing in her eyes, and the sense of having given up on something. Had she come here looking for adventure, like me, and then stayed so long that life off the rez had become foreign and disagreeable to her? Or was she desperate to get out but found that her résumé had become unsuitable to schools elsewhere? From the viewpoint of many mainstream schools in the United States, public and private, the line between teaching in foreign lands for experience and adventure (and I must include American Indian reservations as foreign lands), and teaching in foreign lands because something about you isn't quite right or isn't quite mainstream, or perhaps because you sabotaged your professional reputation with some unsavory activity, might be drawn at about five years of teaching and about twenty-eight years old, maybe thirty. After that, school administrators seem to regard such experience as questionable. Suspect. A little weird. Did Louise wake up one morning and find she was stuck on the rez? Or did she live here by choice?

Still, Louise knew her business at the school, and she obviously cared about these kids. And that, as any teacher will affirm, is all that matters.

Lauren came into the office and greeted us all. She asked me,

"How have you been? You need anything? Is everything going okay? Do you need anything?"

"That's what we said," Deena said.

"I'm here," I said. "Just settling in. Everything's all right."

"You're probably overwhelmed with all this new stuff. It'll calm down soon. You can ask me for anything anytime," she said.

"Thank you. I will."

Except for the principal and the school board, Borrego Pass School was run by women. The majority of the teachers were women, and women ran the kitchen, the purchasing office, and the payroll and drove half of the buses. And I would discover that the girls far out-performed the boys in the classroom. This corresponded, to my mind, with the fact that traditionally the Navajo social structure is matriarchal. It's the wife who controls the family home, or *hogan*, and the land, which is often passed down from her family. She is said to "own" the children. They become part of her clan, rather than her husband's, so that descendants are traced through the woman's line. She owns her jewelry. She owns the sheep from which she spins her wool, as well as the income from the sale of the blankets and rugs she weaves. In the old days, a Navajo wife was far more liberated than women of white America. Later, due to the influence of white people and white inheritance laws, matriarchal practices atrophied until it wasn't so uncommon for a Navajo woman to live on her husband's land, if he had any. Still, the matriarchal structure runs as an under-current through Navajo life and seemed to influence everything that happened at Borrego. I felt at all times in the care of women.

"Lauren," I said. "I do have one question. What about a textbook?"

So far I had gotten by without a book, but I was running out of ideas. I didn't need a text to teach writing, but it was the reading I needed most, some kind of story and essay collection.

"Right," Lauren said. "I've been thinking about that. I want to order individual books for my classes, so I won't be using my textbooks. Would you like to look at them?"

"Look at them? I'll take them," I said. "Whatever they are."

"But there is also the option of me keeping the textbooks and you using whole works," she said.

"No, no. You go ahead with your plans. I'll take the texts."

"Oh, good," she said. "Good then. I prefer to teach whole works anyway."

"When can I pick up the books? In a week or so?"

"Anytime. Right now. Today," Lauren said.

"That would be so great. Can I send my class over to pick them up?" I asked.

"That would work great."

After breakfast, the sixth-grade class formed an orderly line behind me at the cafeteria door. I had been sitting with the same group of sixth-grade boys from that first morning, listening to them talk and joke. This was a critical part of the school day: most of the students at Borrego didn't get breakfast at home because there wasn't any, and some of them came to school just to eat breakfast. The school certainly couldn't expect the students to be attentive in class when they were hungry.

When the line quieted down a little, and all the kids looked at me ready to go, I led them down the hall to my classroom, the boys' hair shining and wet from the bathroom sink and swept back with the liquid soap they put in there to look like Chicano gangbangers in Albuquerque. But they weren't Chicano gangbangers. They were Navajo boys, and they spent a lot of time outside in the sun and they were always talking about their dogs and killing rabbits to feed them, and how they'd hunt half the morning for their horse wandering somewhere out there in the desert, and when they found it, they'd have to catch it, and then they'd leap on it with no saddle and no bridle and ride and ride and ride.

"I heard you come from China!" Shane Yazzie said as we stepped into the classroom.

"You remember the rule," I said. "You have to raise your hand if you want to say something."

Shane sat down. His hand shot up.

"Yes, Shane?"

"I heard you came from China!"

"No. Not China. I'm from Oregon. But I worked in Japan for a few years."

"That means you're Chinese?" Shane said.

"No, Japanese," said Kyle Bigfoot.

"You have to raise your hand," I said.

Kyle raised his hand as high as he could, and so did Shane.

"Kyle?" I said. "Yes?"

"That means you're Chinese!" Shane said, then he clapped his hand over his mouth to stop himself.

"No, it's mines," Kyle said. "I'm next. I raised my hand."

I never knew if this was a carryover from the Navajo language, or just a glitch in understanding English, but most of these kids added an *s* to pluralize words that didn't need it. "Mines" was one example. And "reals" was another. "For reals, Mr. Caswell?" they would say. And when they said goodbye it came out, "See you laters, Mr. Caswell." One of Mary's students over in Ganado told her that his family was headed out to cut firewood that weekend. He said, "We're goin' to the woods to get some woods."

Shane still held his hand over his mouth and puffed out his cheeks like he might explode.

"Yes, Kyle, you raised your hand," I said.

"You're Japanese," Kyle said. "From Japan, way over there."

"No. I'm still American. I just worked in Japan."

"Hey, you gotta Japan-girl?" asked John George.

"Your hand," I said.

"Oh, yeah," John George said. He put his hand up and said, "You gotta Japan-girl?"

"We have to get to work," I said. "First I need five of you to go over to Mrs. Sittnick's room—"

Every hand went up.

"—to get our textbooks," I said.

All the hands went down.

"Naw. We don't need no books," said Shane. "Let's just go outside and play around."

"Yeah," said John George. "Let's just go out there and do nothin'."

"We have to study," I said. "We have to practice reading and writing."

"No way," Shane said. "Let's just do nothing."

Leanne Yazzie raised her hand. "I'll go do it," she said. "And Valeria and Gay will come with me."

"Is that right?" I asked.

Valeria and Gay nodded their heads.

"And pick me, Mr. Caswell," John George said. "I can do it."

"Okay," I said. "And I need one more volunteer."

The room went still. No one said anything.

"Just one more volunteer," I said. "Then we'll have this job done."

Still no one moved.

Then Leanne slowly raised her hand. She looked around the room. "What's a vol-lun-teer?" she asked, almost whispering.

"I mean one more person to get books," I said.

Six hands went up.

"Okay, Kyle," I said. "Why don't you go."

"Yeah!" he said.

I put everyone else to work making room on the shelves for the books. Lauren advised that I assign each student a textbook but that they leave the books in the classroom rather than taking them home. We opened up a space, and the five volunteers began filling the shelves with books, big, heavy hardback books, each with a softcover workbook. They brought in the books for the seventh and eighth grades too.

"Here you go, Mr. Caswell," Valeria said. "We're almost done now."

She hefted her pile up on the shelf, and I noticed blood leaking out of her left ear.

"Valeria," I said. "Your ear is bleeding." I could see the circle around the ear on the side of her face where something had struck her.

She put her hand there. "No it's not," she said, disgusted with me.

"Yes it is," I said. "Did you fall or something?"

"No."

"Do you need to see the nurse?"

"No," she said.

"Let me see it," I said.

She pulled away. "No," she said. "Just mind your own beeswax."

I had obviously invaded her space, but it seemed necessary. "May I just take a look?" I said. "You might need to see the nurse."

"She got hit," John George said.

"Shut up, stupit," Valeria said.

"I'm not gonna touch it. Just let me take a look," I said.

"Yeah," John George said. "He hit you right there on your ear."

"No," said Valeria, jerking back again. She made a fist and waved it at John. "I'll hit you."

"No," John George said, " 'Cause you're crazy and too slow!"

Valeria went after him then, moving fast around the desks, and John George leaped away as she went for him, crashing back into a chair that tipped and clattered on the floor, both moving faster now, around the edge of the classroom along the windows. John passed the blackboard and ran out the door. Valeria followed, and I heard them running down the hallway at top speed.

"Jesus," I muttered.

"Jesus!" Shane said.

"She's gonna beat him up," Kyle said. "And she hits real hard, too."

I looked down the hall, but they were both gone. I saw Lauren stepping out of her classroom. I waved to her. She waved back and then looked down the hallway toward the front office. We heard the double doors that led outside onto the playground shut.

"It's recess time, Mr. Caswell," said Kyle. "Let's go! Hurry."

"Yeah," said Shane. " 'Cause maybe they're gonna fight."

"No fights," I said. "Don't let them fight."

Shane grinned. "I like to watch a fight."

"All right, you can go now," I said. "Don't run in the hallway."

They all ran down the hallway as fast as they could and out the front doors into the sun.

I met Lauren outside watching over the playground.

"What was that all about?" she asked.

"Have you seen Valeria today?"

"Valeria Benally," she said. It sounded like she already knew. "No, but I heard about it from Leanne."

"About her ear?"

"Yeah," Lauren said. And then Lauren told me the story.

Sometimes Navajo children have problems with their ears because they sit in the back of pickup trucks wherever they go, the winter and summer winds speeding across their bare ears. It often causes hearing loss. But that's not what happened to Valeria. A bad uncle took drunken liberties with her younger sister. He raped her. Valeria might have been next, but she fought him and hit him and struggled to break free, when he clapped her on the side of her head with his hand. She ran to get her good uncle to help. The drunk uncle shot the good uncle in the chest with a pistol. Valeria escaped into the hills with her little sister and they lived out there for two days. They did not eat anything for two days. By the time Valeria's grandmother returned from Window Rock, the bad uncle was in jail. He stole a car in Gallup, and the police chased him all the way to Albuquerque.

"What do we do?" I asked Lauren.

"Well, Bob King knows about it. And so does Louise. I don't know what we do. We don't do anything. We just teach them. We can't do anything."

"We can't do anything?" I said.

"Well, I think we've done everything we can, I mean. Someone reported it, and I think they're making sure she's staying somewhere safe right now. That's about as far as it goes. From here, we just teach them."

We stood there looking out, the playground awash in children running and shouting and playing like children, and I saw where the desert fell away into the morning sun and a red-tailed hawk rode the currents there along the rocky edge headed south and stretching out into the flats where the hunting was good in the mornings.

Here, then, were the two opposing forces at Borrego—its austere, clean beauty, and its belligerent, ugly darkness. I had only been here a couple of weeks, and already I felt utterly helpless and broken in the face of it. This was a violent world, one that stole energy and hope from its people, beat them down, and then kept them down, possibly forever. There must have been something else here too, something soft and caring, something safe and loving, something good that held this community together. If so, I could not, as yet, see it. Perhaps in time I would. But why, I had to ask, did I so readily witness the cruel and violent face of Borrego, and nothing of the other side? Why would a community like this one show me, a stranger, this dark part of itself, and hide its best qualities? Was this an American characteristic, or was it specifically Navajo? Whatever, I began to wonder what effect living and working in such conditions might have on me. Would I too find my energy and hope stolen away? Would I give up on my students, my fellow teachers and friends, myself?

Not much later, I moved out of the duplex. Fifty years of tree roots growing through the underground sewage lines brought the maintenance man, Everett, to my place every couple of days, the days when shit backed up into the bathtub while I showered. He carried the big electric snake up onto the roof and drove it down some pipe and ran the motor. It thumped and whined up there like a great pterodactyl in amorous display. I stumped around in the kitchen below with dark remnants of the event still outlining my toenails. Everett came again and again, hauling that heavy machine up a ladder onto the roof, until he tired of it, and left it up there. At last the maintenance foreman, Dean West, decided that it wasn't going to end and he'd have to dig a trench and replace the sewage line. That would take, he told me, oh, maybe a week or two. I should move into the empty trailer near the fence across the way. I could easily walk everything over. It wasn't far.

"I can wait a week or two, no problem," I said. "Until you get it fixed."

"Well, maybe it'll be a little longer," Dean said.

"How much longer?" I asked, recalling my conversation with Navajo Communications. "I like the place I'm in. I don't really want to live in the trailer."

"A bit longer," Dean said. "We're on Indian time, remember. You'll be happier if you move into the trailer."

In other words, instead of two or three weeks, it might be two or three months before he got to it, or even two or three years. What was the hurry? So I moved. The rent for the trailer was $150 a month, almost double what I had been paying for the duplex, but since it wasn't my fault about the tree roots, Dean said my rent would remain $80 a month.

"That's a good deal," he said. "You get all those rooms for half the money."

But I didn't want all those rooms. I had too much space in the duplex already. Everything I owned fit into the back of my truck. That trailer was going to swallow me whole. Yet, one lazy weekend, I toted everything over.

The trailer was comfortable enough, clean enough, when the wind didn't blow. When it did, the walls bowed and rattled, and sand sifted in through the gaps. I borrowed a vacuum from the janitor closet at school and used it to rake the green shag carpet clean. For the green linoleum in the kitchen I used a broom, and then got down on hands and knees and scrubbed it with a wet rag. I pulled the frosted mirrors off the wall in the main room and painted over the scars on the wallboard (I couldn't stand staring at myself all day).

In addition to the master bedroom with the attached bathroom on the west end of the trailer, I had two more bedrooms and a second bathroom down a narrow hallway on the east end. One of the two bedrooms looked out across Borrego Pass Road onto the low escarpment that rose up along the winter sun in the morning. The desert out there was green and inviting in the fall after the monsoon rains. A soft patch of grass grew up against that end of the trailer. The wind couldn't reach it here, and so whatever moisture the sky gave to the ground lingered a little longer there than in other places. I thought about putting my desk down there, and my books, so that I could watch the sun come up in the mornings, but I couldn't stand the thought of spreading myself out all over the trailer. I wanted Dean to repair the sewer lines and open the cinder block duplex again, though I knew that it was futile, that he'd never get the job done while I lived at Borrego. I felt an uncontrollable urge for something smaller and safer to live in. Someplace smaller and safer. I wanted one room with one door. My feeble response to this impulse was to shut the doors on the two extra bedrooms and the bathroom and hang a towel from the ceiling at the head of the hallway to keep the heat from going down there in the winter. I brought my blue canoe in out of the weather and stored it upside down in the hallway; at least that long corridor had some use. I lived only in the master bedroom and the living room, which was open to the kitchen. I was living scared in Navajoland. I didn't feel at home here, so I lived in a state of fearful readiness. If I had to, I could pack up and get out fast. Moving from the duplex to the trailer revitalized this impulse in me. I didn't want to take my things out of their little boxes again. I lived in a state of preparation for some frightening eventuality, but I knew this state was a measure of me and not of the place. Huddled in my little rooms in the trailer, I felt an overwhelming agitation, a fear of the place that crept up into my chest and knocked at my heart like the wind.

In that new space, in that new feverish agitation, I sat at my desk, placed sidelong to the living room window, and wrote long, wistful letters to Sakura. I ached for her. I imagined her there in my trailer, sleeping in my bed in the early morning, and cooking with me in the evenings. I imagined her face so close to mine, and her smell, the beautiful presence of her, that deep female way she blossomed in my nose. As a parting gift she had given me Yukio Mishima's *The Sound of Waves*, a novel about youthful love in a fishing village. I kept it on my desk beside me, because inside she had left a note card graced by a flower she painted in watercolor and scented with her perfume. I would open the book as I wrote to her, and draw in her memory from those fragrant pages.

"Where we goin' now, Mr. Caswell?" Shane asked. "We goin' to China?"

"Hey, yeah, let's go over there to China," Manny said. "They got a lot of cool stuff over there."

"Naw, naw," said Kyle Bigfoot. "Let's just go outside and mess around."

"You guys!" said Leanne Yazzie. "Stop it. Ssshhh. Or we won't get to go."

My sixth-grade class was lined up against the wall in the cafeteria after breakfast that October morning, following standard procedure. Every class lined up this way before leaving the cafeteria, and the rule was that everyone had to be quiet and stand at attention before we could go. This didn't seem to me like a rule anyone would want to follow, because the reward was going to class. But no matter. When my class had lined up that morning, I had told them I had a surprise for them. We were not going to the science room for class; instead, we were going on a journey.

The journey I promised wasn't much of a journey at all, and yet I hoped it would improve my teaching life at Borrego. I had grown tired of sharing space in the science room. One of the portable classrooms at the edge of the playground went mostly unused. A double-wide manufactured building, it featured two main rooms, one on each side of the median; a small reading room with a collection of books; two bathrooms; and a kitchen. It housed some old computers that functioned well enough but had been forgotten when the school invested in new computers that were networked throughout the main building with access to two CD-Rom towers housed in the library. I needed only to arrange a classroom on one side of the portable, and leave the other for the computers that no one wanted. Bob King agreed to my proposal, and I moved my classes out there right away. I had already moved my living quarters from the duplex into a trailer. I might as well teach in a trailer too, I thought.

"Yeah, for reals, Mr. Caswell. Let's go over there to China," said Shane, swinging his little rooster tail back behind his shoulders. "I want to be a China-man." He stretched his eyes out sideways.

"Hey, Mr. Caswell," Manny said. "Michael stepped in dog shit, I think. It smells real bad, too."

"Ooh, yeah," said Kyle Bigfoot. "I can smell it."

They laughed out loud.

Michael stood there grinning like he'd done it on purpose. He was a quiet, small boy, but I came to think of him as a master of deception, inventing little pranks and tricks which he unfolded daily, and for which someone else would be blamed.

Shane breathed in deep through his nose to take in the smell. "Ooh, yeah," he said. "Ooh, yeah! Smells so good."

The other boys giggled and breathed deep through their noses too and made farting sounds with their lips.

"C'mon, you guys," Leanne said. "We can't go unless we're quiet. I want to see where we're goin'."

"That's right," I said. "I'm just waiting for you to be quiet."

"Ahh, we ain't goin' nowhere 'cept over there to language arts," said John George.

"No, no, we're gonna go outside and mess around," said Kyle Bigfoot again. "Then we're gonna get a big truck and drive all the way over there to Gallup and drink some whiskey."

"Yeah, for reals, Mr. Caswell. Let's do it," said Shane.

"Yeah, c'mon!" said Charlie Hunter.

"Shut up, you stupit boys," Leanne said.

"Children!" Louise barked at them. "Mr. Caswell is waiting for you. And I'm waiting for Mr. Caswell. My class is ready to line up. So be! Quiet!" she said.

"I'm ready," I said, about to break the golden rule. "Let's go!" And I led my class out the front doors and into the sun.

I wondered what would happen next. The previous spring, when Lauren was hired, she had used this same portable as her classroom. That first morning, she lined up the sixth graders along the wall in the cafeteria, just as I had done. She demanded their attention and waited until they got quiet, just as I had failed to do, and she led them out the front doors into the sun, just as I was doing now. It was February and cold then, 40 degrees, maybe 30, and the sky was clear and too perfectly blue to be possible, the sun so bright it wanted to be warm, but it wasn't. When those sixth-grade boys hit daylight, they bolted, or five of them did. Lauren heard them behind her as the line broke apart into an amorphous pack of testicular whir and speed, and the boys came by her on both sides, their heads tilted back like Edwin Moses, their knees rising and pumping in the sprint, and they hit the corner of the building and disappeared around it. Lauren sauntered casually on, not worried at all about their prank, opened the door, went in, the girls following her, and prepared to begin the lesson. The boys would be along soon, she thought, just as soon as they got cold and tired. But Navajo boys like these are tough, and used to the cold, and they were not going to give up on their fun without a fight.

Well, they didn't show up, and they didn't show up, and they didn't show up, until Lauren felt she'd be remiss if she didn't go look for them. So she did. She went out with the girls onto the front porch, and one of the girls suggested that the boys might be hiding underneath the portable. And they *were* hiding underneath the portable in that cool, dark silence. They had crawled under through a gap in the skirting, and there they were, hiding in that happy darkness. She called for them to come out, but they wouldn't. She called again for them to come out, but no, they were not going to come out. Why should they? This was much more fun than reading class. So standing outside like that, Lauren began to talk with the girls about what nasty things lived under portables like this one—rats, she said, and black widows, real big fat ones, and poisonous snakes. Three of the five boys came out right away, but the other two were not afraid of anything. They stayed under there for the entire class. All Lauren could do was turn their names in to the front office.

The next day Bob King gave those boys what-for before they went outside to the portable. Lauren thought that would do it. It didn't. Those same two boys, those brave boys, those foolish boys, once they hit daylight, they were under the portable again, quick as weasels. This time Bob King came out to help, but they wouldn't come out for him either. At least not right away. Then some strange urge came into them, perhaps that same urge that drove them underneath in the first place, and they crawled back out. A teacher has two choices at such a juncture: rule by force, or rule by reward. Lauren chose reward. She developed a system founded on offering stickers for good behavior, for staying with her through the lesson, for trying hard. At the end of each week, anyone with ten stickers earned a little pack of peanut butter crackers. It seemed to work.

I heard the front doors of the school close behind the end of the line, and as we made our way out into the parking lot, I expected something out of the ordinary to happen, something wild, something I could write home about. But nothing happened. Everyone stayed in lockstep, and in fact, Shane, who liked to make things happen, began to walk in lockstep behind me, his right foot hitting the ground as mine did, and then his left foot hitting the ground as mine did, right, left, and so on. Was he mocking me? It didn't matter. Kyle Bigfoot picked it up behind Shane, left, right, left, right, and then Manny behind him, Michael, Leanne, even Leanne, Joseph Jones, Charlie Hunter, and right on down the line. Shane began to sing it out as we walked: "Left! Left! Left! Right! Left!" he sang. "Left! Left! Left! Right! Left!" And that's how we came to the portable.

"Remember what we learned last time?" I asked, as everyone found a seat. The room was small for the twelve to fifteen students in a typical Borrego class, but we could make it work. I had arranged the tables and chairs in a semicircle so everyone could see everyone else, and there was plenty of open space in the middle of the room. As I waited for a response to my question, I propped the outside door open to let the sun in.

"Does anyone remember what we learned last time?" I asked again.

"Nope," said Joseph Jones.

"Me neither," said Manny. "I'm stupit, Mr. Caswell."

"I know. I know," said Leanne.

"No, you're not," I said to Manny.

"Yeah, real stupit. My grandma even says so," Manny said, smiling big.

"That's 'cause you are," said Valeria.

"Just like you," said Manny.

"Anyway," I said. "I'll remind you. Last class we talked about the six steps in the writing process. Does anyone remember all of them? Or just one of them?"

"Yeah, Kyle Bigfoot said. "Hamburgers and french fries."

"I know one," said Leanne.

"No, it's going all crazy like this," said Charlie Hunter, and he shook his body like a madman and let his lips flap against his teeth.

"Aawww," said Manny, laughing. "That's crazy, isn't it, Mr. Caswell."

The girls in the room, most of them, except Valeria, were not amused at all. They rolled their eyes and stared at the ceiling.

"Okay! Okay. Okay." I said. "You need some paper. You're going to write this down now."

Everyone got out a sheet of paper or borrowed paper from someone else, and then waited, quiet and ready. This seemed always to work best, to have the class, especially the sixth graders, active. If they were not physically doing something—writing notes, writing in their journal, reading aloud, answering questions about the reading—the class was a bust.

"Number one," I said.

"I know one . . ." said Leanne.

"All right," I said. "What is it?"

"Drafting," Leanne said.

"Rafting!?" Joseph Jones said. "What?"

"Oh, I know, Mr. Caswell," Manny said. "That's when you go around in a big boat and crash through the waves."

"No, that's rafting," I said.

"Is it?" Manny said.

"Leanne said 'drafting,' which is right, but it's not the first one," I said. "It's the third one. We'll get to that one in a minute, okay? The first one is—"

"Prewriting," Leanne said.

"Yes, yes. Good," I said. "Prewriting. Write that in your notes."

"How do you spell it?" asked Michael Benally.

"Just a moment," I said. "I'll write it down for you on the board, if you give me a moment."

"Yeah, okay," said Michael, and he nodded his head in approval.

"What's that mean?" asked Valeria.

"Yeah, what are you talking about?" asked Charlie Hunter. "What's a process?"

"I'll explain that too," I said, speaking very slowly and calmly, "after I write it down on the board."

"Oh, okay," said Manny. "Let's hear it. Tell us then."

I wrote the word on the board. "You see," I said, "if you're going to write a paper or a report or something for one of your teachers, you have to go through six different steps. The first one is prewriting. Prewriting is when—"

"How come you gotta do it?" asked John George. "You don't need steps. You just write it."

"Yeah, just write it anyways," said Valeria.

"Or don't write nothin'," said Kyle.

"I can't write it, Mr. Caswell. My pencil's somehow," said Manny.

"Somehow?" I asked. "What do you mean, somehow?"

"I don't know," Manny said. "It's just somehow. It doesn't work."

"Here, use mine," I said.

I would hear this usage of the word "somehow" routinely after this, for anything that didn't work, or anything new or out of the ordinary. "Mr. Caswell, my stomach is somehow. Can I go to the nurse?" or "Mr. Caswell, your hair looks somehow," or "My boyfriend is somehow."

"All right. Let's focus," I said. "Yes, you can just write it, but if you follow these steps, it helps keep you organized. You can write a better report this way."

"I don't care about no report," said Valeria.

"Me neither," said Shane. "I don't care. But I like low-rider bikes, Mr. Caswell."

"Yeah, that's cheap anyways," said John George.

"Let's just go outside and mess around," said Kyle Bigfoot.

"Okay, okay," I said. "Look, here's the thing. I'm going to give you these six steps—they're just six words. You don't have to understand them, just remember them. Just write them on your paper and what they mean. Then you can look them over, and then I'll give you a quiz. Okay?"

"Okay," Leanne said.

Everyone else just sat there, staring at me.

I wrote out all the words on the board with little definitions next to them, like this:

1. *prewriting*—write some ideas as fast as you can
2. *organizing*—organize prewriting ideas that are the same into groups
3. *drafting*—write a report using these groups to make paragraphs
4. *revising*—read your report and make it better
5. *proofreading*—check for spelling and grammar mistakes
6. *typing*—type your report and turn it in

"For now," I said as I wrote, "you don't need to understand everything. Mostly you need to know that writing happens by taking these steps. These steps make it easier, and you'll get better grades."

"Are you from Mars or what?" Valeria said. "What are you talking about?"

"Yeah, you're actin' all crazy," said Kyle Bigfoot.

I noticed then that Michael had gotten up and was wandering around in the back of the room, looking up at the ceiling.

"Hey, Mr. Caswell," said Shane. "What do they eat over there in China anyways?"

With the exception of team teaching in Japan, I'd never taught the sixth grade. I didn't really know much about sixth graders—what worked, what didn't work; what they knew, what they didn't know. I couldn't determine whether the material was too difficult, I was being unclear, or these kids were trying to drive me insane. I was just doing my best with what limited information I had. The obvious signals coming back to me from the class were that my best wasn't working, at least not yet. But it felt good that we were at least talking about the course material, and not every jab and joke was directed at me. I looked at the clock. Twenty-five minutes left. An immense span of time, I thought, with total chaos imminent. I needed to move them on to something else, and fast.

"I think we're about done with this for now," I said. "Did everyone write down 'prewriting'? We'll talk about that next time."

"Yes," everyone said, which was a complete lie. But no matter.

"Shane. Why don't you choose a book from the shelf back there. I'll read it to you."

"Yeah!" he said. "I'll get one."

"A short one," I said.

"Can I get one too?" Gay DeLuz said, speaking for the first time all period.

"Yes, why don't you," I said. "Maybe we have time for two books."

"If we need three, I'll get one, Mr. Caswell," Manny said.

And that's how the day ended.

On some ordinary day, cutting vegetables in my trailer kitchen, I discovered a bottle connected to the water line beneath the sink. I was just leaning over to put something in the garbage, and I leaned over a little farther than usual. It looked like an oxygen tank for scuba diving. Why hadn't I noticed it before? I asked Bob King about it, and he told me it was an ion exchange filter to even out the spiking radiation levels from so much uranium mining in the 1950s and 1960s. The same technology is useful for stripping arsenic from drinking water.

Later I learned that a cattle dip vat site at Casamero Lake, the Navajo community five miles south on Borrego Pass Road, is listed as a Superfund site by the U.S. Environmental Protection Agency, along with dip vat sites at nearby Crownpoint and Thoreau. What is the danger of living near dip vat sites? Arsenic poisoning in the soil, and the ground and surface water. For the better part of the twentieth century, arsenic was part of the recipe for pesticides used to combat parasite infestation in sheep, cattle, horses, mules, and goats. Because such pesticide solutions required large volumes of water, they were constructed near wells or good surface water. Ingesting arsenic in high volumes through water, food, or the air causes death, and in low volumes causes nausea and vomiting, abnormal heart rhythm, damage to blood vessels, and low production of white and red blood cells. And, of course, arsenic can cause various cancers: skin, lung, bladder, prostate, liver, kidney.

I discovered other nearby Superfund sites: the Blackjack Mine at Smith Lake, the Doe and Santa Fe Blue Water Uranium Mines near Prewitt, and the Brown Vandever Mine and the Febco Mine, also at Prewitt. In McKinley County, where Borrego is, I counted thirty-seven Superfund sites in all. In neighboring Cibola County another eighteen sites are listed, including the Kerr-McGee Nuclear Corporation and the Anaconda Company Bluewater Uranium Mill, both at Grants, and the Poison Canyon Mining District in Milan.

I began buying bottled water in Gallup. I collected a half dozen empty milk jugs and routinely filled them at a water station at Wal-Mart or at Smith's grocery store. I kept this up for three months, but, living in the desert, I began to feel trapped by this meager water supply. I used the bottled water only for drinking. I cooked with water from the tap, and bathed in it, and drank water from the drinking fountain at school sometimes. I asked Bob King again, and he assured me that the water was safe. And then he said, "Well, at least it's easier just to drink it. Everyone else does."

I started drinking it too.

The Grants Mineral Belt in the vicinity of Grants, New Mexico, is one of the largest uranium ore deposits in the world. During the Cold War, uranium mining became increasingly profitable as it was tied to issues of national security. The local people, mostly Navajo and puebloan people, became increasingly alarmed about this mining because of the potential health risks, which would persist for what amounts to forever. They held meetings, issued statements, tried to resist the poisoning of their ancestral lands. It did them little good. The mining companies, primarily Kerr-McGee and the Vanadium Corporation of America, extracted what was profitable and then pulled out, leaving behind deadly radioactive tailing piles, poisoned water and soils, and a Navajo labor force unemployed and infected with cancer. On July 16, 1979, an earth dam ruptured near Church Rock, off I-40 near Gallup, spilling over 95 million gallons of radioactive wastewater into the Puerco River drainage. Many experts consider this spill the largest nuclear accident in U.S. history, larger even than the accident at Three Mile Island. The media mostly ignored it, and as a result, few people have ever heard about it.

So here I was, breathing, drinking, eating, living a few dozen miles from the greatest radioactive spill in my country's history. The ground I walked on, the air I breathed, the vistas I marveled at, had all been poisoned. Along with all the people I worked with at Borrego and the students here, along with everyone living in the region—Navajos, whites, Zunis, Hispanics—I was part of the generation that was inheriting a poisoned land. But there was one primary difference between me and the Navajo people at Borrego: I planned to leave, eventually, and they did not. Not ever.

I heard a knock at my front door. It was a Saturday, and the last thing I expected was someone at my door.

"Hello," I said, crossing the room. "Just a minute."

"Hello?" I heard from outside.

I opened the door to Gay DeLuz, one of my sixth-grade students. Her long black hair was tied into long black braids, and her eyes were dark and direct. She looked happy to see me. A big car waited for her with the engine running.

"You wanna buy a cherry pie?" she asked.

"No," I said.

"How 'bout an apple pie?" she asked. "Only one dollar. I made them myself. I baked 'em last night at my grandma's."

She pulled back the red-and-white-checkered cotton cloth covering the basket she held in the crook of her arm. It was full of little handmade pies wrapped in cellophane, little pies like Mexican empanadas, browned and golden, with fork marks around the edges where she had pinched the crusts together. I could smell them now, and they smelled real good.

"No," I said again. "I don't have any money."

She knew I was lying and frowned.

My response was automatic, I think, and rude, even cruel. During my travels I had adopted "no" as a standard answer when offered anything from anyone I didn't really know. Especially food. Better to decline something likely good than accept anything potentially bad and end up with a crampy stomach or diarrhea or worse. Besides that, I had begun to build an attitude against the many Navajo children selling jewelry and trinkets in restaurants in Gallup. In the beginning, these children all looked so sad and needy that I wanted to say yes to every one of them. They would file by my table with a bright display, everything laid out beautifully. "You wanna buy some?" they'd ask. When I was with Mary at, say, the Eagle Café on Route 66, she would straighten her face, shake her head, and wave the poor children away. So callous, I'd thought at first, but it came to happen so often. I learned that a parent, or an uncle or aunt, or even an older sibling or cousin waited outside while the little ones went in to make the sale. Mary's hardened position was more about survival, not stinginess or cruelty. You buy from one little salesperson and a whole flood of them break through the door to get at you. Down here on the rez, we white folks were trying to survive too, if even in a different way. And besides, how many pairs of cheap earrings does a guy need?

Had I not been so guarded, I might have said yes to Gay. In truth,

I might have liked a couple of those pies for breakfast. They certainly smelled good. But I was a traveler trying to look like I fit in, an outsider posing as an insider. What escaped me in that moment was that my policy worked in reverse: saying no kept me outside, because I hadn't considered being neighborly.

Gay didn't say anything more to me, but her countenance fell. She turned and walked back to the car. I watched her get in. The car drove away, fishtailing a little in the gravel and raising an angry plume of dust down the sad road.

THREE

THE ROAD TO CROWNPOINT

Rain fell softly across the windshield of my truck as I crossed the cattle guard at the school entrance and drove out the empty dirt road northwest to Crownpoint. The sky was light over there, dark over here. Sun pulsed in and out of the truck windows. The rain lasted only a moment, but the air was wet and electric. A thunderstorm was brewing.

I just wanted to use the telephone. I would have used the pay phone inside the school, but the doors were already locked tight for the night and I hadn't been entrusted with a key. I was restless, lonely, tired of being alone. I wanted to hear the voice of someone I knew. Sakura's voice from across the sea in Hokkaido. Mary's voice. My parents' or one of my sisters'. Anyone's.

A mile from campus I came to the Borrego Pass Trading Post. I pulled up in front of the squat brick building. It was tucked in close to the big sandstone mesa, and other buildings grew out from the sides and behind it, including a little barn and corral right up against the rock where it came down along the road. Deena, the receptionist at school, had told me that I should introduce myself to the managers, Merle and Rosie Moore. They were good people, she said, very friendly and helpful. They lived in a house behind the Trading Post and were almost always there. They sold gasoline from the pump out front and a little bit of hay from the barn. Inside the store, the Moores stocked canned goods and dry goods, basic hardware, ice cream, soda pop, and candy. They also sold and traded silver jewelry and other traditional arts, like kachina dolls, mostly made by local Navajo artists.

A kachina is a wooden doll carved and adorned to represent one of hundreds of Navajo and puebloan spirits (primarily Hopi and Zuni in these parts). These spirits are not gods; they are intermediaries between the people and the gods. They often live in the mountains, and they come to dance and restore harmony between all living things. The men who perform these ceremonial dances wear elaborately decorated masks and are said to become the kachina spirits they represent. The dances are especially important for fertility and for bringing rain.

I spotted a pay phone outside the front doors of the Trading Post. Maybe I wouldn't have to go all the way to Crownpoint after all. I got out and walked up onto the front porch. The sign in the window read "Closed." I peered in through the glass. A pale darkness covered the interior and the front counter of the little store. I could just make out the great collection of kachinas arranged on shelves along the back wall. They seemed to be looking at me. And in the glass case in front of them, rows of beautiful silver things—rings and bracelets, pendants and concho belts—gleaming a little in the low light.

When I got the job offer at Borrego, I had called Sakura to tell her the good news. I was employed again, and off on a new adventure. We had parted in Hokkaido on good terms, making our vows to each other, our promises to see each other soon, and perhaps never again to part.

"Do you think," she had said, when I told her the good news, "I could stay with you there in New Mexico? They have one of silver artists there," she said. "I want to learn more about making silvers."

She was an artist without specialization who loved to work in all kinds of mediums. She loved to paint, she loved textiles, and mostly she loved to explore.

"You want to come and live with me?" I asked. "Really?"

"I don't have much here," she said. "Just my little job and my families. I miss the States, and I could learn how to make those jewelries. I have some little money saved."

"Yes, you could apprentice with some Navajo silversmith, maybe. Or learn weaving. Or paint every day."

"And I could help you make a home there," she said. "We could loving each other all the time."

"Sounds like a dream," I said.

I felt something cool across my back. The wind had picked up, and it had begun to rain again, lightly but steadily. Large round drops dotted the dusty ground around my truck. I remembered the pay phone. I put the receiver to my ear. Nothing. The line was dead. I hit the cancel lever several times. Still nothing.

I drove on. The road crested and started down the northwest side of the pass. I wound my way through the stands of layered rock and earth, along a long deep canyon where the road fell away. From the driver's seat I could not see the bottom of it. Bob King had told me that this narrow section of road along the chasm was not so narrow a few years back. During a thunderstorm, a big pickup truck carrying four Navajos up front in the cab, and a couple of children in the back under a tarp in the rain, came through this place as the sky cracked and blew. Water came down from the mesa and flowed over the road, washing under the truck and floating it up, carving a path beneath it. Perhaps the truck remained suspended there for a moment or two, the water unsure of how to handle such a big thing, and then just as someone might have realized the danger they were all in and made motions for the door—"*Get out!*"—the water surged and dragged half the road, the truck, and all those people over the edge. No one survived. The truck is down there still. Later on one of my

long walks through the desert, I went down in search of it, and found
it, at least I thought I did, mostly buried now, frozen in the mud by
years of storms, the doors cracked and lifted like the shell casings of
a desiccated beetle.

I drove alongside the canyon there and down through the sharpened pass, through a narrow opening in the mountain's face and out
onto the long, bumpy flats. I passed a few scattered hogans, dilapidated things, some with a mongrel dog or two tied off at a post or a
makeshift shelter. House-sized stacks of firewood, not cut and split
and stacked neatly, but whole trees leaned up against each other,
standing like a pyramid. I noted the shiny new pickup trucks next
to these sad dwellings, domestic mostly: Ford, Chevy, an occasional
Dodge. A cluster of well-kept trailers rose up out of the desert, the
rooflines dotted with tires to keep them from rattling in the wind.
And as a companion to the empty land, a satellite dish, like a great
ear, listening.

Like a good horse in the old days, my new pickup truck—a 1994
Dodge Dakota extra-cab, four-wheel drive, silver with black trim
and seven thousand miles on the odometer—was both an essential
tool on the reservation and a personal trademark. A truck defined
the man who drove it, and many Navajos put their resources in their
vehicles to the detriment of everything else. Electricity, running
water, sometimes even groceries were optional, while a good truck
was fundamental to Navajo life, a constant like the speed of light. It
was the truck, not the telephone or the television or the radio, that
was the real source of communication in Navajoland. If you wanted
to know what was going on in the world or even next door, you had
to travel, move, roam around until you found out. This was a world
measured spatially, rather than temporally—here you might as well
measure your age in miles as in years. To revise an old aphorism: a
man without a truck ain't a man at all.

Navajos travel great distances in their trucks, back and forth across the reservation, visiting family, shopping for supplies in town, attending powwows and ceremonies and rodeos, or just out seeing the country, going from place to place, covering ground. Several people might sit abreast in the front seat of a Navajo's truck, with a few children huddled in the back, or a few hitchhikers catching a ride to the laundry or to the hospital or to drinking, in all kinds of weather. A good truck is like a Navajo family's blood, and the roads are arteries connecting them to every corner and to the heart of Navajoland.

All this wandering about originated in the myth-time when the "air-spirit people," who become the Navajo, made a series of migrations from the First World to this world, the Fifth, where they finally claimed a home. These migratory journeys were not completely voluntary, as the people were content enough in the First World until they began to quarrel with each other and commit adultery. The chiefs of the four directions complained, and eventually told them to go away, to leave the First World and never return. Away they went, up, up into the Second World, where yet another set of problems plagued them, and they moved on again, and then again, and so on. The Navajo story of creation is a story of migration from that primal First World deep inside the Earth to the Earth's surface, where the "air-spirit people" evolved and changed into "earth surface people," the Navajo. The story's meaning and the great achievement of the Navajo is that through migration, through movement, the people seek for *hózhó*, a state of harmony, balance, and beauty between male and female, between self and community, between the community and the universe.

This mythical migration is paralleled by the anthropological story of the Navajo, who, along with the Apache, are relative newcomers to the Southwest. Both are Athabascan peoples who migrated southward from western Canada along the Rocky Mountains as early as AD 1100. By the time they reached the Southwest, they had splintered into several smaller groups, one of which became the present-day Navajo. Going deeper into the past, the ancestors of these Athabascan peoples migrated to North America over the Bering Land Bridge from Asia somewhere between twelve thousand and fourteen thousand years ago. There is mounting scientific evidence for other scenarios as well, including multiple migrations of different peoples at different times, an earlier entry into North America, and other scenarios that are not yet understood. But the basic premise is still intact: the ancestors of the Navajo came to the Southwest from Asia by a series of migrations, and the Navajo are a traveling people.

Though widely accepted among anthropologists, these ideas have been rejected by many Navajo anthropologists and cultural experts. They believe the Navajo people have always been here, in residence between the four sacred mountains. But this belief does not negate the overwhelming energy and passion for movement in Navajo life.

The Navajo language, too, is grounded in movement. The core verb in Navajo is "to go," whereas the core verb in English is "to be." One scholar worked out 356,200 variations of "to go" in the Navajo language. This linguistic footnote parallels a Navajo cosmology of dynamic change, a vision of the universe based on events in process. Nothing is static, especially not the self, which is continually changing, shifting, moving.

I felt like I too was continually changing, shifting, moving. I had never lived anywhere for very long, and each new place I lived or traveled in felt like the unveiling of a part of me I did not know. My father's army days and tour of Vietnam and then his career in the U.S. Forest Service kept us moving every few years, from one beautiful land to another, mostly in Oregon. I came to depend on moving on, even at a very young age. Perhaps it was acculturated into me, or maybe I was born that way, but my dad's announcement that he had taken a new job and we were packing up so roused my spirit that I came to live for those fresh, unborn moments when we flew off into another where and another when. I didn't give our life of movement any thought—it wasn't tragic or romantic or sorrowful to leave my friends and familiar country. We moved on, as we always had. I did not know anything else. Only later, only now, did I begin to see that those early days had come to define my life. My thirst for new places, new experiences, new people was both a blessing and a liability. I learned a great deal in each new place we lived, but it always came to feel stagnant after a time, and I yearned to move on. And when we finally took flight, and all my relationships with people, and places, and things fell away, then, only then, did I feel hopeful and free.

The sky grew increasingly ominous, black clouds and the deep belly-rumbling of thunder in the distance. I dropped out onto Highway 371 and pavement again. I was at the edge of Crownpoint, New Mexico, and the Eastern Agency of the Navajo Nation. I drove the soft mile into town, my tires rolling soundless over the civilized world.

Crownpoint is a village of some two thousand Navajo people that grew around the establishment of the Pueblo Bonito Indian School in 1909. The Navajo name for this place is T'ííst'óóz Ndeeshgizh, which means "Narrow-leafed Cottonwood Gap," after the collection of tall cottonwood trees that cool the streets in summer. A coal mine once operated here, as well as a radio station and a U.S. Weather Bureau station. From the highway, Crownpoint looked to be in decline, a sleepy little burg huddled close to Hosta Butte with the wind blowing through it. Trash and tumbleweeds collected against fence lines, and what trees I could see looked sad and thirsty for love. I drove by what appeared to be government offices, likely those of the Eastern Agency, and maybe somewhere in there was the tribal hospital. A small complex of government houses lined the highway, each painted a different bright color, blue and red and yellow, a couple of gas stations, a Bashas' grocery store with a laundry next door, and a household supplies store where I would later buy four cheap forks and spoons that cut the corners of my mouth when I used them.

Hosta Butte, a couple of miles to the south, is visible from great distances and was likely a landmark along the ancient south road leading in and out of Chaco Canyon, that ceremonial center of the Anasazi people. Also sacred to the Navajos, Hosta Butte is the home of two deities, Mirage Stone Boy and Mirage Stone Girl. It is said to be fastened to the sky with Mirage Stone and covered over by dark clouds and thunderstorms.

I turned into the wide parking lot at Bashas' and found a pay phone outside. Who was I going to call? I didn't know.

I wanted to call Sakura in Hokkaido. I wanted to hear her voice and tell her I loved her, tell her I should never have left Japan, tell her I should have stayed to make a life with her there. But I wasn't sure. Maybe this surge of passion for her was more about my little hardships here, and the growing loneliness inside me that I did not know how to handle. I was so frazzled by my first week, I wasn't certain I could trust these feelings. I wasn't certain I should be making overtures of love when I felt so weak and vulnerable, so out-of-sorts and lost. It was too risky. Not just for me, but for her too. I had to be careful. Why put her through the trials of my indecision? Before I call her, I thought, I need to settle in a little at Borrego, settle out, settle down.

I called Mary instead. We made plans to see each other over the weekend. She would drive out Friday afternoon. Maybe we'd make a long hike out into the mesa country around Borrego. We said good-bye, and the phone went silent except for a low buzzing sound I heard first in the receiver, and then somewhere behind me and above me. It was the charged desert air. The storm was building.

I went inside Bashas'. The store was outfitted for the local life-style. Camping equipment and household items lined the shelves: lamp oil, shovels, canning supplies, white gas for cookstoves, mon-

IN THE SUN'S HOUSE

strous cans of green chilies and pinto beans, and great sacks of sugar and flour, Blue Bird flour from Cortez, Colorado. I selected a few things I thought I might need over the next several days and made my way to the checkout counter.

"You the new teacher up there?" the woman at the register asked me. She was tall and heavy, with a wide, friendly face, a smile beneath her sharpened, hooked nose. She wore her bangs cut just above her eyebrows so that they seemed to tickle her, annoy her.

"Yes," I told her. "I started just a couple weeks ago."

"I gotta daughter goes up there," she said. "She's in the sixth grade. You might know her."

"What's her name?" I asked.

"Marcella," the woman said. "That's her."

I did know Marcella. She was hard to miss. She took a lot of grief from the other kids at Borrego, especially the sixth-grade boys. She weighed at least twice what they did, and she had wide, powerful shoulders. I had seen the skinny little boys taunting her at recess, staying just out of her reach, fast and quick on their feet, as she swung at them and grunted and steamed in her anger. They would call her "grandma," perhaps because she wore little pink glasses that forever slipped down her nose, and to mock her they would stoop over as if with age and hobble around as if leaning on a cane. This dynamic had probably been in play as long as Marcella could remember. Even so, she still responded just the way those boys wanted her to, and they likely never tired of this terrible game. Meeting her mother, I felt a little closer to her troubles, to understanding how she must feel about being taunted as the school fat girl.

"You her teacher?" the woman said.

"Yeah. Her language arts teacher," I said, and I gave her my name.

"I'm Betty Brown," she said. "Why don't you take care of her up there, okay?"

"Yes," I said. "I'll look out for her. Especially for her studies."

"Thank you," she said. "She's real smart, you know. Maybe you know that?"

"Yeah. I can see it."

Betty finished ringing up my order and packed my things away in a paper sack.

"It's gonna rain," she said. "You better hurry back up that road. It can get real nasty out."

"How nasty?" I asked.

"Well, really nasty," she said. "You don't wanna get caught out on that road under a sky like this." She looked up into the ceiling of the big store.

"Okay," I said. "I'll get going. Nice meeting you."

She nodded at me as I left the store.

Outside, the sky rumbled deep earth sounds. The tone of it, the rhythm was somehow comforting, familiar, old. I imagined that the people in this dry country had always lived inside a daily hope for rain. This impending storm was a blessing, but I was rather hoping to get back to Borrego before it broke and showered the forsaken desert. After I was safely indoors with supper cooking and an afternoon cup of tea, then it could rain all it wanted.

"Yá'át'ééh!" I heard behind me. "Hello."

"Yá'át'ééh!" I returned.

"Oh!" he said. "You speak Navajo?"

"No. But I know that word."

He smiled and laughed. "You should learn it," he said. "Like me. You can talk like me."

This fellow who had walked up behind me stood near the open passenger-side door where I loaded in my groceries. He seemed to be moving toward me like he was going to get in, but he caught himself, and staggered back the other way, taking a step to keep himself right. His cropped hair went in all directions. His clothes were clean, but tattered and unkempt. He was visibly drunk. He leaned in, and I could smell it on him.

"I'm Charlie Hunter. Charlie's father," he said. "Charlie Hunter? You know him up at school?"

"Yes. Nice to meet you."

We shook hands.

"So you're both Charlie Hunter?"

He grinned, showed me his perfect, white teeth. "Charlie told me about you," he said. "I figured you were you."

"I am," I said.

He looked into my truck at my sacks of groceries. "You wouldn't be able to spare a few dollars?" he asked. "I mean so I can get something to eat?"

I didn't want to give him anything, but I had a few dollars in my pocket, change from my purchases. "All right," I said. "For something to eat, right?"

"Right. For food. I'm not gonna go out an' buy beer or nothin'."

"Of course not," I said. I gave him all of it, three ones and a few coins.

"You're a good neighbor," he said. He reached to pat me on the shoulder, but the distance was farther than he expected. He patted the air a few times and then pretended he was waving. "Goodbye, then. So long. Laters," he said, walking away. Then he turned back. "That's English," he said. "Laters."

I waved to him. "Laters."

"Teach them boys good up there," he called back to me.

"All right, I will."

I wondered where he would spend the night.

I scanned the sky. It was immense and dark and still, an ominous nothing readying to break open and wash everything away. I considered that I might be wiser to wait the storm out here in the parking lot. Of course, I risked getting stuck in Crownpoint for the night. I didn't know if the roads would be passable after such a storm, and how long it might be before they dried up. The sky hung there close over my head as if waiting for me to decide. Nothing happened. I climbed into my truck and headed up the long dirt road toward Borrego.

All roads leading in and out of Borrego were dirt, and so there was no avoiding the hazards of desert driving. In August and September in the Southwest, the great monsoon clouds roll in to crack and blow at the earth, turn the washes to raging rivers and steam and charge and carry away trees, old car bodies, sometimes horses, cattle, and unfortunate people. To the Navajo, these violent thunderstorms are known as male rains, and they live in the East and the West. In winter, I was plagued by stories of stray, drunk Navajos who broke down and froze to death in the desert night. Such stories didn't seem to worry the people who knew this land because they motored on through the greatest of storms. Or maybe worry wasn't it at all, but rather, a proper life was trusting yourself to the desert. When Navajos put a car, a truck, a school bus even, into the muddy ditch, they just got out and walked home, or maybe caught a ride from someone who was faring better that day. They would return to get their vehicle the next morning, or in a few days when the mud dried up.

The sun was another problem with the opposite effect. On a dry day with the quiet sky stretching on forever, you can drive for hours, even days, lost in the maze of dirt roads that run helter-skelter across Navajoland and nowhere find water. Or your truck might be tested by a rogue sand trap piled in the roadbed by the wind. Still another hazard was the debris that rose to the surface of the road after the grader came through. The big blade churned up nails and broken glass and shards of sharp steel, artifacts of the modern world. The grader smoothed out the track and improved the ditches for drainage, but it also ensured that a certain number of tires would go flat.

For my part, in anticipation of the unanticipated, I took to carrying two gallons of water in my truck at all times: one for the radiator (it was a new truck, but I took no chances) and one for me. I kept a pair of boots in the extra cab, a fleece jacket, and my sleeping bag. I never knew when or where I might have to spend the night.

I drove on past the hogans, the chickens scratching freely in the roadside ditch, the sad dogs lying out in the dirt chained to posts. A few derelict cars parked forever at the end of a trailer. No one stirred anywhere. I was the only vehicle on the road. Was that a bad sign? Ahead I could see the steeper, narrow slot that was Borrego Pass, and ahead of that was the sky, a blue wafer at the front of the storm. Behind me, black thunderclouds closed in, so black and close it was hard to know where the sky ended and the earth began. I turned on my headlights. It was that dark.

The rain came softly, just a few drops at first against the windshield like the intermittent wreckage of summer insects. I rolled down the window and breathed in the fresh metallic smell of the desert in the rain. I hung my head outside in the open air, catching raindrops in my hair. I heard the wind rushing past, and the desert seemed to say: Who are you? Who are you?

I didn't answer.

The rain momentarily stopped (a drawing in of breath), and then it came all at once. The black cloud consumed my truck as the rain broke over the dry land. In an instant, the road was awash in flowing water.

The dirt road transformed into a wide swath of clay and mud. It stuck to my tires and built around them as they turned. The mud grabbed at the wheel wells, caught and released, caught and released and spun off, kicking up waves of heavy mud that arced and splattered the side windows. For a moment it was fun. I was four-wheelin'! The truck was doing me right. I bore down on the accelerator, picking up speed, then slid sideways in the road, slowed, leaned, and turned into the slide to keep the truck straight. The fun passed as I realized I wasn't sure anymore if I was on the road or in the ditch. What would I do if the truck stuck fast in the ditch? Curl up and go to sleep until the sun returned to dry up the world? Or would someone in one of these hogans open their door to me for the duration of the storm? I didn't want my truck in the ditch, that most of all. Not because I was afraid for my safety—I wouldn't mind a little adventure. Rather, the truck was my lifeline in and out of Borrego, my connection to the outside world, my safety net, my stability. The truck was all I had.

I motored on, the mud catching and giving way, building and letting go. I crossed the flats and started up the steeper grade. The storm was ahead of me now. I could no longer see that thin blue line of sky. It was all black clouds and rain woven with lightning. I drove straight into the belly of the storm.

Up along the deep canyon now, the road bent around the arm of the mesa and narrowed into one lane. There was no room here to pass another vehicle, and on a corner like this, I couldn't see ahead of me. If I met someone here, someone else foolish enough to leave home in this storm, I'd have to back down the steep incline and risk sliding over the edge.

I rounded the corner as carefully as I could, but pushing hard enough so as not to lose momentum, and there, pouring off the cliffs on my right, was a river of rain speeding over the road. I stopped, the engine humming under the sound of the pounding rain. This didn't look good. It didn't look good at all. The water flowed fast, carving a path for itself in the roadbed as I watched it, a great gap widening and deepening before my very eyes. I thought of Bob King's story. This is it, I thought, this is how it happened before. I watched as great boulders came down, stumps, clumps of vegetation torn from their moorings, rusty man-made things dropping off the road cut, and all of it washing over the edge into that monstrous hole.

Rain slammed the windshield in waves, the wipers cranking at a furious pace. I had two options: back down the precipitous road to the flats and wait for the water to subside. Or go for it. I couldn't sit here any longer. The whole mountain seemed to be coming undone. Another boulder, a chunk of something, came over the cliffs through the air, hit the roadbed in front of me, and was swept away over the edge.

I jammed the truck into four-wheel drive, engaged the clutch, and, lurching forward, gained as much power and speed as I could. The truck hit the rushing column of water, and mud splashed up on both sides, mud and water and noise. The engine whined. My hands clutched at the wheel. I felt the force of the water pushing the truck sideways in the road toward the canyon edge as it seemed to reach up to swallow me. I cranked the steering wheel over toward the wall, turned the truck against the force, and pushed, pushed, pushed forward through the flowing mess until I felt the water against me soften, then release, and I slipped out safe on the other side.

I drove the rest of the way in and parked in front of my little cinder block duplex. It was still raining hard. I stepped from the truck into the pooling water on the asphalt. My legs were weak, adventure-woozy. Was I standing on dry ground? Water flowed down the road-way in front of my place and dumped into the ditch at the cattle guard. I took up my bags of groceries and hurried inside.

Leaving the bags in the kitchen, I returned to the front windows to watch the storm. My big blue canoe, a college graduation gift from my father, lay upside down in the hallway. The irony of hauling my boat into this desert was not lost on me, yet somehow I felt comforted by it. I had grown up in a country of water and green trees, and just because I lived in a waterless place right now didn't mean I had to give up hope. Good thing, too, because for the moment, there was water here. There was water everywhere.

I stared out the windows at the flowing water, water flowing out the drive, deeper and deeper moment by moment, faster now, and more powerful. I watched as it gathered around the rear wheels of my truck, pillowed up against them, pushed at them as the truck vibrated and rocked with the water's force. A river! A real river with waves that curled back and frothed into white caps, right in front of me, flowing down the road. A big pickup truck appeared in front of my windows, the water up to the running boards. I could see the driver at the wheel, Dean West, the maintenance supervisor. He drove out to the cattle guard, and then turned the truck around and motored back up against the current. The berm behind the school must have given way, and now the rain collected by the big mesa behind us flowed through campus instead of around it.

I watched as the water rose higher and higher, almost to the top of the rear tires on my truck. For a moment I wondered if the whole truck wouldn't be dragged out and swept away. I saw pieces of plywood borne off down the road, a Styrofoam cooler and its lid, a broken lawn chair tumbling in the current. I panicked, opened the front door, and looked on helplessly. What could I do against water like that? Hours passed. Minutes went by. A raven flew overhead. The water slowed. The waves settled out. And soon that river flowing down the road smoothed into a broad plain of trickling water, washing the desert clean.

FOUR

WALKING

I left the windows open all night listening for coyote songs across the moon. Black beetles crept in without invitation, making foot trails over the butter I absentmindedly left exposed on the kitchen counter, and the land, too, sifted in on the wind, covering everything in fine dust. That dust, I knew, was the blood and bone of that great mesa, the refuse of an ancient seafloor laid down eons ago. It didn't look possible to climb to the top of the mesa. It looked like an impenetrable fortress, a place only ravens and vultures could know. In my mind, it loomed large and dangerous, but also inviting, and voices from my reading urged me to venture out:

> Above all, do not lose your desire to walk: every day I walk myself into a state of well-being and walk away from every illness; I have walked myself into my best thoughts, and I know of no thought so burdensome that one cannot walk away from it . . . but by sitting still, and the more one sits still, the closer one comes to feeling ill . . . . If one just keeps on walking, everything will be all right.
>
> —Søren Kierkegaard

What gives value to travel is fear. It is the fact that, at a certain moment, when we are so far from our own country . . . we are seized by a vague fear, and an instinctive desire to go back to the protection of old habits. This is the most obvious benefit of travel. At that moment we are feverish but also porous, so that the slightest touch makes us quiver to the depths of our being. We come across a cascade of light, and there is eternity. This is why we should not say we travel for pleasure. There is no pleasure in traveling, and I look upon it more as an occasion for spiritual testing.... Pleasure takes us away from ourselves in the same way as distraction ... takes us away from God. Travel, which is like a greater and graver science, brings us back to ourselves.

—Albert Camus

The morning came, a Saturday, and I put on my hat to shade me from the sun, and my favorite boots, and took up my walking stick. The boots I had bought in Rome on a three-month tour in Europe. I selected them for the rugged sole and the figure paddling a canoe pressed into the leather near the ankle. Made by Sisley, "for town and country walks." I had put them on at once, and had passed off my old boots at midnight on a friendly bum in the Marseilles train station who claimed a former life as a salvage diver on wrecks off Gibraltar. He'd spent so much time at depth, he told me, that he had developed a particular problem with his bladder, which required him to piss about every fifteen minutes. To affirm it, he did just that, off into the empty tracks, looking both ways for trains and policemen.

How did my students spend their weekends? Not doing their homework, I was convinced of that. Did they stay indoors and work in the kitchen? Did they help the family with wood-getting and pinyon-gathering? Did they roam the restaurants in Gallup selling turquoise and silver? Did they play? For my part, I wandered.

I walked out of my trailer home at Borrego and into that vast wild land. I came by a row of three trailers. A dog, short and powerful, came fast out of a little wooden box next to a pole, snapping and snarling and barking as it lunged, its teeth a white menace. I jumped, for I hadn't seen it. I watched as the dog came to the end of its chain, hung there a moment against the force of it, and then fell back, barking as it regained its feet. The adrenaline went through me like a tornado and I stood there a moment, panicked and pissed off, while the curtains at the window fluttered where someone had taken a look outside. I walked on, doing my best to act like I knew where I was going, like I belonged here, and like the dog was nothing to me.

I slipped through the gap where the two chain-link fences met behind the school, just enough room for me to pass, but not the cows grazing out on the wide flats to the south. I walked out into the stone forest in the New Mexico morning, a collection of rock and juniper moving into pinyon and ponderosa pine at higher altitudes. The monsoon clouds would build fat and purple all day, and later, the sky would come down and lay flat against the barren earth. But I had hours yet to explore this land before the storm. From here, I entered a deep inlet where the great mesa drew into the shape of a C, and where the water poured off in heavy rain and flowed like the Columbia out of the wash onto the flats below. I walked in, and deeper in where the mesa wrapped silence inside itself at the edge of an echo and rose and towered burnt umber over my head. I leaned back and looked up. The light, stuck fast against the stone, caught my eye, ruddy and soft, and, arching my back to see the high edge of where I was going, I exposed my chest and throat and face to the sharp sun. Standing between these sunburned walls, I listened to the greatest silence I had ever known. No birdsong. No insects chirping. No wind in the conifers. Nothing at all, and in that empty nothing, a presence too, unknowable, indifferent, and sad. Yet I felt happy indeed to be out here walking, out here and away from the impossible world of my classroom, which each weekday morning I woke to face with dread. I took a step, and that one step, my boots on the hard rock and course dry grass, was a clamor in my ears. It crashed against the walls and rebounded in the hollow air.

Inside the shade of this deep inlet, the moister air made me feel a little more at ease, safer, somehow in the middle of something blue. I could taste moisture on my tongue. I knew if I knelt and dug with my hands like a badger into the soft dry sand at the bottom of the wash I would find water, maybe enough to drink. I followed the dry wash lined on either side with scattered yucca, the plant Edward Abbey supposedly called "bayonets in the night," and short, leather-leaved plants, intensely green, I could not identify, greasewood maybe, up into the thickening trees in the protection of the mesa's shadow. I had to duck under a juniper branch here, around a boulder there, and along a long collection of debris: metal roofing, torn stumps and branches of trees, a few tires stowed here and there by rushing water in a storm. Had someone hauled this stuff out here to dump it? Or did someone live up this wash at one time, and had these remains of that life come rushing down the arroyo with the water?

In the depths of the shaded grotto, the mesa loomed like a curtain around me, dark and huge and edged in yellow light. It seemed I had two options. I could scramble up the southwest side, up the steep track of boulders through the thick trees where the water washed into the wash when it rained. The boulders looked bigger than I was tall, and it looked like I would have to negotiate each one, up and around them, or balance as I climbed over. Or I could take the northeast face, which looked easier, a broad, sandy slope with only intermittent boulders and trees. I went that way, and walking out and up it, I happened onto a trail of easy switchbacks all the way to the top. It looked like the daily route of deer, given all the cloven tracks in the trail. I walked alone in my comfortable boots, back and forth across the slope. My foot hit a loose stone and I rolled it back and almost fell. Regaining myself, I watched the stone come out from under me, rolling, rolling, and tumbling over the edge. Chink, chink, chink, chink. Gone. I moved around the scaly branches of juniper, brushing against the fragrant olive green berries, the scent of gin blossoming in my nose. Switching back again along the trail, sweat warming and cooling my back and brow, focusing on my feet to keep my footing, I stepped up and over a sun-twisted stump, raising powdery puffs of fine dust beneath my boots. Then there I was on top of the world.

Looking back, I surveyed the trail I had followed, winding down into the arms of the shaded inlet. The trail flowed back through geologic time, down through the ages of the Mesozoic, 245 to 66 million years ago, during which the great continent Pangaea was breaking apart and spreading over the face of the earth. That era is made up of three periods: working back from the most recent, the Cretaceous, the Jurassic, and the Triassic. The mesa top, where I stood, was the floor of an ancient sea during the Cretaceous; the red sandstone cliffs that line Interstate 40 to Gallup mark the Jurassic; and the Triassic lies beneath that, marked by a layer of soft mudstone that erodes relatively easily, undermining those great cliffs that crack and sliver off into the Puerco River Valley. This ancient sea was alive with swimming monsters, such as the snake-like mosasaurs and the long-necked plesiosaurs. On land, reptiles ruled, among them turtles, snakes, lizards, and dinosaurs—*Apatosaurus* and the fabled *Tyrannosaurus rex*. People at Borrego said that I would find dinosaur tracks up here, but in all my wanderings, I never did.

During the Cretaceous period, the North American continent was inundated by water. The sea came from the north, out of the Canadian Rockies, and filled the world with water as far south as the Gulf of Mexico. You remember Noah's story? Fossil cephalopods and clams are visible up here on the mesa, even to an eye as untrained as my own. Cephalopods were snail-like swimmers with highly complex chambered shells. By the end of the Cretaceous, the inland sea had retreated, and with the exception of the nautilus, which has a shell of simple, smooth partitions, the cephalopods died out.

I wanted to see the lay of the land to the south, the view from on high. I followed the edge of the grotto around. I cruised over the smooth tanned rock as fast as I dared, almost running, the ground a clean field of sand and crumbling sandstone punctuated with boulders, and I leaped sometimes over dark gaps and across fissures, my body warm and sweating and fluid so near the mesa edge. Weird shapes carved by wind and rain rose up out of the rock as I negotiated around or over them, my boots comfortable and stable on my feet, the sweat broken over me like holy water, my wide-brimmed hat shading my ears and eyes from the sun. I wasn't thinking at all as I walked, at least I didn't think so—not worrying about anything, anyway. I felt like a cloud flowing over the hard ground. I felt good, happy for the first time, maybe, since I'd come into Navajoland.

> I haven't got any special religion this morning. My God is the God of walkers. If you walk hard enough, you probably don't need any other God.
>
> —Bruce Chatwin

I stepped down off the higher ledge into the final flat leading to the end of the road, the far southwestern edge of the mesa. At that place, I would be able to walk no farther in this direction. As I bent low to pass beneath the crowded branches of a village of juniper huddled together against the sometimes wind, the underbrush exploded. It was the streaking tail-end of a coyote, gone before I could see it, or after, I wasn't sure. Before I could think, I broke into a run. I ran as fast as I could in my heavy boots, leaping sun-rotted logs and cacti, and bursting through juniper boughs. I followed the delicate foot marks in the soft soil, catching one in my view every few steps. I saw it again, a streak of silver-gray, coming around a copse of trees, as I chased it out onto the narrow peninsula of rock, out to the very edge. I didn't know why I was running after a coyote, or what I would do if I cornered it against the sky where the cliff dropped away. I was just running across the roof of the world, the sun pouring in like honey, my boot-sound fading into the moment, into the distance behind me. I couldn't hear anything anymore, the noise of the world dropped away with all my troubles, all my worries, all strife, everything and nothing but the running rhythm of my boots and my breath and my heart. I broke out at the edge of the mesa, the extreme edge where beyond there was only air.

The coyote was gone.

I looked down over that edge, two hundred feet below, three hundred, maybe more, to the sandstone talus turning to sand, and beyond that the broad expanse sweeping out in every direction. I half expected to see the body of the coyote down there broken on the rock. But there was nothing. Where that coyote went to, I could not tell. The cliff face was sheer except for a narrow ledge of rock a few dozen feet down. Yet to jump down and balance there without going over, even for a coyote, appeared, to me, impossible. And once down, what then? Maybe it circled back along the edge of the mesa, then behind me, and off into the trees. Or perhaps it was hidden in some little crevice I could not see. Or did it vanish the way birds do, flying off into the distance?

I stared out across the great landscape from the mesa top. I could see the tiny school below to the southeast, the great white water tower, my cinder block duplex, and my silver truck. Was that my silver truck? Looking out northwest, I saw the long thin dirt road winding away, past the Trading Post, forking and running out across the dusty land to Crownpoint. To the east, the mesa top led away through the trees and cactus. I felt a great sense of relief, and even power, knowing that this mesa was not a fortress after all, and I was not a prisoner. In later months, I would come to depend on this mesa

behind the school as I would on a companion, a dark sentinel standing watch as the harsh sky swept in around Borrego and buried it in
white snow. Walking here would become a kind of religion for me,
the place where I sought refuge from long days in the classroom, from
the tragedy and poverty of my students' lives, from loneliness and
from being alone.

I found Kuma on a little ranch near Los Lunas south of Albuquerque.
He cost me fifty bucks. I kept that part secret, as no respectable Navajo
would pay money for a dog, I had been told, because as one man said,
"Anybody can have a dog on the rez, and sometimes you have two or
three, even if you don't want 'em. There's always plenty of 'em about."
And few Navajos kept dogs as companions, at least not here at Borrego.
Dogs were for working, mostly for herding sheep, maybe cattle, or
perhaps tied forever to a sad tree to guard a house or hogan. Any dog
left to its own designs was vermin to be kicked and cast aside where
it lived out a life of hunger and disease at the edge of a Navajo town,
haunting gas stations and tourist campgrounds for handouts. It was
unlikely that these wandering animals lived very long, for everywhere
in Navajoland, dead dogs lie wasting on the roadsides.

Kuma was an Australian cattle dog, or blue heeler, a mixture of
collie stock from Scotland and the wild Australian dingo. Bred for
working cows, heelers have great endurance in hot, dusty conditions.
They are also known for their intelligence, loyalty, and speed. They
are fine guard dogs too, very territorial. Their ears stand straight up
like coyote ears.

I called Sakura in Hokkaido to tell her about the dog. I wanted to
name him Kuma, I said, the Japanese word for "bear." She suggested
Tsuki, which means "moon," because it matched the place where I
got him, or Kaze, which means "wind." The name Kuma was over-
used and clichéd, she said; maybe it was like naming a dog Fido or
Rex. But in Hokkaido I had known an Ainu dog named Kuma, and

the word brought back memories of that place and of the indigenous Ainu people whose cosmology was defined by the Hokkaido brown bear. I missed living in Hokkaido, and having a dog named Kuma would be like carrying with me a piece of that experience, a piece of that landscape. Besides that, when I took him to Ganado for the first time, another teacher who worked with Mary said, "Oh, he looks just like a little bear!" and that was enough for me.

Kuma was only five weeks old when I got him, too soon for him to leave his mother. His instinct to herd and guard meant that he loved to chase cars and trucks down Borrego Pass Road. And once he learned that my truck was also his, no one could touch it without his permission. His ears did not go coyote-up the way they should have, and his temperament was wary, aggressive, deeply pessimistic. He loved Mozart. I played all kinds of music for him, and he paid no mind. But when I played Mozart, and especially the overture to *Le Nozze di Figaro*, he raised his ears, cocked his head, and sang and howled and wailed. He was a good companion despite his love for fighting and biting whatever or whoever crossed him. He seemed to me more a part of the desert than of any human community. In the company of most people he appeared anxious, agitated, overly wary, and when we went out walking in the wilds, roaming from sunup to sundown, he was at peace at last, and we were the best of friends.

The first time I saw Kuma lose control was when he attacked my shovel. I bought it at Bashas' in Crownpoint to pick up the dog shit around the trailer, and I thought I might keep it in the back of my truck to dig myself out if I got stuck in the sand or mud or snow. Kuma was intelligent and attended to detail, as most heelers do, and he noticed and inspected even the slightest change in his environment. The first day I used the shovel, I loaded the blade and pitched the shit over the field fence far out into the desert wastes. Kuma watched me do it, and before the second load left the blade, he leaped up into the space in front of me and had the sharp steel in his mouth. He crashed into it, not sure of what it was, and the shovel blade tilted and knocked him on the head, and his own waste rained down on top of him. I calmed him and had him sit and stay, but he could barely hold himself back. I finished up fast, leaned the shovel against the side of the trailer, and then released him by command. The hair on Kuma's back rose up as he stalked the idle tool, nosed it, and pressed it away with his nose. When it gave and moved and threatened him, he bit at it, clamping his jaws down across the angle of the blade. His jaw caught there, and for a moment the shovel had him, and it cut him a little in the mouth. When he broke free, he lunged at the metal edge again, snapping and biting and barking until the shovel came toppling down and he stood over it, his body rigid as a board, his hackles standing up across his back, growling and bleeding and frothing in his mouth. That was the first time I considered that he might be more dog than I could handle.

I made walk after walk after walk out behind the school, so many walks that I came to know the land out there like I knew the placement of my books on the shelves. The poetry all together and organized by poet, my favorite poets on the same shelf next to each other: Keats next to Wordsworth next to Coleridge, Thomas, Yeats, Frost, Pack. Travel narratives too, the same routine: Chatwin and Theroux, Byron and Thesiger, Matthiessen and Lopez, O'Hanlon and Least Heat-Moon. A span of books on Asia and by Asian writers. A string of writers who love the natural world. Each time I went walking, I found some subtle difference in the arrangement of things. A fallen branch leaving a track across the sand after the wind. A stone fallen from the mesa top. A piece of trash I hadn't seen before. A burrow dug out at the side of the wash. A new shining thing in a pack rat nest.

I went walking out through the fields of late fall desert flowers, the yucca and stunted pinyon pine, the soft sandstone labyrinth. I rarely found surface water, and I usually carried none. It was a moderate risk. My trailer was never more than a few miles away, and I didn't fear getting lost. In this open country, I could always climb up onto something, a great sandstone shelf or spire, and see how to get around and which way was home.

I happened upon Manny Spring one day behind the water tower where the rock face rises sharply up. A sixth-grade Zuni student in this otherwise all-Navajo school, he was soft and round, a little plump, a little shy. Manny's grandma worked at the school. The other teachers told me that if Manny got out of line, I just had to say so to his grandma, and she'd grab him by the ear with her strong fingers (I saw her do it), and drag him off home for a lickin'. Such a fate I never wished on him. I wasn't quite sure what Kuma would do when he met Manny—attack him or lick him—but he ran right up to the boy and sniffed at his ankles and hands. Manny reached down and petted Kuma's head with one hand, and in his other he carried a CO_2 pistol pointed at the ground. I noticed three colorful songbirds stuffed headfirst into his pants pocket. He explained without a prompter: "My uncle's gonna use the feathers." Kuma stood up on his rear legs then, sniffing at the birds in Manny's pocket. Manny turned away and put his hand between the birds and the dog, and Kuma licked his fingers. That seemed to me a good sign, the side of Kuma I wanted to encourage. Yet I knew that Kuma felt free and open out here on the desert, and if Manny had approached him in my truck or trailer, the scene would have gone a different way.

Merle Moore, from the Trading Post, kept his cattle on parts of the land over which Kuma and I ranged, long-legged creatures that lived on rocks and sand. We came through places tramped out by cows, and, in their wake, a minefield of beautiful green bovine splats. Kuma would make a run for it and lie on his back to roll in the fresh spoils. By the time I caught up to him, it was always too late. He got himself in so deep he wore a great green cape over his shoulders and back, and a cap on his head to match. The sun dried him, and by the end of the walk, he sported a spotted shell of cow shit, which slowly cracked and shifted off in clean slabs. The only thing left was the smell.

He was a fine dog, indeed.

I took to walking with Kuma early in the morning, often before light, because he needed an outlet for his great energy. One long walk a day was not enough. So we'd creep out along the edge of the school in the dark, making our way between the juniper and sharp yucca. Some of the maintenance men came in to work early, and I didn't want to be seen moving so slowly and carefully in that weird light because of what they might say about skinwalkers. About me. They would offer me a warning against going out in the dark, but to their neighbors they would offer a warning because they had seen me going out in the dark. I avoided detection for a few weeks until one morning, passing behind the maintenance building back inside the low trees, I stopped and fumbled with my fly to take a piss. I moved forward onto a yucca and lanced my shins. I cursed and leaped back and cursed again.

Everett heard me as he was getting out of his truck. "Who's there!" he said into the dark.

Kuma barked at the sound of him, a sure sign to most Navajos that a skinwalker is nearby. Some Navajos who keep dogs tied outside their hogans do so for just this purpose, and when they rise up in chorus in the night, it means "Beware, the witch people are coming."

"It's just me," I said.

"What you doin' out here in the dark?"

"I'm just taking my dog out," I said, which made no sense to him at all.

"Well, don't be whistling out here," he said. "That brings in the witches."

Of course I hadn't been whistling, or at least I didn't think so. "All right," I said. "See you later," and I walked off into the dark.

Soon after that Shane Yazzie said to me in class, "Hey. Mr. Caswell. I seen you in a sheepskin last night goin' a hun-dret miles an hour!" And he almost died laughing.

Skinwalkers are Navajo witches, and they work their witchery wearing the skin of an animal, usually a coyote or a wolf, or, in my case, a sheep. They prepare a potion of powdered human flesh and feed it to their victim or blow it into their face. A skinwalker will utter a magic incantation, or shoot someone with a small object, like a splinter of bone from the dead, or ash collected from an abandoned hogan where someone has died. People who get a bump on the head are said to have been infected by a skinwalker in this way. Skinwalkers will also use narcotic plants to subdue their victims, and often this technique is employed for seducing women, and for winning at gambling or in trading. Even the boldest Navajos are terrified of skinwalkers.

Most of my students had a story to tell about an encounter with a skinwalker. Usually it happened when their parents were away from home. "Mr. Caswell," they might say. "Guess what? I was home with my sister and my cousin-brother. And at night the dogs started barkin'. We were real scared, and so we blew out the lamps inside and looked out the window. It was real dark out there, and then we seen it. It was a skinwalker goin' real fast. But we were so lucky it didn't see us 'cause we blew out the lamps. And we were real scared too."

The only way to defeat a witch or skinwalker is by use of medicinal plants and certain ceremonials. A successful ceremony is said to effect the death of the witch, and some sudden or strange deaths in a community are explained this way. Witches are also frequently said to be killed by lightning. If a community can get someone to confess witchery, it is said that their death will occur magically within a year's time. Or in the olden time, a confessed witch might be ritually and brutally killed.

Skinwalkers are not dead, but they use the dead. And everything about the dead terrifies most Navajo people. Even to look at a dead body, unless it is an animal killed for food, is considered dangerous. Many Navajos these days will dispute this fact, and it's true that Navajos, like all peoples, leave some beliefs behind and acquire new ones. The old ways don't disappear from a culture, however—they just go underground. You'll find plenty of individuals that believe or don't believe one thing or another, but the currents from the olden time still flow beneath them. The dead are associated with ghosts, which return to the world from the north, the land of the dead, usually to seek out some revenge. This is why many traditional Navajo people avoid Anasazi ruins, which are in such abundance in Navajoland. Ghosts can appear as animals such as mice, coyotes, or owls, and they can appear as whirlwinds, flame or fire, or even strange dark objects in the night. And ghosts can change shape, usually under the cover of darkness, right before one's very eyes.

I wonder if to Everett, that morning, I didn't appear as a strange dark object in the night. Or if when he called to me and I answered, what he saw was a skinwalker that metamorphosed into a long-haired white English teacher with a dog.

Such soft asylum is the sun, and that day in late October, that cool, happy day in fall, I needed sanctuary like I needed nothing else, sanctuary from my classroom, from my trailer home, from Borrego Pass School. I had just seen Caleb Benally ride away in a police car after he threatened someone with a knife at lunch. He likely always carried that knife in his pocket, but somehow on that day, he'd decided the situation demanded he use it. He was a scary kid, and he didn't like me at all. I wondered how long it would be before he decided to use that knife against me.

I drove to Ganado to see Mary. We planned to make a Saturday hike, just the two of us and our dogs—Kuma, and Mary's dog, Ranger—down Three Turkey Canyon to a ruin there, Three Turkey

Ruin. Mary had talked about this place when I arrived at Borrego, a nineteen-room cliff-house dated between AD 1266 and 1276, located about six miles south of Canyon de Chelly. Somewhere on a wall in that ruin we'd find three white and red pictographs that looked like turkeys, though they have also been identified as handprints and as gourds. We might also find more recent habitation in that canyon, parts of hogan walls that predate the Long Walk of the Navajo in 1864. There was little else to note about this place—the ruins at Chaco Canyon are far more grand, Mesa Verde is far more famous, and the hike to White House Ruin in Canyon de Chelly far more dramatic. Yet we needed none of that. Few people knew about this place, Mary had said, and even fewer bothered to make the hike to it. We'd likely have the entire canyon to ourselves. That sounded ideal to me.

From Ganado we drove west on 264 to the junction, and then took 191 north toward Chinle. Driving that happy highway, the morning breaking bright about us and talking together about everything, something, nothing at all, some amorphous cue appeared in the land, appeared in Mary's mind, and I slowed and turned east onto a little dirt road where she called it out, and we started toward the rising sun. We drove my truck, bumping along that dusty gouge that passed as a road through the desert, because Mary's truck didn't have four-wheel drive. We'd need to cross several washes, Mary said, and who knew how much water might be flowing. Maybe too much for Mary's truck. Maybe too much for any truck. Maybe none at all. The road was deeply rutted where water had carved its passage, storm after storm. I aimed my wheels up along the edges on a high track where other vehicles had gone before, and we tilted this way and tilted that, following the dirt rail-line. Ranger stood on the seat in the extra cab behind us looking out, with little Kuma pressed up against his front legs, jockeying for position, and they both whined a little, kneaded the seats with their front feet, they so wanted to run. If we slipped off, or slipped in, the tires would likely jam sideways, and the nose of the truck jam forward so that whatever power came from the wheels would only move the truck deeper in. We'd have to dig our way out then, and I didn't have a shovel. At the first wash we found only a flat slick of water moving across the wide sand flat. We pushed fast over it, and water flared up alongside us, onto the hood a little, splashed the windows. Mary smiled and laughed and loved it, and on we went through the rock and sand, up and over humps of ground shaped by the wind, and along cactus patches and juniper, a rabbit striking for cover, a scrub jay flittering across. Another wash came into our path, and here there was more water, deeper water, flowing over a rocky wash bed. I stopped, hesitated.

"We can make it, easy," Mary said. "That looks pretty solid."

I engaged the four-wheel drive and drove in. Water rose up around us as my truck slipped and spit stones out from under the tires. Mary rolled down her window, put her hand outside, and wet it in the wash spray. We touched the opposite bank and the front tires pulled us up, up onto the sand ramp, and away we went over the hump and across the shining desert.

"All right!" Mary said. "This Dodge can ford." And she looked at me and laughed.

We arrived there where the road met the head of the canyon, and I pulled up under a juniper into the shade. We bailed out, took up our packs, and, with Ranger and Kuma already gone off in front of us, walked in.

The cottonwood and gambel oak were turning, the leaves gone golden and red. Leaves lay scattered about on the pebbly wash bed too, and in the morning, in the secret corners in the shade, we found frost from the hard, cold night. The air felt fresh, smelled clean, and we began a walking rhythm that carried us, razzmatazz, for an hour. We spoke very little, the morning was so quiet, with Mary in the lead, her hair curly and bouncing over her daypack. Ranger was a streak of white and black through the juniper and cactus and brushy shrubs.

He'd appear, quite suddenly, walk along us for a bit, nose Mary's hand as if to say, like Abraham, "Here I am," and then vanish again into the Arizona morning. Kuma, like a little brother, was forever a bit behind, tracking Ranger with his nose and ears, coming in from the side of the trail to find where Ranger had been, and, looking at me and mewling in his disappointment, he'd run alongside until Ranger flashed across the path out in front, and away he'd go barking and squirting up the dust.

It felt so good to be away from the school, away from all my fears and doubts. Here I was free and happy and complete, just walking the canyon as the canyon unfolded to walk it. I weighed no choices and made no decisions. I was not in conflict with anyone or anything. My legs carried me along as if without my consent while the canyon, the path water takes, led me on my way. If nothing more, if nothing less, perhaps this was why I came to the Southwest. If the whole school year was a bust, if I failed as a teacher, at least I'd have this walk with Mary and the dogs on this exquisite morning through new country.

No clouds anywhere in the crack-line sky view out of the canyon, and time moved the cool flat morning on into noon. It warmed up, but not much, Mary still comfortable in her shorts and long-sleeve poly-pro, me in my long cotton walking pants and T-shirt. I noted how little we said as we walked, how little needed saying. Ranger appeared, disappeared. Kuma found him and lost him. A canyon wren called from the cliffside.

Up ahead of us now we could see it, the dark, solemn overhang where the ruin endured the ages. "Three Turkey Ruin," Mary said, as if the words were waiting for her at that place.

We dropped our packs and sat in the shade looking up. The sandstone overhang shaded the little collection of dwellings up there, and we could see how pleasant it must have been way back when, the rooftops alive with people grinding corn, mending baskets, talking in small circles; the canyon bottom where the children played, young girls bathing in the shallow stream, and men gathering near a cottonwood to walk out together on the hunt. What could we say to each other in that perfect moment, the ruin suspended in time, the breeze in the cottonwood tops trembling the leaves, and Ranger and Kuma panting and lying on their sides now, a puff of dust where they breathed? What would we say? I wanted to say that it was beautiful, but Mary knew that. I wanted to say how fine it was to feel the hard canyon under my feet and the cool, high elevation air, but Mary knew that. I wanted to say how grateful I was, how happy to have a friend like her in a place like this, but Mary knew that too. So we sat there looking up, taking in the morning turned to day, thought about our lunch because we had walked ourselves into an appetite, but we didn't want to spread that lunch out yet—the breads and cheeses and pepperoni, the canned oysters, the little sweet things we carried with us, the fresh fruit. We let that moment go on, and on a little longer still, until nothing at all was going to happen, and then something did. Something startled Ranger from his rest, and his head popped up, his lip on the left side tucked weirdly in his teeth, his ears twitching and alert. He got up, listened, and then rose and drifted off to inspect the here and there.

"I'm going to see if I can climb up in there," Mary said, at last. "You want to come too?"

We approached the steep sandstone face together and stood there looking up.

"Man," Mary said. "How'd they get up there? I mean, we could get up there, now, this one time, maybe, but they lived up there. Went up and down all the time. Looks treacherous to me."

"It does," I said. "Where'd they put their feet? I hardly see any place to put your feet." Then I asked, "You count nineteen rooms up there? Doesn't look like that many."

"Nope," Mary said. "Doesn't look like that many at all."

"There's supposed to be nineteen. Maybe this isn't Three Turkey."

"I think it is," Mary said. "I was here last year, and this is where we came."

"Yeah, you were here, but maybe here is somewhere else."

"Good point," Mary said.

"Maybe this is One Turkey Ruin," I said, trying for a laugh.

"Three Turkey, One Turkey, whatever," Mary said, not much amused. "We're here. Let's climb this thing."

And up she went, her right foot leading, her left hand finding a hold to pull up on, her left foot going out to the side and a bit above her right. She paused there, seemingly stuck, unsure about what to put where, next. I came up under her and offered my hand. She put her right foot into my hand and I pressed up until, at my arm's length, she took hold of the lip of the ledge and scrambled into the ruin.

"All right!" I said.

"Kinda cool," Mary said. "Kinda nifty."

"Is it worth my trying to get up there?"

"Hmm. Not really. It's not that impressive. Plus I don't know if I can pull you up. Maybe this is One Turkey Ruin."

From below I watched Mary roam a bit through the little ledge house, bending to inspect this, pausing to look at that. Ranger joined me there, and whined and paced and scratched at the rock. Kuma whined too, put his front feet on the rock, peered up, whimpered and cried, and barked out loud. I wanted to try to climb it, to scramble up and see the canyon from the dwelling, see the dwelling, but with Kuma acting that way I couldn't bear to leave him. Is this what parenting feels like, I wondered, when your attachment is so great you cannot imagine leaving home?

"The dogs want to come up," I said. "Or you to come down."

"I'm comin' down," Mary said.

I put my hand up again as she stepped into it, the other foot fixing friction against the wall, her hands with good holds, as she down-climbed back to the canyon floor.

Soon we were sitting in the sun at the bottom of Three Turkey Canyon, sunlight filling the air around us, the canyon walls warming, the day breaking just so. Mary opened the oysters and we put out the crackers and cheese, all of it, for our lunch. The dogs came in close to pick up the scraps, and, getting nothing for a time, they lay down, Kuma curled next to my leg into a little ball in the dirt, then stretching his head up and across my knee where the cheese hovered over him in my hand. He had so far not been corrupted, and now in his goodness, I wanted to corrupt him. I handed him a little cheese, and up he sprang, seated now, staring at my hand, hoping for it all. I had that troubled, happy feeling that comes when you know the perfection of the moment cannot last, and what will come later is going to be hard, painful even, perhaps a kind of trial you might just fail. I didn't want to go back to Borrego. I didn't want to go back and stand there in front of my classes. Yet I knew I would. And it was this moment, this quiet rest out here on the land, this friendship with Mary and with the dogs, that made it possible, that makes everything possible. I felt grateful as we shared the lunch between us, and the best thing about gratitude is that you don't have to do anything with it.

Like me, Kuma was more at home in the truck than in the trailer at Borrego. We almost lived in it together, lived in the truck out on the road. I was happiest at the end of each week when I packed the truck with a few basic necessities and then drove out the dirt road into the outer world. I had bought myself a three-watt bag phone in Gallup, like the one Bob King kept in his office, and that always came along too. That little piece of technology gave me a renewed sense of safety and peace, if a false one. From I-40 in my truck, the phone worked great. I set it on the dash and made calls to friends and family back home, to Mary when I made the journey from my place to hers, to anyone I could think of. Out roaming around, I felt in touch with the wider world, not so isolated, not so alone. Up in the trailer, however, I got a signal maybe half the time. In all my months at Borrego, I would only once receive a phone call coming in. The rest was silence.

Loaded and ready for the road, Kuma would sit next to me in the passenger seat, or he'd sit just behind me in the extra cab with his head and front feet thrust forward on the armrest, his butt on the seat back there, his back legs down in the well like a little man. He seemed to like that position best because he had a space all his own, and yet he was next to me too, and he could see the sky out the front window. He'd force his nose under my arm until I slung my arm around him and we'd go shooting down the highway the best of pals, feeling like the great southwestern desert was a blossom that would never fold. I could leave him inside the truck in cool weather for any length of time and he seemed mostly content. Sometimes I'd buy him a few dried pig ears at the feed store in Gallup. When I left one for him in the cab, say, when I went in grocery shopping at Smith's, he wouldn't touch it until I returned. My cart loaded with groceries, I'd put the key into the truck door and open it, and there Kuma would be with the pig ear between his front legs. He'd cock his head as if to ask if it was all right, and I'd tell him, "Okay. Go ahead." And only then would he begin to gnaw. I admired his good manners.

He had some bad manners too, some of which had to do with two dogs at Borrego chained to a clothesline pole behind one of the cinder block duplexes. It happened one evening when Kuma was still very small and he was roaming out around the trailer. I was inside cooking. I had the back door propped open to let the sun in, and Kuma burst through and hauled himself into a corner and curled up so small he almost disappeared. I called him to me and he came reluctantly, hunched up and slinking and shaking. I found a deep puncture wound on his soft belly and knew he'd gotten into something out there. Alice, who managed the school supply trailer on campus, came to the door then and said, "Those dogs got loose and they was chasin' your puppy." I dabbed the wound with Bag Balm against infection, and gave him a good taste of bacon grease over his dry kibble.

After that, every Friday afternoon when we drove out of Borrego, we passed by those two dogs chained to the end of their lives, and Kuma would leap at the passenger-side window and bark and snarl and tear at the glass with his front feet, which I took to mean: "FUCK YOU! FUCK YOU! FUCK YOU!"

I thought of Kuma as kindred to both coyotes and bears. In Navajo mythology, Bear is one of the guardians of Sun's house, the father of the world. It is also said that Bear was given to the people by Changing Woman to protect them on journeys. In the myth-time, Shash, the Fearless Bear, was one of the five pets who traveled with the people during the gathering of the clans. He was revered for providing protection, food, and good company. But the people knew that Shash was wild and would not be happy among them forever. They decided they had to let him go. Grateful for his freedom, Shash wandered off to live with his own kind. Despite this story, Navajo people fear bears, and they are more commonly a symbol of evil. Changing-bear-maiden exemplifies evil: she was the perfect Navajo woman who became a bear when she was corrupted by Coyote's deception and lust. Her snout grew long, and her nails changed into claws. She grew thick hair all over her body, except on her breasts. The beautiful maiden transformed into the most horrible part of herself—a bear, the beast within—and Coyote was to blame. The stories of Yellow Woman from Laguna Pueblo, just east of Grants, echo those of Changing-bear-maiden, only the transformation into a bear is effected in marriage and centers on sexual and personal liberty for Yellow Woman. For her husband back home, who says something like, "Where have you been these past months, and how do you explain these two children," Yellow Woman fell prey to some evil. But in her own mind she seeks out such an experience, an encounter with Bear-man, to free her from the bondage of tradition. Navajo people also say that Bear has a sheen over his hair that is akin to the sheen in pollen, that sacred symbol of life and light and regeneration, also of peace and happiness.

Coyote does not get as much respect as Bear. His name in Navajo can be translated as "First-to-get-angry" or "First-one-to-use-words-for-force." Coyote's anger is an essential force in war. Indeed, Coyote is force, combined with the elements of deception and knavery. Coyote's lust began in the lower worlds, where it went uncontrolled. It is said that he lay with the women constantly and licked them between their legs, and this is why coyotes and dogs lick each other there to this day. Dogs are considered dirty, sly animals too. They are little more than property to most Navajos. Adults do not stop children from torturing or abusing them. They laugh at the dogs' misery and misfortune. Traditional Navajos do not allow dogs into their homes because they are seen as dirty, vile, dishonorable. When Vanessa Angel, an eighth-grade student in my language arts class, learned that I had a puppy, she said, "I bet you sleep with that dog like other white people. That's sick. It has ticks and things."

Coyote is the great trickster figure in Navajo mythology, and seeing a coyote usually means bad luck. A Navajo warrior on his way into battle might turn back if he sees a coyote cross his path. Coyote is both good and evil, in that he aligns himself with whichever side suits his fancy. In the assembly of Navajo gods, there are two options: the gods representing good on the south side, and the gods representing evil on the north side. Coyote sits between them near the door so that he is at once on both sides and on no side. It is said that he buries his vitals in the ground to protect them, his heart and blood, his breath and lungs, so that the rest of him can wander the earth doing foul deeds without fear of vulnerability. It is also said that Coyote keeps his life force safe in his nose and tail so that when the rest of his body is killed, he can come to life again. In her book *Navaho Religion*, Gladys Reichard writes of Coyote: "He is sneaking, skulking, wary, shrewd, tricky, mischievous, provoking, exasperating, contrary, undependable, amusing, disarming, persuasive, flattering, smug, undisciplined, cowardly, foolhardy, obstinate, disloyal, dishonest, licentious, lascivious, amoral, deceptive, sacrilegious, and, in a sense, persistent." All this ill news is counter to Coyote's poetic beginning: in the myth-time, the sky bent down as the earth rose up to meet it. At the moment and the point of contact, sky and earth, Coyote sprang out.

Walking in the desert with Kuma, I remember a day watching the light find its way into the horizon. A coyote appeared on the edge of the next rise. Kuma took flight. He became a whirr of speed and motion, and I heard his high-pitched barks rising and falling with the shape of the land. He went far, far away, out into the place where the sky squatted on the desert. I stopped and scanned the distance for him, and called to him, and called again. I wondered if he was ever coming back. He did, after a long time, and I thought then that Kuma wasn't *like* a coyote, he *was* a coyote.

One day in the spring at Borrego, Kuma and I traveled out into the open country, walking softly and surely among the scattered cows. Several miles of desert lay between us and our trailer home. A light wind blew crosswise, delivering the scent of fresh manure as we walked. We might have gone on around the foot of the entire mesa, a long walk that would take us behind the Trading Post and over the hill that Merle claimed was the site of some not-so-ancient massacre. On days of exceptional rain, he said, the bones of Navajo children washed into his garden. I loved long walks, but this walk had gone on long enough. The sun was falling into the western lands and I felt hungry, thirsty, weathered, and ready for something else. So we turned up a little wash that seemed to promise a shorter path over the mesa again and back home.

The wash steepened as we went, the slope on either side coming up around us like ribs over the belly of a great animal. I had never been through this little slot before, and even here at the end of the walk, the landscape promised something new. We skirted boulders and roots of pine perched on the edge of life in this rocky, scorpion-tail country, pulling ourselves up by tooth and claw. At one point I hefted first the dog and then myself onto a ledge and crawled across a fallen tree as a bridge between us and the crack of doom.

I wondered if we wouldn't get caught inside this little canyon and have to go back the long way around, which meant perhaps walking part of it in the dark. But I could see the top now and thought we would make it.

Kuma stopped. The hair on his back and tail rose up, and he growled low in his throat. I stopped too, and crept up cautiously behind him. He nosed the air, pumping his body forward and back in hesitation like a snake, which is what I thought he'd found. Deep in the chasm between two great stones, the wreckage of a horse lay wasting in the sun.

The lips were laid back from the teeth and the eyes were empty hollows. The neck was twisted up at too sharp an angle, and the legs, broken and bent under the body, seemed to be coming from every direction. The ribs curved up and around where the insides were supposed to be, but the cavity was empty. The hide, tanned by the sun, looked stiff like wood. There was nothing wet about this death.

In the land I read the story of where the horse had broken down, the hoofprints marked its turning point in the sand. A juniper tree showed the dramatic plunge where it fell and tore some branches away and dragged them down. I saw them now jutting from beneath the animal's cavernous belly. And there I saw more markings of horse feet, probably before the fall, the horse coming up the trail out of the wash, stumbling where the marks were many, here dropping its panicked shit, dark and ill, then stumbling again, shuffling across the dirt, skidding here, tripping up there, whirling in an unbalanced dance, sick maybe, or old and blind, lost and dehydrated into delirium. All of it came to the edge of these rocks, the edge of its life, and in a final effortless grace, the horse fell in and out of this world.

I thought something needed blessing, so I said, "Amen," and then, with Kuma, scrambled up and over the mesa to the other side. We walked on home in the failing light.

Back at the trailer, I discovered that absolutely nothing had happened in my absence. Everything was as I had left it. Did I expect something more? I let Kuma in, bent to remove my boots, then went in, and shut the door.

FIVE

THE TRADING POST

The Navajo children at Borrego said that a great horned owl lived in a juniper tree behind Mr. Wiseman's house. Owls, they told me, can perform strange magic. Sometimes this magic is good, but most of the time it's bad. Owls can make people go to sleep, and they are harbingers of evil and death. When you see an owl, especially a big owl, bad luck is on its way. The word was not that Mr. Wiseman was in danger because the owl lived behind his house, but that he himself was danger—that he was a witch, a skinwalker, or possessed by a devil.

Raymond Wiseman was a tall man with a soft pear shape. His narrow shoulders sloped into his round, gentle middle, and he wore his gray hair buzzed like a soldier. He laughed a lot. He wasn't a teacher at Borrego, but his wife, Jane, taught the third grade. She had a son, Miles, by another marriage, who was in the fifth grade. Miles was the only white kid at Borrego and, with the exception of Manny from Zuni, the only non-Navajo. Mr. Wiseman (only Jane seemed to call him Raymond) said he had been a professor at the University of Indiana, but I never clearly understood what it was he professed. Sociology, maybe, or political science, or anthropology, or something. When I asked him about it, he somehow got all those words in there together, so that I was never sure if he taught all of it or nothing. Jane had been one of his graduate students. At least that was the story going around. She was younger than he, but not that much younger. They made a fine couple, and I rather liked them.

I wondered why they lived at Borrego. With all the choices in the world, why Borrego? When Mr. Wiseman and Jane fell in love in Indiana, I mused, maybe they had broken something else up, Jane's marriage, for example, or Mr. Wiseman's. Or perhaps their union violated some ethical code in Mr. Wiseman's department and now they were on the run? Or did one of the families reject their union, and so they lived in exile in New Mexico? When I asked Mr. Wiseman about it, he pointed out the front window of his house to the wide, wild country opening before us. "We got tired of the Midwest," he said. "We want to be living here, inside of that."

Because Mr. Wiseman claimed to be a seasoned teacher, he sometimes filled in for teachers when they were gone, like the time the art teacher, John Yazzie, went turkey hunting and didn't bother to tell anyone. A few of his students wandered out to my classroom to see what I was doing. "John's not here," they said. "And we have nothin' to do." So I called the front office, and they called Mr. Wiseman.

Perhaps his retirement gave Mr. Wiseman greater freedom from the stress and sometime-chaos of teaching at Borrego Pass. He'd already put in his time, and so any teaching he did at Borrego was just fun and games. Like me, he rarely had control of his classroom, but unlike me, it didn't seem to bother him. As a substitute, he could leave bad behavior for the regular teacher to deal with; the substitute's mantra is the eternal "Just wait until your teacher gets back!" Mr. Wiseman floated through classes, day after day, seemingly unaffected by the hardness of his students, the sometimes disturbing and tragic stories of their lives, the pervading sense that the great hope that education would heal all social ills was an illusion, that book learning would take these kids nowhere except to a monthly government check. I was plagued by my failure in the classroom, while Mr.

Wiseman seemed unaffected by his. "I don't mind a loud classroom," Mr. Wiseman told me once. "As long as everyone is in the room and no one gets hurt."

He exaggerated himself in the classroom to the point that he seemed crazier than the students he taught. Probably he was. One day in the cafeteria Jerry Valdez, an eighth grader who held an alpha position among the boys that rivaled Caleb Benally's, said something nasty to Mr. Wiseman in Navajo. Mr. Wiseman latched onto his arm as he passed, pulled him in close, cradling him, and said, "Jeerrryyy. Honnneeeyyy. Come sit on daddy's lap." Jerry ran away shrieking.

The owl that lived behind the Wiseman's house told the kids that Mr. Wiseman was a skinwalker. He wore big eyeglasses that darkened in the sun, so that sitting in a classroom in front of a sunny window, the kids told me, he looked like a skull with cavernous black holes for eyes. And they were sure he could take himself apart, which he proved by removing his false teeth and clacking them together in front of the classroom. In addition to these powers, the boys at school had seen Mr. Wiseman out behind his house crawling around on all fours like an animal, collecting hairs and bits of bone, they said, to use in dark spells.

I knew, however, that Mr. Wiseman wasn't collecting hairs. Every time it rained he went out to collect the potsherds that washed down into his backyard. He laid them out like puzzle pieces on a table in the kitchen and fixed them together where they would go. He had several ancient Anasazi pots emerging at once, a slow, steady resurrection.

Even so, to the Borrego boys, Mr. Wiseman was a witch. It only reinforced their position when the maintenance man, Everett, put his rez dog down after it broke free of its chain and attacked Miles. I first heard the story when Everett offered me a doghouse for Kuma. I accepted it, then asked why he was giving it away. I heard the story again at school when Charlie Hunter told me to be careful around Mr. Wiseman, that dogs like Everett's only attacked witches and their relations.

Miles showed me the bruises and puncture wounds under his right arm and along his ribs. He wore these wounds like a badge of honor, proof of his hardiness, and made them available to anyone who wanted to see. As the only white kid in school, he'd been taking a lot of shit from the other boys, and no one, not even his good friend Tom Charlie, could defend him. It was about this time he started karate lessons in Gallup.

Mr. Wiseman's growing reputation as a necromancer gave him increasing power in the classroom. He knew it and seemed to like it. No matter how unruly, how crazy the kids became in the classroom, he challenged them by acting crazier. It didn't seem to calm them down any, but perhaps it allowed Mr. Wiseman an outlet for the inevitable frustration, and even anger, that might arise out of working in the center of such madness. His other tack was one of assuming a royal air. Students in Mr. Wiseman's class could do or have whatever they desired as long as they acknowledged his special birthright: "Yes, Oh Great One," they called him, and he would then grant their wishes.

Mr. Wiseman also loved to say, over and over, the phrase "As Shakespeare said." He used it as a prefix or a suffix, depending on the situation. "As Shakespeare said, it was fuckin' awful," he would say. Or, "The dirty sons-of-bitches, as Shakespeare said." Once he told me that his secret to solving discipline problems in the classroom at Borrego was to pinch these Navajo kids on the soft underside of their arms, hard—except the girls, don't touch the girls, he said—and that would take care of the little shits, as Shakespeare said.

Beyond substitute teaching and crawling around on all fours like an animal—which seem somehow related—Mr. Wiseman spent a lot of time hanging out at the Trading Post. I found him down there a number of times sitting on a stool behind the counter like he ran the place, while Merle stood in front of the counter like a customer, sporting his usual Wranglers and cowboy hat. Mr. Wiseman would sit there all day, if Merle let him, and neither of them would get anything done. It seemed to me that Mr. Wiseman wasn't really the kind of guy who would sit around at a Trading Post telling amazing stories, a kind of barfly without the bar, but that he wanted to be, so he went down there regularly as if in training. I think he was lonely, too, spending day after long day alone in his house fitting potsherds together while Jane worked and Miles went to school. The Trading Post offered him a much-needed distraction.

On a late fall day at Borrego, I walked down the cow trail to the Trading Post for something, a nail, or a can of beans, or to relieve the monotony of a lonely day. The little bells on the knob jingle-jangled as I opened the front door. I noticed a flyer posted there that read "Gospel Teardrop God Ministry Banquet. Evangelist Samuel Begay. Next Sunday, 10:00 a.m. to whenever."

"Mr. Cas-well! Welcome," Mr. Wiseman called out from his bench behind the counter.

To which Merle added, "Yá'át'ééh!"

Merle spoke pretty good Navajo, as he'd been dealing with Navajo artists and traders, not to mention customers, for years.

The Borrego Pass Trading Post opened in the 1930s under the leadership of its owners, Don and Fern Smouse. They set up a silversmith operation there and employed dozens of Navajos who made hundreds of pieces of silver and turquoise jewelry: belt buckles and pendants, rings and watchbands, bracelets, earrings, far more than they could sell. Years later, Smouse tapered off production and stored most of the jewelry in a room beneath the Trading Post. He and his wife retired and hired Merle and Rosie to run the place. Every now and again, Mr. Wiseman told me, Smouse drove up to Borrego and rummaged through the jewelry collection. He'd take a box with him to exotic places like Albuquerque and Santa Fe and sell it all. Because the craftsmanship of those early years was far superior to the work of today, that jewelry was worth quite a bit of money. "Well,"

Smouse said to Mr. Wiseman one day, "that last box was worth ten thousand," or some big number like that.

"What can I do for ya?" Mr. Wiseman said. He paused a moment to reconsider. "I mean, what can Merle do for ya?" he said. "Or Rosie," and Rosie smiled.

Her face, wrinkled and beaten by the New Mexican sun, evened out when she smiled, and I could see that she had been a beautiful woman in her youth, or rather she was a beautiful woman even now. She wore her light brown hair in tight curls against her head, and large squarish glasses. I felt a confidence and stability in her that made coming into the Trading Post a pleasure.

Merle was a Korean War veteran who had taken shrapnel in his left arm and leg when a mine exploded, killing the soldier next to him. Merle carried his arm around like it didn't quite work, and it probably didn't. After I got to know him a little better, Merle told me that his fighting team had had to walk from Pusan in the south of Korea all the way to Seoul just to get to the war. Now when Rosie asked Merle if he wanted to go with her on an evening walk out behind the Trading Post or up Borrego Pass Road, he always responded the same way: "I had enough walkin' in the goddamn war."

"The gate back there against the wall was open," I said to Rosie. "So I latched it."

"Oh, that," said Rosie. "That latch doesn't quite hold anymore. Thank you anyway."

"Maybe 'cause that damn wall winds around like a snake," Merle said.

"Oh, it does," said Rosie. "But I'm rather partial to it."

"It's falling down in places," Merle said, "because those Navajos who built it weren't worth a damn."

Mr. Wiseman laughed. He'd heard this story before.

"You see," said Rosie, as if on cue, "those men who built that rock wall kept a bottle hidden in with their lunch. They didn't start drinking much until after lunch, usually, but the drunker they got, the longer they worked, and the longer they worked the more that wall began to sag back and forth. They were good boys and they did their best to keep it straight, under the circumstances. They didn't mean no harm."

"Jesus," said Merle.

"It looks more natural like that anyhow, to me," Rosie said.

"Christ," said Merle.

"Wasn't that one of them who came in here just the other day?" asked Mr. Wiseman.

"I don't know," said Merle. "Was it?"

"The one who went back there and drank part of that bottle of Pine-Sol?" asked Mr. Wiseman.

"Could have been, I guess," said Merle. "Did he pay for it?"

Mostly Merle and Rosie tried not to enable alcoholics, especially those who resorted to all kinds of elixirs for a fix: drinking cleaning fluids or cologne, huffing hairspray or gasoline, and the like. Therefore, it wasn't proper or legal to fill anything at the gas pump but your truck. Once in awhile, though (maybe Merle would be sorting through nails or bolts or cans of tomatoes), someone would pull up, run a pint of gas into a Mason jar, real slick-like, screw on the lid, stow it, and then fill the truck.

"I don't remember if he paid for it," said Mr. Wiseman. "Maybe he did. Maybe he didn't." Then Mr. Wiseman said to me, "Isn't it right that you come from Idaho? We were just talkin' about Idaho. Isn't that right, Merle?"

Merle nodded.

"You know I knew Mr. Hemingway," Mr. Wiseman started in. He had lived in Ketchum, he said, while working on his dissertation. He became friends with a certain medical doctor in town, and they had a practice of drinking together at various Ketchum and Sun Valley bars. It was about ten one morning when Mr. Wiseman ran into his friend on the street. The doctor carried a guitar case and walked with a purpose.

"Morning," said Mr. Wiseman.

"Morning," said the doctor. "Where you headed?"

"To such and such," said Mr. Wiseman. "I didn't know you played guitar."

"Forget that," said the doctor. "Come with me."

"Where are you going?"

"To the such and such bar," said the doctor.

"At ten in the morning?"

"Yes. C'mon. You won't regret it. You'll see why."

"I never drink in the morning," said Mr. Wiseman.

"You should make an exception," said the doctor.

So Mr. Wiseman followed the doctor to the bar. Of course there was Hemingway, leaning expertly over a pitcher of iced daiquiri already half empty. He wore a dirty sportsman's cap. His gray beard was twisted and parted like he hadn't slept well. The doctor introduced Mr. Wiseman, and the two men sat down.

Hemingway said, "Have a drink, gentlemen."

And so the gentlemen did.

Mr. Wiseman was about my age, he told me, and because he was working on his dissertation, he counted himself something of a writer. "Hemingway," Mr. Wiseman mused in the middle of his story. "I never knew a man so attentive to detail. So clear and focused in his mind. If you had a flower in your hand, Hemingway wouldn't stop until he knew everything there was to know about it."

"Hmmm," Merle said. "Everything."

"Oh yes," Rosie said. "Everything there was to know."

"Right. I know," Merle said. "He was very attentive to detail."

Obviously they'd both heard this story before.

Mr. Wiseman continued. Then Hemingway said, "Have you got it there?"

"Right here," the doctor said, patting the guitar case with his hand.

"Let's have it, then," Hemingway said, taking the guitar case across his lap. He opened it. "Isn't she a beauty," Hemingway said. He reached in and lifted the shotgun out. He set the case to the side and stood the shotgun erect in his lap with the two barrels pointing at the ceiling.

"I lost a bet," the doctor told Mr. Wiseman.

Hemingway asked Mr. Wiseman, "Do you hunt?"

"No," said Mr. Wiseman.

Then Hemingway said, "Well, if you did, you'd know that you're looking at such and such a shotgun with a such and such and a this and that. And a real fine one, too."

Then Hemingway broke the shotgun open and sighted through the empty barrels. "A real beauty," he said again. He reached into the breast pocket of his shirt and took out a shotgun shell. He set the shell into the right chamber, snapped the barrel back, set the stock firm against his thigh, and blew a hole in the ceiling of the bar.

Then Hemingway said, "Yes, a real beauty. Thank you, doctor." And he poured all three glasses full.

Mr. Wiseman told me that if I was ever in Sun Valley, I should go to that bar and see that hole in the ceiling. "They never repaired it," he said. "Instead they made it into a monument."

That was the day that Leonard Angel came to class drunk. I quite liked working with the eighth grade. They were no kinder, no more accepting of me, but we moved faster, seemed to accomplish more, and could sometimes hold together a discussion about our reading. I hatched a plot to read *Romeo and Juliet* with them in the spring, maybe with the seventh grade too.

I had fast grown bored with the textbook, its dull patterns and predictability, its simpleton stories and stupid review questions,

questions that seemed to close doors to the story, close doors to the world, rather than opening them. I couldn't imagine bothering with such dross. Wasn't one of the prime values of literature, of all the arts, that it opens doors to a larger world, that through it we are allowed into an experience or world foreign to us, and after wandering around a bit, we discover the foreign is not so foreign after all, that we are in fact reading a story about ourselves? Review questions like those in our text allowed very little room for discovery because they circled too close to an answer, a literal and pedestrian understanding from which students walked away thinking Now I get it, and all that's left is the final exam. It occurred to me that such textbooks are written not for students, but for teachers who lack inspiration, creativity, energy, maybe interest. For teachers who used such textbooks when they were in school and so came to believe that art is a little puzzle that must be solved. For teachers who didn't know what else to do and really didn't want to do it in the first place. For me, reading our textbook was like living in a plastic house with a plastic family who sat together to eat plastic food—you think you can live on it, but you can't. Or maybe I was just feeling grumpy.

"What's goin' on, Leonard?" I said.

"Nothin'," he said, with a big grin on his face. His cheeks were flushed, and he stared off into the ceiling. He wore dusty black Levis and that light winter jacket he always wore over a blue T-shirt. The jacket, gray with snap-down chest pockets, bore a dark greasy ring around the bottom about halfway up and around the inside of the collar. The coat was in good condition, it just hadn't been washed.

"You sure?" I asked. "You look a little too happy." Too happy? I thought. Who can be too happy?

"Yep," he said, giggling. "I'm too happy."

"Leon-nard," Tom Thompson said, smiling big.

Tom didn't have anything to say, he was just laughing with Leonard.

"What's on your mind, Leonard?" I asked again. "You got a story to tell?"

I wanted him to talk a little. It was obvious to me that he was drunk, or buzzing on gasoline fumes, but I wanted him to give it away with his voice.

"Yeah," Leonard said. "A story."

"Go ahead, then," I said. "Let's hear it."

He put his head down on the table then, rolled his forehead back and forth over the table.

"You all right?" I asked.

"Ahhh," he moaned. "I think I'm sick," he said.

"Git away from me, then," said Mary Jane.

"Me too, you stupit," said Victoria Angel, his younger sister. "You're always so stupit."

"Shut up," he told her. "You shut you up."

Then Tom started laughing, laughing so deep inside himself he couldn't hold it in. "You shut you up!" he said, laughing. "You shut you up!"

Leonard was laughing too now, only he was also moaning in pain, "Oohhh, I'm sick. I'm gonna get sick."

"Go outside, then, you ugly dog," Victoria said.

He did go outside then. He got up and dragged himself around the tables at the edge of the room as fast as he could, keeping his head low and his hand on his stomach. Tom leaned back in his chair and pushed the door open for him, and as Leonard crossed over the threshold, Tom pushed him outside and let the door swing closed. We heard him retching out there against the side of the building.

"Oh god," said Renee Benally. "That's sick."

"Yeah, Mr. Caswell. That's too gross," said Victoria.

"I'm sorry," I said. "Give me a minute here. I have to call Frank, you know."

"No, you don't," said Mary Jane. "Frank won't do nothin'."

"Yes, he does," said Victoria.

"Yeah, he does too," said Renee.

"Hey, Mr. Caswell," said William Brown. "You like to get all crazy like Leonard too? Maybe you drink too much too," he said, grinning big through his missing teeth.

That probably would have made me mad a few weeks ago, or under different circumstances, but I didn't have time for it now. I used the phone there in the classroom to call Deena at the front desk, who would then patch me through to Frank. Deena was Frank's wife, and it was her position at the school that helped Frank get the detention monitor job when Dallas West resigned amid charges that he was too rough with the kids, especially the boys. The story I heard was that a teacher had caught Caleb with a knife in class and sent him down to spend the rest of the day with Dallas. Caleb didn't just have a pocketknife in his pocket—he had been waving the knife around in class boasting that he might do something with it. Dallas asked Caleb to give him the knife. Caleb refused. Then Dallas gathered the front of Caleb's shirt in his fist, picked Caleb up with one hand, and slammed him hard against the wall, held him there, hurt him a little.

I rather liked Dallas. He invited me into his office during my first week of work to explain how he could help me with discipline. He wore a sharp little beard on his chin, rare for a Navajo, and thick, dark eyeglasses. He wasn't tall, but big, heavy, and powerful-looking. He told me that he had been a Navajo cop and that he had specialized in investigating occult activities on the reservation. Navajo gangs were cropping up all over, he said, mostly boys with little to no home life, and they were practicing the dark arts, sacrificing animals and sleeping in coffins. He was presiding over a Navajo ceremony in the coming weeks, he told me (he didn't say what ceremony), and if I wanted to participate, not this time, he said, but sometime, I should let him know. Shortly after that he left the school and I never saw him again.

Frank brought a much-needed positive force to school discipline.

Younger than Dallas, Frank had a kind face and a gentle, soft voice, yet he commanded space and respect. He made a point of visiting every classroom his first day of work, especially the classrooms of the white teachers. In the middle of my class he stood up to interrupt me and addressed the class like an angry father. First he spoke in Navajo, then he repeated what he had said in English so I could hear it. He told the students that they should be more respectful and that I had something to teach them. That I was living way out here in this place that was not mine and maybe they could appreciate my efforts to bring them a piece of the outside world. And he didn't want to hear anymore cussing and carrying on in Navajo because they all knew that I couldn't understand and they were taking advantage of me. And he was going to teach me a few Navajo words and phrases to recognize. If I heard them, he would expect me to report back. Then he would come to the class again and make it stop.

Since coming to Borrego, I had hardly heard a positive word about my work. From Lauren, yes, whom I looked up to as a teacher, and from Bob King, true enough, but I couldn't quite believe him. My confidence in the classroom was tenuous at best, and over the past weeks I had come to believe very deeply that I was a failure as a teacher, that I had nothing at all to offer these kids, this school, this community. I had come to believe that I was not wanted here and that everyone, but for a few, perhaps, was patiently waiting for me to leave. Frank changed that. For the first time I felt that I wasn't alone, that someone on the inside valued what I was working for, that if Frank cared, then so could I. Not only did I have a new ally; I also had a new friend.

When I called Frank and told him that Leonard Angel was drunk, he came right over. Leonard was still outside, stooped over with his hands on his knees. He moaned a little, opening and closing his mouth like a fish.

"You been drinking, Leonard?" Frank asked.

"No," he said.

"I said, you been drinking?"

"No," he said. "I'm just sick, that's all."

"You ain't been drinking, then?" Frank asked.

Leonard shook his head.

"Go inside," he said. "Wait for me inside. Tell Tom to come out."

Leonard went in. Tom came out.

"Has Leonard been drinking?" Frank asked Tom.

"No," Tom said.

"You sure?"

"Aoo'," Tom said, this time in Navajo.

"Go back inside, then. Tell Jerry to come out."

Tom went in. Jerry came out.

"Has Leonard been drinking?" Frank asked Jerry.

"No," Jerry said. "I don't know."

"You sure?" Frank asked.

"I don't know," Jerry said.

"You don't know."

"No."

"Go back inside," Frank said. "Tell William to come out."

Jerry went in. William came out.

"William, has Leonard been drinking?" Frank asked.

"Yeah, I mean, I don't know," William said.

"So he has been drinking?" Frank asked.

"I don't know. He's drunk, anyway."

"All right," Frank said. "Go back inside. Tell Victoria to come out."

"Has Leonard been drinking?" Frank asked Victoria.

"What do you mean?" Victoria said. "You can see he is."

"Yes, but I want to know if you think he's been drinking."

"Course he is. He's always drunk like that," Victoria said. "Anyone knows."

"Thank you," Frank said. "You can go back in. Tell Mary Jane to come out."

It went on this way until Frank had talked to everyone. I wondered why he needed to talk to everyone; after William and Victoria, it seemed he knew enough. But he made sure no one was left out. Meanwhile, my class was held prisoner inside the portable, and it became clear that today's lesson wasn't about reading and writing, but something else. What, I didn't know. No one complained, however; perhaps they were bored with our textbook too. Finally, Frank asked for Leonard again.

He came outside, negotiated the steps well enough, looked a little better.

"Leonard," Frank said. "You've been drinking. And you came to class today drunk." It was clearly a statement now, a verdict, and Leonard accepted it.

"Yes," Leonard said, his head down.

"What you been drinking?" Frank asked.

"Nothing."

"I asked you a question."

Leonard reached into his coat pocket and handed Frank a bottle of cologne. A green squarish bottle with a black cap, maybe about seven ounces. It was mostly empty, except for the bit of residue that settles in the bottom. Frank held it up in the light and looked through it.

Borrego Pass had a long contraband list, which included the usuals: chewing tobacco, cigarettes, alcohol, and all recreational drugs. It also included cologne and hairspray, and all sorts of cleaning products, because kids would mix them with water and make a weird cocktail to get drunk. They also huffed gasoline, so, like the Trading Post, most gas stations banned filling any container but a fuel tank. Such substances were highly toxic, of course, but it was a cheap, easy way to get high.

"Where'd you get this?" Frank asked.

"Nowhere," Leonard said.

Now Frank was losing his patience. He wanted to cuss, I could tell, but he held himself back. "Leonard," he said, and then he spoke in Navajo, something forceful, something aggressive, something uncontestable.

"Wal-Mart," Leonard said. "In Gallup."

"Did you pay for this?"

"No."

"Is this the first time?"

"No."

"I have to take this, you know."

"Yeah."

"What else you been drinking?" Frank asked.

"Gas," Leonard said. "Huffin' gas. They make me do it."

"Who makes you do it?"

"My brother, and my cousin-brothers," he said. "Every day," he said, and he started to cry.

"It gives you a bad headache, doesn't it, Leonard," Frank said.

"Yeah," Leonard said, wiping his tears with the back of his hand.

"Okay," he said. "That's enough. I have to take this to Bob King, you know."

"Yeah."

"And you'll have to do detention."

"Yeah."

"And I'm gonna get you to a doctor."

"Okay," Leonard said.

The front doors of the school were propped open, and the little ones, the elementary grades, were streaming out onto the playground.

"Go to your next class," Frank said. "Thank you, Mr. Caswell. We'll talk more later." Then Frank walked back inside to his office.

Later Frank told me that Leonard had gone down to the Eastern Agency hospital, and the doctor there confirmed that he had about 40 percent of his lungs left.

After that morning when I turned down her pies, Gay became one of the angriest students in all three of my classes. Far angrier, even, than Caleb Benally. She stared at me with a deep hatred. If I asked something of her in the classroom, she answered a hot, sharp "No!" or sometimes "Yes!" and that was all. One day, working through a story in our textbook, I called on Gay to read aloud. She was one of the best readers in the sixth grade. I often relied on her to take the lead. Many of the other students were reluctant to read first, or at all, but not Gay. She had no fear of all those words on the page. With her success, other students became willing, and we would cruise right along to the end of our story. But this time when I asked her, Gay pierced me with her eyes and said, "Don't talk to me!"

Gay was just one hostile voice among many in my classroom, and I didn't think much about it at first. I certainly didn't connect her anger with my refusal to buy her pies. That seems obvious now, but maybe I was so absorbed in my own troubles that I was incapable of stepping outside myself. Whatever made her that way, I thought, was her problem. There was little I could do to fix it, or to fix anything in her life. In fact, I came to believe, there was nothing I could do to fix anything in any of these kids' lives. I didn't know what my students wanted or needed, or where to look for common ground, or even how to talk to them. I didn't know if the gap between us was about age or language, or about race, about me being white in a Navajo world, or about something else that I couldn't identify.

How do I teach these children, I asked? How do I manage them in the classroom? How do I live in this place with them? How do I earn the respect of young Navajos who seemed to believe that all their problems were the fault of rich white people, like me? Of course, I wasn't really rich—I was just barely paying my bills. But to these kids, I was wealthy beyond anything they might ever know in their lifetimes. This was not a money-in-the-pocket kind of wealth, but the kind of wealth that comes from the privilege of having choices. I could work in Japan, as I had already done. I could move back up to Idaho. I could find a job in Albuquerque or Seattle or New York City, if I wanted to. I could seek a law degree, study to become a doctor, a businessman, a real estate tycoon. I was rich because I had the power to choose to pursue wealth. I had the potential that came with a childhood in which most people I knew told me that I could do or be anything I wanted.

The kids in my classroom, with few exceptions, probably never heard from anyone they respected that they had a wide range of choices about how to live their lives. Many of my students at Borrego did not consider high school an option. At so young an age, they already believed that one of the few options they had was to stay home, which meant to have children and collect a government assistance check. I might say, "What are you going to do when you finish school?" To which someone would answer, "I'm gonna stay home."

It wasn't that Navajo people didn't value education. They did. But life at home was an education too, a better education in how to be Navajo, perhaps, than any classroom could provide. In talking to some of the parents at the school's quarterly Open House, I sensed that they didn't wholly trust that what I was teaching was in the best interest of their children.

Still, I expected compliance in the classroom. Some days that expectation seemed unrealistic, hopeless, naive. I felt plagued by where to draw that line between bending to my students' circumstances and challenging them with standards I brought from a world they seemed to want no part of. So often I could not get through a lesson. I would spend the entire class period working on discipline, trying to teach these kids to pay attention, or to take notes, or to write an exam in silence. After weeks of effort, it all seemed a futile endeavor. So I fell into a kind of sleepy indifference, moving on with my lessons, day by day, week by week, trying to help my students improve their reading and writing skills, and trying not to care whether they ever did.

"Where's my grade book?" I said. "It was right here on my desk a moment ago."

"Of course we don't know," Valeria said.

"C'mon, people," I said. "I just set it down right here. We walked into the room. I collected your papers. I took out my grade book and set it down here on my desk. Where is it? Who took it?"

I knew I should not have made an accusation like that—innocent until proven guilty, of course—but this wasn't the first time, and it probably wouldn't be the last. The thing was, this sort of prank was a daily feature of teaching at Borrego, especially with the sixth grade. Lauren told me that on one of her first days at Borrego, someone poured all the water from her water bottle into her waterproof school bag. All her things, including her new grade book, were sloshing around in there like little toys in a bathtub. That bag was supposed to keep water out, not in. She hadn't considered it might work in reverse.

"Maybe you lost it," Shane said.

"No, I didn't lose it. I told you I set it down two minutes ago right here."

"We don't have it," Valeria said.

"That means we all get A's," Michael said.

"You can't be serious," I said.

"Yeah," John George said. "I'm gonna get an A." Then he smiled and laughed, because he prided himself on getting F's.

"No," Valeria said to John George. "You couldn't get an A anyways."

"Yeah, I can," John George said. "I can get an A, 'cause I'm too smart."

"You're too stupit," said Valeria. "Like a sheep."

"No," said Shane. "He likes sheep. He likes 'em so good."

Then they were all laughing, even John George.

We seemed to go through this same routine every day—a prank or a wild comment from nowhere, followed by an insult, which resulted in the refutation, followed by a joke, until everyone ended up laughing. I should have learned by now that if I only lightened up a bit, didn't take myself or my precious lesson so seriously, if I joined in on the joke, I'd have a much easier time in the classroom.

"So where is it?" I said again.

No one said anything.

"If you don't tell me where it is, we're all just gonna sit here and do nothing."

"Hey, yeah," said Charlie Hunter. "Let's do nothing."

"Yeah," said Kyle Bigfoot. "Let's go outside and mess around, since we're doin' nothing."

"Can we, Mr. Caswell?" Leanne said. "Can we for reals? I didn't take your grade book."

Had everyone lost their mind?

"All right!" I said. "Everyone who wants to learn something, stay here. Everyone who wants to learn nothing, go in the next room and do nothing."

At first, they seemed stunned. The class didn't seem to think I was serious.

"I'm serious," I said.

"For reals?" Shane said.

"Yes, for reals," I said.

"For really reals?" Leanne said.

"Yes, yes, yes. For really reals."

A few of them got up and went to other side of the trailer. "No computer games," I called after them. "You just have to sit in there and do nothing."

"Okay," someone called back. They sat in there for the rest of the class. A few students remained at their desks, and I went on with the lesson. It was the best class I'd had to that day.

As class ended, I called over to the kids who had opted to leave class. "It's recess time," I said, but no one came out. When I went to the doorway, there they sat with sour faces, dejected and sad, looking at all those idle computers, as if it were my choice, not theirs, that had brought them to this state. It turned out to be no fun at all doing nothing. I thought I'd stumbled onto the perfect trick to get my students into their studies.

A week or more later, I tried it again, but it backfired. This time everyone except Leanne Yazzie went into the next room to do nothing. I started in on the lesson anyway, but Leanne looked very uncomfortable, maybe because there was so little of her in the room against so much of me. She raised her hand shyly and asked, "Mr. Caswell. Can I go over there too?"

"Okay," I said. "Let's both go." Only this time, instead of doing nothing, everyone played number and word games on the computers, including me. And we had a great time.

Juan Carlos Morales lived in the trailer next to mine. He worked as the Gifted and Talented Education (GATE) coordinator at Borrego Pass, but mostly he seemed to wander around the school all day poking his head into classrooms. He was about my age, athletic-looking, with an evolving belly. He wore his hair greased tight into a little ponytail high on the back of his head. He wore gold jewelry. His face, pitted from youthful acne, was rugged and rather handsome. He only wore black Levis, a black cotton T-shirt with the sleeves rolled up, and a black leather jacket. He looked like a gangster.

Many of the boys at Borrego admired Juan Carlos. They all tried to dress like him. They slicked their hair back like his, with dish soap from home or hand soap from the school bathrooms. One morning Samuel Smith, a seventh-grade student in my homeroom, boasted, "I got so much soap in my hair it took three pitchers of water to wash it out." Juan Carlos's cousins, Clemson and Caleb Benally, especially admired him. They formed a little trio with an obvious pecking order: Juan Carlos reigned as a kind of mob boss, while Caleb ordered Clemson around, and Clemson in turn bullied all the boys in the seventh grade. Caleb had such power among the boys at Borrego that he rarely got into fights. Clemson wasn't very imposing; his power stemmed from the fact that everyone knew Caleb would support him, and Juan Carlos would support Caleb. I had heard that Juan Carlos had an uncle or a cousin on the school board, so whoever that was must have supported Juan Carlos.

The day I interviewed for the job at Borrego, Louise caught Juan Carlos in the hallway and asked him to give me a tour of the school. We shook hands and began a little walking tour of the hallway and grounds.

"This is the hallway," Juan Carlos said. "And all these doors are the classrooms." He spoke like he had trouble breathing, or he was overly excited and trying to catch his breath, or perhaps this added duty was a great strain on his day. He didn't appear to be put off, but friendly, rather, and quite happy to tour me around. His breathlessness I took to be a style of his, like the way he carried himself, something from the street to go with his black outfit and pimped hairstyle.

I asked him what he did and how he liked working at Borrego.

"I'm the GATE coordinator," Juan Carlos said. "My job is to get as many kids qualified for the GATE program as possible. Then I fill out a lot of paperwork and send it in. The more kids I get qualified for the program, the more money we get. It's just paperwork, really. It don't mean nothin'. So if you come here, you'll work with me some, and your job will be to find kids I can qualify in the paperwork. Sometimes I help with Special Ed too."

"Do you live here?" I asked.

"I gotta place here. A trailer over there," he motioned the direction with his chin. "But I stay over there in Albuquerque a lot too. Mostly every weekend. It's a good job because nobody bothers me. I can do what I want."

That turned out to be true. One afternoon the eighth-grade class was working on individual reading projects, and Renee Benally looked out the trailer window and said, "There goes Jerry with Juan Carlos again." Several of the girls frowned and got up to look out the window. I looked out, too. We watched Juan Carlos lead Jerry across the parking lot and out into the residential part of campus where students were not allowed to go. They went up the steps to Juan Carlos's trailer, went inside, and closed the door.

Jerry had started the semester in my language arts class, but Juan Carlos had him qualified for Special Ed, which meant he spent his language arts and reading class periods out in the Special Ed trailer, where he would receive focused instruction. It was true that Jerry read below grade level, Lauren had confirmed that, but I doubted the attention he got from the Special Ed teacher would help him. Maybe I didn't know what I was talking about, but in my estimation she didn't speak English well enough herself to teach reading and writing to a struggling student. To Juan Carlos, qualifying Jerry for Special Ed brought in funding for the school, improved job security for him and, more important, gave him access to Jerry anytime he wanted. Juan Carlos often pulled kids out of classes during the day to take them to medical appointments in Crownpoint or down to the school nurse (who was his sister) for medication. Sometimes he took students for "testing." Testing for what, I didn't know.

"What are they doing in there?" I asked.

"You know," Renee said.

"I don't know. What do you mean, 'You know'?" I said.

"You know," Renee said again. "They're doin' it in there."

"Doing what?" I asked.

"Maybe Jerry's payin' for it in there," Renee said.

"Renee!" Vanessa Angel said.

"No, Renee," someone said.

"What's he paying for?" I asked.

Of course I thought "it" was either sex or drugs or maybe both. Maybe drugs paid for with sex? But I wanted to hear her say it. I wanted to know what was going on. I hadn't decided what I would do with this information if I got it, but I knew I had no information until someone spoke clearly about it. No one did.

"Maybe I don't know," Renee said, and she sat down.

Everyone got real busy as if suddenly classwork meant everything to them.

From my classroom window I observed Juan Carlos leading kids away to his trailer several more times. Jerry went regularly, and Vanessa's brother, Leonard Angel. One day Clemson and Caleb went into Juan Carlos's trailer together without Juan Carlos. They just wandered out into the forbidden residential zone at recess and went in. I didn't see the boys come out. But just before recess ended, Juan Carlos opened the door and walked out. He came across the parking lot looking cool as ice and went in the school's front doors.

Frank Lee and Deena Bell invited me to dinner. They lived in the duplex just across the drive from the one I had moved out of. I could smell the food from Deena's kitchen through the open door as I came up the concrete walkway. Inside, handsome wool rugs covered the bare floors. Clean, comfortable-looking furniture warmed the living room, a couch and an easy chair. When I knocked, Deena's son, Kestrel, came running out of somewhere and slid around the end of the couch in his socks to get the door. "I got it. I got it," he shouted, and let me in.

Kestrel looked small for his age, a little thin and frail. Maybe he was seven or eight years old. He had much lighter skin than most Navajos at Borrego. I came to understand that he was Deena's son from a previous marriage, and maybe her husband had been white. That didn't seem to matter to Frank, though. He treated Kestrel like his own son. Deena prepared something simple and wholesome for dinner, chicken baked on a bed of wild rice. For dessert, Navajo tea and apple pie. Frank told me again and again that whatever I needed, I should just ask him. He would help me, if he could, and so would Deena, if she could.

After that night, Deena and Frank invited me over every couple weeks. One evening after dinner, while Deena and Kestrel dished up dessert, I followed Frank out to the front step, where he was working on a kachina doll to fill an order from a buyer on the East Coast. He had made most of his living this way before he was hired on at the school. He didn't think of himself as an artist, but I considered him one. We generally avoided talking about school when I came for dinner, but I burned to tell Frank about Juan Carlos. When I did, Frank nodded and said, "Hmm," and continued working the sandpaper over the wood. "I'll look into it," he said, but I sensed in his voice that Juan Carlos was well protected, and Frank knew there was nothing he could do.

One Sunday afternoon Juan Carlos knocked on my door and invited me over to his trailer to have a look at a leather chair he wanted to loan me. He didn't have space for it, he said, but he didn't want to sell it or give it away either. Since I didn't have any furniture, it sounded like a reasonable arrangement to me. He pointed out a box of marine fossils sitting on his front steps that he had collected up on the mesa.

"Tourists in Albuquerque and over there at Santa Fe love these things," he said. "I can get a few bucks apiece for 'em."

The interior of his place was dressed in black like him. A black leather couch and easy chair. A black rug in front of the couch with a black coffee table. Black stereo equipment with huge black speakers. Black curtains over the windows. He showed me the chair, a heavy oak rocker with a brown leather cushion and back. It was the only thing in the room that wasn't black. I could have it on loan, he told me. I accepted, and thanked him.

"In fact," Juan Carlos said, "I'm selling some things. Not this chair I'm loaning you, of course, but other things. Is there any *thing* you want to buy?"

I took this to mean he had drugs for sale, probably pot. I told him no thanks, and then thanked him again for the chair.

"You're not from New Mexico, are you?" Juan Carlos asked me.

"No. I grew up in Oregon," I told him.

"I was gonna say California," he said. "I grew up in Albuquerque."

"So what're you doing way out here?"

"I was gonna ask you the same."

"Well," I said. "I'm just trying to work as a teacher. Making a living, you know?"

"I know," he said. "Me too, I guess. I don't know. It's a good job, you know. And I got family out here. But when I was growing up, I didn't know I was a Navajo. I thought I was Chicano or something. So later I decided maybe I should know something about what being Navajo means, so that's why I came out here. Anyway, I got family out here," he said. "You know Caleb and Clemson are my cousins."

"Yeah," I said. "I do know that. You like it out here?"

"I don't know," he said. "Maybe okay. Enough anyway. Mostly I like it over there in Albuquerque. That's where most of my friends are."

"So why stay here?"

"Maybe 'cause I'm Navajo," he said. "This is Navajoland. This is my ancestral place, you know. The old people say Navajos gotta live inside these four sacred mountains. And I'm Navajo, so seems like I should live here, and I should know something about it."

William Brown was a very simple boy. He was in the eighth grade, and he was big, the biggest kid in school. His hair was cropped close and stuck up on top of his head. He lived with his grandma in a little hogan not far from the school. He seemed to be a natural Zen man: among his favorite things to do in the world, he said, were splitting wood and carrying in the water. He spoke with a kind of lisp and whistle because a week before I arrived at Borrego, he got into a fight with Tom Thompson, and Tom broke three of his front teeth out.

I heard that story not too long after I had an encounter with Tom myself. That fall, I coached the seventh- and eighth-grade cross-country team with the second-grade teacher, Lorrain Puente. She worked mostly with the few girls who wanted to run. I worked with the boys.

I had been running since I was twelve. When I was in the eighth grade at a small school in western Oregon, I broke district records at both 800 and 1,500 meters. In high school, I competed at the state level. My high school track coach, Mark Ferris, was a tough retired air force officer. His father was a retired air force officer too and had survived a German prisoner-of-war camp during World War II. Sometimes before a hard workout or a race, Mr. Ferris would step in front of me, look me in the eye, and say: "Get your game face on!" and he meant it. And so I did. I admired him for it and loved him like a father. One day before I ran the hardest and best workout of my life, he put his index and middle fingers together, made a hard missile out of them, and thunked me in the middle of the sternum. "Get your game face on!" he said. It hurt and I shrank back, but I felt tough knowing that I could take it and that he did it because he wanted me to do well.

To my mind, these Navajo boys had no work ethic when it came to running. Most of the best runners quit, like Caleb Benally, because they said it was too hard and wasn't any fun. The team dwindled until I was left with just a handful of boys, boys who kept with it because they were a little hardier maybe, or they had individual goals, like Will Brown, who said he was running to lose a little weight. Miles Wiseman and Tom Charlie said they'd try anything, and they were best friends, so anything they tried, they tried together. And Tom Thompson. He kept running because he was good; he was the strongest runner in the school.

I pushed them all too hard, I know. They didn't have dreams of grandeur, they just wanted to do something, to be part of something that would open their world a little. And I should have admired them for that, but I wasn't very happy at Borrego in those earlier days. Maybe I wanted to punish them for it. Or prove to them how tough I was in order to regain control of my classroom. So one day when the whole team was just fucking off, I lost my cool.

Will Brown was tearing off the branches of the little willow tree that grew in front of the school. Miles and Tom were giggling and laughing like girls, but minding their own business. We were waiting for John George, who was always late, and Jerry Valdez, who could never remember to bring his shorts. (I kept loaning him mine until he owned more pairs of my shorts than I did, but still forgot them, and sometimes ran in his pants.) And that's when Tom went after Will again. Will started something near the willow tree, an argument about nothing. He was a clown. He didn't like fighting because he often lost, and he always lost against Tom, but his clown nature always seemed to trump his fear. He said something to Tom and teased him and laughed and then ran. Tom ran after him. And I ran after Tom.

I caught up to him somewhere behind the school. We were running fast, and I grabbed the back of his neck and jerked him back and stopped him and turned him around. I was inches away from his face, and I shouted obscenities at him and waved my arms in the air and threatened and shouted and cursed.

"You want to run hard?!" I yelled. "You want to do well?!"

"Yes," Tom said.

"Well, you can't fuck off like this if you want to do well!" I sputtered.

"Yes," Tom said.

My face felt hot and I felt my hands clenched into fists. I could see he was scared, at least a little, but he didn't back down. He stood there against me and took it.

"Goddamn it!" I yelled at him. "All you gotta do is run. Nothing else! No fights. No Will Brown. No nothing. Just run!"

"Aoo'," he said, speaking in Navajo this time.

"That's it!" I yelled. "That's all there is if you wanna do well. Just run. That's all."

"Aoo'."

I didn't know what else to say, but I hadn't cussed out my anger yet, so I kept saying the same thing over and over again. I wanted to hit him. I felt it in my hands, in my arms, in my face. I knew from the way he stood there, a little hunched over and leaning into me, that he expected it. He'd been hit before, probably by his father, or an uncle, and at the very least, I knew he'd been in a lot of fights. I had to stop. I had to back down. Tom looked me hard in the eyes, and I wondered if he wouldn't hit me. If he did, at least I'd have a reason to hit him back. But that was crazy thinking. I was twenty-six and he was probably fifteen. I took a step back, and that softened the space between us. We stood there, that great anger cooling a little in the silence.

Then Tom said, "Aoo'," in acknowledgment and contempt.

"Let's run," I said, and stormed off. The whole team snapped to attention, with Will Brown in the lead, and John George just getting out of the gym doors, and Jerry Valdez running in his pants again, and Miles and Tom together as usual, and they all followed me, and I ran them hard and fast up the dirt road past the Trading Post because I was going to run them until they puked, until they couldn't run anymore, until they bitched and complained about how tired they were and how this sucked and how they hated it and hated me and I'd hate them back, so I led them on and up into the higher pinyon pine country beyond the derelict hogan where someone a long time ago had died, and the family had boarded up the door and windows and left the place behind forever.

When vice principal Louise Fairchild called me in to Bob King's office a few weeks later, I knew it was about Tom. She sat next to him at the long table where just a few months before I had interviewed with the school board for this job. I didn't know why Bob was out, but on this day Louise steered the ship. Another teacher had busted Tom for fighting again. To take the heat off, he had told Louise about how I had assaulted him during cross-country practice.

"That doesn't sound like you," Louise said to me. "Can you explain what happened?"

I sat down at the table across from Tom. His eyes met mine and then he looked away. I sensed that he wasn't going to forgive me for this. And I couldn't think of a reason that he should. Maybe I could tell him about the world I came from, about my years running and racing, about my coach and how he pushed me to make me stronger. Maybe I could tell him that what I did was for him, that I yelled at him to encourage him to excel. Maybe I could tell him that I wanted only to protect Will, which was part of my job. Maybe I could tell him . . . But I knew anything I told him was a trifle compared to the humility he must have felt and the anger he held back. What could I say?

Louise looked at me expectantly. Tom looked down at his hands. Instead of explaining to Louise, I spoke to Tom.

"Tom," I said. He didn't look up. "I'm sorry that I yelled at you. I went too far. I'm sorry I did it."

He didn't respond. Louise looked on, waiting for more.

"You're a good runner," I said. "I want you to do well. I was frustrated by you and Will, and I didn't want you two fighting again. But mostly I'm just sorry I yelled at you."

He looked up at me for a moment. I thought he looked sad, maybe a little hopeful, maybe a little desperate. We had come so close to blows, a line over which, had we crossed it, neither of us would have been able to return. Likely I would have lost my job, and perhaps been unable to find work as a teacher for a long time, maybe forever. Maybe that wouldn't have been so bad. I didn't feel like I was cut out for teaching anyway. But I knew I would have packed a lot of guilt around for years, and Tom would have one more reason to hate people, maybe everyone. He was already so angry.

"Now, Mr. Caswell has said he's sorry, Tom," Louise said.

She sounded condescending, but I didn't trust my judgment on that. I waited for Tom to respond.

"Tom, were you fighting in cross-country practice?" Louise asked.

"Aoo'," he said.

"And you're in here today for fighting."

"Aoo'."

"Tom. We can't have this," Louise said. "Maybe we'll need to meet with your parents again."

"Aoo'."

I knew a parent/teacher meeting wouldn't do any good, and so did Tom. It might even make the situation worse. I'd recently attended a meeting with John George's parents, all of John's teachers, and Louise and Frank. After we had presented the problem, said that John was unmanageable in class and was failing everything, his father stopped us. He said that he thought the problem wasn't John, but us. The school. The teachers. The administration. We did not discipline John properly, he said. He would shape up in class if we meant what we said, if only we would be a bit harder on him. If we hit him, that would do it. It seemed to work at home. Silence went around the table. We asked about another solution. How could we work better with John? John's father insisted he had given us the solution. The conference ended with Louise explaining that we couldn't use that kind of discipline, to which the father shrugged and said that if we didn't, John would continue doing what he was doing.

I was guessing, but I suspected that meeting with Tom's parents would produce the same kind of stalemate.

"Anything else, Mr. Caswell?" Louise said.

"No," I said. "Just that I'm sorry for yelling at you, Tom." I offered him my hand. He took it. We shook hands, which meant something, but it didn't mean that Tom forgave me.

Cross-country season ended, and Tom did very well. At the district meet, he placed in the top twenty. We rode the bus home that Saturday afternoon. Tom's father could not pick him up at school, as he usually did. The driver turned east on old Route 66, passed the turnoff to Borrego, and went on through Prewitt past the gas station and laundry. She turned down a dirt road that wound south toward the freeway. It was potholed and dirty, littered with rubbish. We stopped at a hogan where a couple of dogs lay in the sun. Smoke trickled from the stovepipe, and the few windows had been boarded up against the coming winter. Tom got out. I watched him walk across the road in his big shoes, the laces left untied and sloppy, his shoulders slumped forward. The dogs didn't move. No one greeted him at the door.

Shortly after that, Tom dropped out of my class and began working with the Special Ed teacher for language arts. Whenever I saw him in the hallway, I said hello, but he had nothing to say to me. He would stand straight and tall, square his shoulders, and walk by staring past me as if I wasn't there.

After the monsoon rains in October, the desert bloomed with wildflowers. It was still warm and wonderful outside, and so I took my classes out to write in their journals. I led the eighth-grade class out behind the school and through the gap in the fence beyond the berm that held the water back when it rained. I had been walking here every day now for weeks, and the flat was littered with garbage—old tires and tin cans, pieces of roofing, rusted metal and broken glass—but today most of that was hidden by colored flowers. Purples and reds. Yellows and oranges. And our feet brushed a trail through the colors as we walked out to the foot of the mesa. Here the juniper crowded into a city of rocks fallen from high off the sandstone cliffs. A red-tailed hawk passed overhead along the edge of the mesa top, and William Brown said, "That's a ret-tail hawk!" Everyone looked up. "I seen 'em when I get water for my grandma." We watched the hawk draw a line out into the distance until it became a black spot against the sky.

I instructed everyone to find a place to sit. Pick a good place that you'll want to spend some time in, I said. We'll come out here often and write in our journals, and over time everyone will get to know their spot. In a moment I was alone.

I walked down around this great collection of boulders and found a place up against one just inside the sun with a view of the green and colored land spread out before me. The warm sun settled over my page as I scribbled away in my own journal, partly to set the example for the kids, but also for myself. I wanted to mark this moment, to record a piece of my life here. A little bluebird—the Navajo call it the bluebird of happiness—came flittering by and paused a moment in a juniper tree. It bounced on its tiny legs, bounced again, and then was off, a blue bolt across the flowers. I took it as a good sign.

I heard voices up behind me, boys' voices calling out in Navajo, words I did not know. Teresa Smith came walking around to discover me in my hiding place; I heard her feet on the dry ground. She stood in front of me, a thin, frail creature, and she looked out of breath.

"They're up there throwing it down," she said.

"Throwing what down?" I asked.

"Throwing down things from up there. Rocks and things."

High in the sandstone cliffs, the boys clung to the rocks like spiders. They were whooping and hollering and calling down to us. I called up to them. I told them to come down. What they were doing was too dangerous.

They laughed and echoed me: "It's too dangerous," they yelled back, and I saw Jerry Valdez hanging from the edge of a great stone by one arm like a monkey a hundred feet in the air. "It's too dangerous!" he yelled down, and everyone laughed.

"It's lunchtime," I called up to them.

And it was. The girls all came out of their places and crowded around me with their journals in their hands to watch the boys, to watch William Brown cast down a great chip of the mountain that he could hardly heft.

"Look out!" said Renee. "He's gonna throw it."

We all stepped back a few feet, a dozen or more, and watched it fall, all of it, whatever it was, soft and fast and slow all at once, until it reached the ground and exploded into dust. "Sorry, Mr. Caz-will," William said. "I'm comin' down now!" And he disappeared beyond the rim.

"Let's go, c'mon," Mary Jane said. "Let's leave those stupit boys."

"Yeah," said Vanessa, "we don't need them. They're actin' all crazy anyways."

We started out the way we had come in, as the boys came down off the mesa and trailed a little distance behind us.

"Did you have to go to college, Mr. Caswell? To be a teacher?" Renee asked.

"I did," I said. "Are you thinking about being a teacher?"

"I don't know," she said. "Maybe. I want to go to high school anyways."

"You'll do great in high school," I said. "And if you want to go to college, you'll do great there too."

"Is it hard to go to college?" she asked.

"Well, it's hard, but if you go to high school, it will help you for college. You just learn a little at a time."

"Is it? I don't know if I can. But if I can I want to do something good for the Navajos," Renee said. "If I can."

"No way. I'm not going to college," Vanessa said. "I'm just gonna stay home and do nothin'," and she laughed and giggled.

"Me too," said Teresa. "Just stay home and make fry bread."

"I don't know," Renee said again. "Maybe I'll go up there to Durango. Or I'll go over there to Albuquerque. I don't know."

"You go over there then," Vanessa said.

"Albuquerque?" Mary Jane said. "They got lots of hot guys over there."

"Is it?" Vanessa and Teresa said at the same time. They looked at each other and laughed.

"Okay," Vanessa said. "Let me go with you, then."

Renee looked back at her and made a funny face. "I'm not goin' for boys," she said. "Boys mess everything up."

"Not hot boys," Vanessa said, and she laughed, and Teresa laughed too and they both blushed, their cheeks like desert primrose.

We walked on a little bit in silence now, Teresa and Vanessa and Renee behind me, and Mary Jane leading the way. When we reached the gap in the fence, Teresa tapped me on the shoulder. "Mr. Caswell," she said. "We got them for you." She handed me a bouquet of wildflowers set into a weathered jam jar she had picked up from the castaway junk piles in the desert.

"Wow. Thank you," I said. "This is beautiful. This is really nice."

"Put it on your desk," Renee said.

"Yeah," said Teresa.

"Right," said Vanessa. "Put it on your desk."

"Okay, I will," I said.

"No. Do it now," Teresa said.

"All right," I said. "You come with me."

We walked to my classroom in the trailer and I set the flowers on my desk.

Then Renee said, "Take a picture, Mr. Caswell," and she handed me a little camera she took out of her bag. "Take a picture of us with the flowers."

Renee grabbed the flowers back off my desk and we went outside. The three of them assembled on the back step, each holding onto the jar, and they posed there with the beautiful flowers in the Navajo sun.

SIX

THE WOLVES OF THE MOUNTAINS

Halfway to Mission: Wolf, the weather turned cold and foul. The little Borrego bus couldn't top fifty miles an hour against the wind, and we slogged north up Interstate 25 out of Albuquerque for hours as night fell around us. Climbing up over Raton Pass into Colorado, it began to snow. The snow fell out of the darkness like rushing stars, and the Borrego girls complained of being cold and hungry because they hadn't eaten all day. Stopping for lunch had not completely slipped my mind, but we were running behind and I was filled with worry about the storm and the distance ahead of us, and how Mary and I had miscalculated the time it would take to get there. She and her students had left Ganado about the same time we left Borrego, which meant we had about a two-hour lead. At that time, the sky had been clear and blue. We planned to arrive at Mission: Wolf about five o'clock, and our two groups would meet for the first time while cooking dinner over an open fire in the high country.

I had no way of getting in touch with Mary on the Ganado bus, no way of knowing where they were, or even if they were still on the road braving this storm, and my bus was on the verge of mutiny. Everyone wanted to go home. Even Redd, the bus driver, a hulking, buzz-cut Navajo with an eternal chew in his lower lip. He had volunteered for this trip, saying he loved camping, but now he was grumbling about the roads and the cold and the snow. "Too cold for camping," he said. And of course he was right.

Kuma was a little pup then, and he wandered the aisle saying hello to the Borrego girls. Now and again he piddled on the floor. "Hey, Mr. Caswell," I heard from the back of the bus. "You're puppy's doin' it again." Earlier that morning, I had pleaded with Redd to let me bring him on the bus. The pup had nowhere else to go, I explained to him. I couldn't leave him in my trailer alone for three days. "Against regulations," Redd had said, and then he gave in: "Don't tell anyone I let you."

The snow fell in great sheets, and the road was a white line through the mountains. The little bus pulled the hill slow and sure, but I was sure the whole trip was a mistake. It was too late in the year to be headed into the high country on a school camping trip. What a foolish dream the whole trip was.

This camping trip to Mission: Wolf, a wolf sanctuary and education center in the Sangre de Cristo Mountains of southern Colorado, originated with an e-mail exchange project Mary and I cooked up. Mary was always asking teacherly questions: How did Navajo communities across the reservation differ, if at all, she wondered? And did those differences affect students as readers? As writers? As learners? Did children from these different communities have different life goals?

Mary's school in Ganado was on the west side of the Fort Defiance Plateau out of Window Rock, the heart of Navajoland. Borrego was located on the remote southeastern corner of the reservation, a region known as the Checkerboard Area because of its mix of federal, state, private, and reservation land. Since our students came from very different parts of the reservation, we decided we could explore these questions by asking our classes to correspond with each other by e-mail. Our project would focus on fostering understanding and friendships among Navajo children with different backgrounds and experiences. As the students developed relationships online through writing prompts and focused discussion topics, we would make a series of outdoor trips together with the hope that meeting in the outdoors would deepen these friendships, opening a dialogue that would color the differences and similarities between the two groups. Perhaps that information would help the students become better students and help Mary and me become better teachers.

During the weeks before we left for Mission: Wolf, the online correspondence between the students had been reserved, a little unfriendly, even slightly antagonistic. Some wrote their introduction letters as if to a machine, as if they didn't understand that a real person waited to receive that letter on the other end. Others wrote aggressively, warily, regarding the unseen online partner as a stranger to guard themselves against. Was it the technology they didn't trust, Mary and I asked, or was this a sign that these kids were so different, so separated by geography and socioeconomic situations, that the project had already given us its outcome? We didn't know. We charged ahead with organizing our first camping trip.

The trip to Mission: Wolf was plagued from the beginning. None of the boys in my classes, who had committed to going, showed up at the bus the morning we departed. We waited for them for nearly an hour. It was just as well, I thought. I had worried over what mischief the boys would bring. I found middle school girls easier to work with. They sat still and listened for nearly an entire class period, while the boys seemed always to be up and around, agitated even, as if something big needed doing and they planned on doing it. On more than one occasion I sat in for a teacher who was out sick, or out turkey hunting, or just down and out, and as instructed, I would plug the class into some action movie in the library. As soon as the lights went out, the boys moved into stealth mode, creeping in and around and behind the stacks on their bellies, and one or two of them would inevitably find their way to the door and slither out into the free world.

On several occasions, I ended up separating a few boys hidden under the tables with their hands down each other's pants. I had no moral position against boys diddling each other, but somehow the school library didn't seem like the right place. Of all my roles as a teacher, I disliked playing cop the most, so I was happy to be traveling with a group of eight girls. They would be reasonable and helpful, I surmised. They would respond if I asked something of them. Among them were all of my best students at Borrego: Vanessa Angel, Teresa Smith, Jolanda Jones, Linda Yazzie, and Renee Benally.

I was especially pleased that Renee showed up that morning. Academically, she led the eighth-grade class, not just in language arts but in all subjects. On any given day when the rest of her classmates were cutting up, bouncing around the room from seat to seat, firing rude questions or answers at me or each other, Renee might be the only student in the room working. She seemed to value what she learned in the classroom. She always finished her homework, always paid attention, always offered to answer questions during discussion, always talked about going on to high school and then to college. I found in her not a desire to please, but a desire to know. She was curious and intelligent. I noticed that when I talked about other places I had lived, she could not take her eyes off me. I sensed in her a deep questioning about the world. She seemed to want to explore, to grow beyond the borders of her life at Borrego Pass.

One day at the end of class, I asked Renee if she wanted to travel. She told me yes, that she wanted to see other places. She wanted to go to school somewhere outside the reservation, then come back home when she was older and give something back to her community. In her words, she wanted to "do something good for the Navajos." That sounded like a rare and mature goal, to be sure, and her motivation came from within. If she had support from her parents and peers, it was likely encouragement to stay home. She would have to defy some of the values of her community in order to give back to it. Where her motivation and energy came from, only she knew. I guessed that she'd had a relatively ordinary childhood for a Borrego kid. She grew up in a modest house with her parents and grandparents. She rarely, if ever, left Borrego Pass, let alone the reservation. Still, her spirit wandered. She knew that a larger world of places and experiences awaited her if she just stepped out the door. This kind of vision was lost on most kids at Borrego. Working with Renee in the classroom, I wanted to champion this energy. She was the first student I found myself rooting for. Perhaps this was a sign that I was becoming a real teacher. I didn't know whether or how I could help her along on this path, but I wanted to try. Maybe the trip to Mission: Wolf was a start.

As we neared the top of Raton Pass, the storm's intensity grew. The snow made the dark sky a whirling white. Redd looked grave as he opened his window just enough to spit into the storm. He repositioned his grip on the wheel and pressed into the big hill.

"Too bad weather for camping," he said, shaking his head. "Too cold and wet. We should go back. That other bus maybe already turned back."

The trouble with turning back was that I was bringing most of the food and Mary had all the cooking gear. If we turned back for Borrego and Mary made it through to Mission: Wolf, her group would have pots and pans, but nothing to cook. If we pressed on and they turned back, the opposite would be true. We needed each other. Yet it seemed like madness to go on. If we did turn back, I could only hope we would see the Ganado bus on the opposite side of the freeway and flag them down. We had a hundred-mile lead on them, but at the slow speeds we had traveled all day, it was possible they might overtake us. Perhaps they had already overtaken us. The question I had to answer was not whether we could make it, but whether Mary was willing to brave this storm. If she had already turned back, then we needed to do the same. From what I knew of her, she was still on the road. Mary would expect the snow to stop and the sky to clear. In fact, I expected Mary to see the storm as a good omen. It would blow itself out, she might be thinking, and we would wake in the mountains to sunshine.

Redd felt certain that no bus driver he could think of would keep going in a storm like this. "No," said Redd. "This isn't busing weather. That other bus? They turned back already."

"Yeah," one of the girls said from the back. "Let's go home."

"Yeah," everyone chimed together.

As we approached the summit, Redd pointed out the big trucks pulling off the road into the rest area to wait out the storm in the parking lot. They gathered there under the big yellow highway lamps, idling and smoking up the swirling snow.

"See," Ray said. "This ain't busing weather."

Both options seemed like defeat to me. Pressing on into the storm to go camping was, as Redd had asserted, a little idiotic, especially with a bus full of hungry children. To turn back felt like betrayal. Betrayal of the project, betrayal of the investment we had so far made in the trip, and especially betrayal of Mary and the students from Ganado. I had to make a decision.

"Okay, okay, okay," I finally said. "Then let's go back."

All the girls cheered.

Redd shrugged his shoulders and spat out the window. "That's what I said anyway," he said. "Too cold for camping."

Redd pulled into the rest area behind a line of trucks and swung around, and we bounced through the snowy parking lot and eased out onto the freeway headed south, back home.

"Hey, Mr. Cas-well," Jolanda said from the back of the bus. "Can we go over there to Apache?"

The Apache reservation was much closer to Borrego than to the little town of Raton, where we were now, but I thought that Jolanda was trying to tell me she didn't want to go home. She wanted to go camping somewhere. Anywhere. She wanted adventure. I hadn't completely given up either. Somewhere in my hopes we would see the Ganado bus headed up over the pass, and we'd turn north again and follow them in to Mission: Wolf.

"Why would we do that?" I asked.

"So we can take their teeth," she said, and then she laughed and everyone laughed with her.

I wasn't sure what to make of that, but no matter. We rounded a great curve in the freeway and on the opposite side, blowing through the snow-covered road, a long yellow bus pushed up the pass and into the night. I read the words on the side as it went by: Ganado Unified School District.

"That's them!" I said, and everyone cheered.

We turned around at the next exit, and started after them. Our little bus was slow and bumpy up the great hill. We chased the Ganado bus all the way to Gardner, Colorado, where they finally stopped for fuel. We pulled into the station behind them. By this time it had stopped snowing and the roads were clear.

"Mary!" I said.

"Hey!" she said, and we embraced warmly.

"You guys made it," Mary said. "We wondered."

"We wondered too," I said.

Mary and I agreed that we had come too far to give up now. We had a cold night ahead of us, and the kids were complaining about everything. But the weather had improved, and we were almost there.

"Let's go," Mary said when the drivers had finished fueling up. "Let's make this happen."

"We'll follow you," I said.

I stepped onto the bus and sat down. We were off again.

"Hey, Mr. Caswell," Vanessa said from the back. "Is that your girlfriend?" All the girls giggled.

"No," I said. "That's Ms. Juzwik from Ganado. She's a teacher over there."

"Looks like your girlfriend," someone else said.

"Yeah," Vanessa said. "She looks like your girlfriend."

"Well, she's not," I said. "I'd tell you if she was."

"Girlfriend! Girlfriend! Girlfriend," they all chanted together.

Redd started up the bus, and we followed the red taillights of the Ganado bus into the dark night.

A few minutes after eleven, we arrived at Mission: Wolf, tired and cold and hungry. Mary and I left the kids on the buses and walked up a dark road to the light in the window of a ramshackle cabin. The ground was bare of snow. The sharp wind blew through our clothes. We passed a series of fences and realized the dark motions behind them were wolves. We knocked on the door. A rush of warm air and smoke blew over our faces. Inside, a half dozen bearded men and one woman crowded around a woodstove. I asked for Kevin, whom I had made arrangements with over the telephone.

"That's me," Kevin said, and got up to shake my hand. He was tall and lean, and his face looked weathered by the mountain air. "We almost gave up on you," he said.

"We did too," I said. "The roads were slow."

"Uh-huh," Kevin nodded. "Well, it's late. You can camp out there on top of the hill. Expect to see me in the morning about ten."

I stood there with Mary in the light of the door hoping he would invite all twenty-seven of us into the warm cabin to sleep on the floor. He didn't. We would have to brave the cold night in our tents.

We parked the two buses in a V to part the wind around our little camp. Mary and I had planned to cook supper that night, but it was late and dark, and we were too tired and too cold. Mary helped some of the kids make sandwiches, but most of them just wanted to go to sleep.

I had brought three big canvas tents from school and two cotton sleeping bags for each of the girls. It was so cold that I suggested the girls all sleep in one tent. "It'll be warmer," I told them.

Vanessa, Renee, and Jolanda helped me with the tent, while everyone else stayed on the bus. The wind blew across our exposed hands, and the aluminum poles numbed our fingers. We struggled to fit the poles through the loops along the tent and then to erect the huge thing in the wind. Renee tried to drive the tent stakes into the hard ground with a stone, but they bent double. We piled big rocks in the corners inside the tent, more on the windward side, and weighted down the rest of it with sleeping bags and pads. Still the wind pressed in on the walls and pushed the tent a little way across the ground.

"It's still movin'," Renee said.

"Okay," I said. "Get everyone off the bus and into the tent. Then it'll stay put."

The girls filed off the bus and through the tent door. I helped them arrange their sleeping bags inside.

"It stinks in here," Jolanda said.

"And it's freezing," Vanessa said. "I'm too cold."

"Yeah," everyone said. "It stinks and it's too cold."

Then Vanessa said, "Mr. Caswell! This sleeping bag's somehow!"

"Yeah, and they stink too," Jolanda said.

They did stink. The bags probably hadn't been used in years. The tent smelled old and musty, much like the canvas tents I used on camping trips growing up. But the girls were out of the wind, and they buried themselves inside their sleeping bags. They looked warmer, maybe happier. I told them good night.

Redd insisted on sleeping on the bus. I had planned to use one of the canvas tents myself, but it was so cold I knew I could never heat that big thing up alone. I asked Mary if I could bunk with her. We were not lovers; we were friends. But we were on a school trip just the same, and we wondered if it would be a problem to share a tent. We talked it over and decided that the circumstances made it acceptable. No one would likely even notice, we thought, and everyone was too cold to care. I crawled into Mary's tent with Kuma and went to sleep.

Several times during the night I woke to the sound of wolves. They howled in chorus, bright notes pitched high, then wavering and falling. Kuma crawled out of the bag and pressed his nose to the zipper on the tent door.

I had read that some Indian peoples believe that wolf howls are lost spirits searching for a road back to the earth. In Navajo mythology, Wolf, like Coyote, is a bad omen. Hunters who see a wolf cross their path will turn back home, lest they meet bad luck or illness or even death. A Navajo could never be sure whether he was looking at a wolf or a wolf witch, a human being dressed in a wolf skin. *Ma'iitsoh*, the Navajo word for wolf, is a synonym for "witch." Wolf is also said to have quarreled with his wife about sex in the myth-time and thereby helped bring about the separation of the sexes. Because the men and women could not get along, they went to opposite sides of the river. Years passed, and the women grew weak and mad with desire. They masturbated and gave birth to monsters that later plagued the world. The men also masturbated in excess, but no evil survived them. After long suffering, the women begged the men to take them back. The men did, but only after the women agreed that men should decide about matters of sex. The story suggests that desire must come into balance with control, that men and women need each other, that the world is incomplete without both their energies. In contrast to Coyote, Wolf is considered the leader of all hunting animals. In that sense he is also dependable. In the puebloan cultures, Wolf is associated with the East. It is also said that a person who puts a wolf's earwax into his own ears will be able to listen beyond his ken.

As I lay half-awake in the tent, I heard a low growl that increased in intensity until it became a diesel engine groaning to life and evening out into a steady hum. I sat up. That's my bus! Our bus! Were they leaving? Had Redd gathered the girls and decided to go home? Would

I have to ride back with Mary on the Ganado bus? It was too cold to go out and have a look, or at least I didn't want to. Or maybe I didn't care. I didn't want to care. Mary stirred next to me, turned over, lay still. If they wanted to leave me here, I thought, then I wanted them to go. I was not going out into the cold to stop them. I lay back down and fell away into a troubled sleep again, my dreams traveling in and out of wolf-song and the hum of the bus engine in the bitter cold.

I rose early to Kuma's soft whimpering at the tent door. I pulled on my pants and warm fleece anorak, a little panicked and curious about the bus. It was still there, and I could see Redd asleep at the wheel. The sky was blue and ever clear, and Kuma headed out to have a look around.

We were camped on a knoll rising out of a broad field that sloped down and away and back up to the foot of the Sangre de Cristo Mountains. I stood for a moment looking out. The world was alive and beautiful. The rocky landscape was softened by pockets of conifers and the tall dry grasses running up the hills and talking in the wind. It came in waves, the wind in the grasses, and they made a soft shushing sound as they folded and moved together like birds. Kuma worked the edges of the camp, tumbling down through the grasses, pausing here, pausing there, and for the moment, at least, I was happy we had come.

I built a fire in the fire pit and went to check on the girls. Their tent was empty. I hesitated a moment before realizing what had happened: they must have spent the night on the bus with Redd. He must have started the engine to keep them warm.

Mary was up now too, and she knelt down for Kuma, who went to her now to say hello. She ruffed him about the ears and chest and shoulders, and she said hello and good morning, and wasn't it beautiful and clear after the storm. We agreed we should get breakfast started, so I needed to get on the bus for the food. I knocked on the door. Redd woke up and let me on. The girls were asleep in there, spread out across the seats near the back of the bus.

Mary and I had the meal sorted out, the stove set up, and the bacon frying when Vanessa, Renee, and Teresa got up. They approached the fire and stood warming themselves.

"Good morning," I said.

"Mr. Caswell," Renee said. "Teresa wants to ask you somethin'."

Teresa stepped forward. She was very thin and wore her hair cut short like a boy. When I met her in class on my first day at school, she asked me if I had taken the Lord into my life, and if not, she said, she could help. I politely declined.

"Yeah," Teresa said. "I have somethin' to ask you."

I waited. She looked guilty, like she'd done something bad and wanted to confess.

"Yes?" I said. "What is it?"

"Hey," she said finally, "can we go over there and get some Skoal? And will you buy it for us? We don' got no money."

Chewing tobacco was one of the many substances on the contraband list at school. A lot of students at Borrego chewed tobacco at home, however, and for some reason, especially girls.

"No," I said. "You can't buy Skoal. Of course not."

"Ahh, c'mon," Vanessa said.

"No. There's nowhere to go anyway. We're in the mountains," I said.

"Yeah," Teresa said. "There's a town way over there. Redd will take us to the store over there on the bus. He said so."

"No."

"My grandma lets me at home," Vanessa said.

"No way," I said.

"You don't even like us," Vanessa said.

"Yeah," Renee said. "And why were you sleeping with Ms. Juzwik, anyway," and they went back to the fire.

They were right. I shouldn't have slept in Mary's tent, but I was going to do it again if only to insist that it was no big deal. And it was true I didn't like them, not at that moment anyway. They had bitched all the way here, and they were bitching now. Their request was unreasonable. I didn't care who let them chew at home. I felt like Redd was in no position to offer them a trip into town for chew. I knew I was being stubborn, defiant, even arrogant, because I felt like the trip was a flop. I felt like I was a failure. But who did he think he was, anyway? He drove the bus. He wasn't a teacher. I was in charge here, not Redd.

After a good breakfast of pancakes, bacon, and fried eggs cooked on our gas stove, Mary and I asked our students to introduce themselves to each other. The Borrego girls huddled together around Redd, but each of them said their name and where they were from and shook hands with their exchange partners. It seemed to go all right.

. Mary and I went to work on the dishes. I heard a couple of the Ganado kids laughing about how the Borrego girls talked. I hadn't been aware of them speaking with an accent, but apparently they did, likely because they spoke Navajo as their first language and English as their second. Most of the Ganado kids spoke English as their first language and only broken Navajo, if they spoke any at all. In this part of the world, it seemed that speaking two languages fluently (English and Navajo) did not indicate intelligence and worldliness; rather, it was a sign of growing up poor in the isolated hills. Most of the Ganado kids had working parents. Borrego families, with the exception of those who worked at the school, mostly relied on government assistance. Every spring, a good number of Borrego kids missed school to harvest pinyon nuts in the mountains with their families. They sold the nuts at roadside stands. For many Borrego families, this kind of extra income was the difference between making it and not making it from month to month, season to season. The Ganado kids had traveled a bit more and spent more time in cities with white influence, like Gallup, and even Flagstaff, maybe Phoenix and Albuquerque. They ate in restaurants and went to movies. Many of the Borrego kids had yet to experience much of the world off the reservation. If they went to town with their parents at all, they might know the inside of a grocery store like Bashas', perhaps a hardware store, and Wal-Mart. Other than that, town life was a mystery to them. Bringing these two groups together was going to be more challenging than Mary and I had anticipated.

Kevin came down from the cabin to give us a tour of Mission: Wolf. We followed him into the warm sun near the wolf pens. Kevin was one of only a few full-time volunteers. The rest of the people living at Mission: Wolf were sometime college students and travelers holing up in the woods. One of them lived in a shelter he built in a nearby gully out of aspen boughs and black plastic sheeting. Mission: Wolf offered him the space to camp out in exchange for volunteer labor.

Kevin offered a short history of Mission: Wolf. Founded in 1986 by Kent Weber as a sanctuary for captive-born wolves and wolf-dogs, its mission is to educate the public about wolves and habitat protection. Over the years, donations have made it possible to buy fencing, build modest housing for volunteers and facilities for visitors, and purchase more land. Kevin told us that Weber and other Mission: Wolf volunteers travel the U.S. with a few wolves, making appearances at schools and in communities to talk about wolves and wolf recovery and about habitat protection. The Ambassador Wolf Program's success is founded on the public's thirst for real encounters with wolves. No film or lecture or book of photographs can compare to meeting a real wolf, Kevin said. When people meet a wolf for the first time, Kevin told us, they discover what beautiful and mysterious creatures they are, and often become wolf advocates.

The need for a sanctuary and education center like Mission:

Wolf coincided with a growing public interest that rose out of efforts by the U.S. Fish and Wildlife Service to reestablish wolves across portions of their former range in the lower forty-eight states, especially in Idaho, Montana, and Wyoming. For Kevin, and for Mission: Wolf, the eradication of the wolf from these lands during the early 1900s is an indication of a much larger problem, that of the desire to subdue and take dominion over nature. If we can learn to respect the wolf, Kevin told us, and all creatures of the wild, we will protect the habitat the wolf needs to survive. The same becomes true the other way around: by regarding wild lands as sacred and worthy of our care and protection, we will also protect the animals that live there.

Kevin led us through the maze of pens and paused to talk briefly about each of the wolves, how they came to Mission: Wolf, and why people should not raise wolves as pets. "Wolves are not dogs," he said. "They don't follow household rules like dogs. People who try to keep a wolf as a pet are often attracted to the cute little puppies. But they soon grow up. And they prove to be wild animals, not pets." Weber rescued a number of wolves that had injured their owners, or their owners' children. "It's not the wolves' fault," Kevin said. "They're just being wolves. They don't belong in people's houses."

We stopped in front of a pen housing a huge black timber wolf called Shaman, one of the first wolves to tour the country in the Ambassador Program. Weber had recently retired Shaman because he had become too aggressive and unpredictable in front of audiences. "He was one of the best for a long time," Kevin said. "Maybe he just got sick of being on display all the time." A smooth path marked the line where he paced back and forth along the fence, hour after hour, day after day. As Kevin talked, Shaman approached the fence, his bright yellow eyes penetrating the group. The kids went silent and still. Then Shaman set to pacing again. Although he had never lived in the wild, something wild and untamable lived in Shaman, as if he sensed there was a larger world beyond the pen.

Kevin led us on to a great mound of road-killed elk and deer parts, wild game scraps from local butchers, and stillborn livestock from area ranches, all donations. The pile was partially frozen and blackened by the cold mountain air. The Borrego girls scowled and whispered to each other, pointing at the weirdly shaped frozen babies in the pile. The boys from Ganado spied the axes and machetes lying about and pushed and poked at each other, enthused.

Kevin told us that it was feeding day and that we could help feed the wolves if we wanted. Everyone agreed to help. A few more resident volunteers came down from the cabin. We used the axes and machetes to break apart the frozen pieces and sort them into buckets, equal parts of fat and muscle and bone. The meat thawed in the sun as we worked with it. Our hands and sleeves became stained and bespattered with blood.

We separated into small groups and followed the volunteers to the wolf pens. A couple of the Ganado girls had made a good effort to connect with the Borrego girls, but there was still little interaction between the two groups. The Borrego girls stayed together to feed the wolves, and I ended up with a Ganado group.

I followed the Ganado kids and one of the volunteers until we stopped in front of one of the high fences. We set the buckets of bloody parts down, and the three wolves in the pen came right up to the fence. They knew what was about to happen. They stood waiting, their eyes looking past us or through us, as if we were not there. One of the wolves, a male timber wolf with a beautifully soft-looking gray coat, stood at least six inches taller at the shoulder than the other two. His head was huge, wide and powerful. He pushed at the other wolves, jostling for position. The volunteer instructed us to throw the meat over the fence. We took hold of huge slabs of half-frozen animal parts, our fingers cold and bloody, and tossed them up and over. The heavy pieces came down hard against the dry ground. The big male seized the first pieces for himself. He collected several in his mouth at once, dropping one piece onto another, and then carried it off. In moments the wolves had settled the issue of who got what. We watched them stand over the bloody flesh and tear and gnaw and swallow huge pieces whole.

Kevin came up behind us. "That's what it means to wolf down your food," he said.

The Ganado kids stood watching. They hardly made a sound.

"C'mon," Kevin said. "Let's get the rest of this into the pen."

They all set to work throwing the rest of the meat over the fence. Some of the soft strings of fat tangled in the branches of the trees. The wolves slowed, and then lay down, looking content and happy to work at the bones in the warming sun. We stood watching for awhile longer, then helped Kevin carry the empty buckets back.

We rejoined the other groups at the still-sizable pile of carcasses. The kids held their bloody hands out, comparing them with each other. Kevin needed to make a trip into town to take care of some business in the Mission: Wolf office. Our tour had reached its end.

"I'll come back this afternoon," he said. "Maybe I can join you all tonight at the fire."

"That sounds great," Mary said. "Okay, let's go. Everyone back to camp."

Mary and I set up a wash station in camp, and everyone filed through to wash the blood from their hands. The kids were buzzing with stories about their experiences. Mary and I noticed that for the first time, the two groups seemed to be interacting on their own. The Borrego kids were talking with the Ganado kids as they told their stories about feeding the wolves. The trials of the day and night before seemed worthwhile now. The friendships Mary and I had hoped to help foster through our project seemed within reach. The sun was warm and the air clear. The trip had had a rough start, but everything was smoothing out.

Then, as Mary and I prepared lunch, a rock fight broke out near the tents. Renee came fast around the end of the bus and Vanessa ran just behind her. Teresa came into view, turned back and punched at the air with her fists, and then ran in fear, smiling and laughing. Sitting near the fire pit, Redd held out his arm and the girls rushed into it, shouting and complaining and making no sense. Three Ganado boys stepped into the circle around the fire and announced that Renee, Vanessa, and Teresa had pelted them with stones. One of them had a bruise on his leg to prove it.

I asked the girls if this was true.

"They're not Navajos," Vanessa blurted out. "They can't talk Navajo!"

The boy with the bruised leg said, "Yeah, well, you can't even talk right."

"That's 'cause we're Navajos," Renee said, and she picked up a stone off the ground.

"Renee!" I said. "Don't."

She clutched at the stone a moment and then threw it down hard against the ground.

"They ripped our tent!" one of the Ganado boys said. And they had. A stone had torn a little hole in the wall of the boy's tent. "That's my tent," he said. "And now it's ruined."

"That's 'cause they were laughing at us," said Vanessa.

"Yeah," said Teresa. "So we're gonna get 'em." She made a motion toward them.

"Wait. Wait. Wait. Wait. Wait," I said.

"Okay," Mary said. "Let's take a break here." She led her group away to the edge of the hill in the sun.

The Borrego girls, even the girls who weren't involved in the rock fight, filed onto the bus and pushed the door closed.

I thought it was best for them to cool off before I tried talking with them, so I finished setting lunch out. Mary came back with her group, and they lined up at the picnic table to make sandwiches. No one on the Borrego bus stirred.

"Let's take them out for a hike after lunch," Mary said.

"Great idea," I said. "I'll go tell them." I pushed the bus door open and stood next to the driver's seat. "We're all going for a hike after lunch," I said.

"We ain't goin' nowhere with them," Teresa said.

"Yeah," Jolanda said. "They ain't Navajos. They're *bilagáanas*. They're white, like you!"

I tried to pretend I hadn't heard it. "Also, it's lunchtime. Why don't you come out and have lunch?" I went down the steps and left the door open. I heard someone push it closed again behind me.

I expected the Borrego girls to come out after all the Ganado kids had moved through the line. They didn't. I waited a bit longer, then went back to the bus. I pushed on the door, but they had latched it. I knocked and waited. I knocked again. No one moved inside. I went around to one of the bus windows. I could see Renee through the glass. She looked trapped, like a fish in a bowl. She stared straight ahead, frowning, as if she didn't see me. Her big glasses made her face look round and sad. I reached up and tapped on the window. She didn't look at me. I tapped again. She stood up and put the window down.

"I hate you," she said, and then jacked the window up.

I had endured all kinds of insults from my students at Borrego, but none of them had so far said anything like that. At least not in English. What's more, it was Renee who said it. Gone was the little spot of joy I had felt earlier in the day when I thought that the trip just might work out. Despite its shortcomings, Mary and I had invested a great deal of time in this trip, in this exchange. I knew at that moment that it was over. The project was finished. I felt disappointed and relieved at the same time. It would be a lot easier not to follow through, and I was sick of being tolerant and open and understanding. Or sick of trying to be tolerant and open and understanding. I had not come to work at Borrego to be treated like this. I didn't want to do it anymore. I didn't want to work with these kids anymore. In fact, I knew then that I didn't want to teach at all. I would finish out the year, I thought, and then try something else. I didn't know what, but if teaching entailed this big an investment with this small a return, it wasn't for me. Then the awareness that I might be overdramatizing the moment flashed into my mind. I would have to be hardier than this if I was going to make it though the year, I thought. I'd probably settle out later, not feel so crushed. Renee, who was a child after all, impulsive and emotional, would eventually take it back. I hoped she would, anyway. I decided she didn't really mean it.

I stood in front of Renee's window a moment. I watched her sit down. Teresa and Vanessa stood up over the seat behind her and patted her on the shoulder. She looked back at them and smiled. Teresa pressed her nose and lips against the glass and made a face at me. I turned away and went back to the group.

The rest of the trip slipped by, almost without incident. We returned from the hike at suppertime. The Borrego girls still sat on the bus. We had made a little loop up and over a knob visible from our camp. From there we had looked out on all of Mission: Wolf, the wolf pens and volunteer housing, and the snowy mountains running north. The Ganado kids had worked up a good appetite. We set to work cooking supper at once.

Redd took the lead grilling up beef patties over the fire. We set out the condiments, heated beans, toasted buns, tossed a huge bowl of green salad, and opened several kinds of dressing. When the food was ready, the Borrego girls filed off the bus, loaded up their plates, and filed back on. They didn't say a word to anyone.

Later that night, while we were all seated around the fire telling ghost stories, Linda came out for a supply of chocolate and marshmallows. She whispered something in Redd's ear as he was nodding yes, and then she slipped her hand into his coat pocket and fished out a can of Skoal. I was about to stand up and confront Redd and Linda, but Kuma was curled against my feet. I looked down at him, not wanting to disturb him, and then realized I risked being a hypocrite. I had asked Redd to bend regulations so that I could bring my dog, so how could I complain when he did the same for the girls? They chewed all the time at home anyway. What good would it do to make a scene here at the fire? In any case, I was angry and beaten and vengeful; I didn't care what those girls did to themselves. Let them chew! I pretended I didn't see it. I let it go and turned back to the group and to the songs and stories at the fire.

Kevin came out of the dark and joined us for a short time. He sat on the ground next to me, and Kuma went right to him. He had brought a small piece of meat and bone from the wolf pile. "You don't mind?" Kevin asked me. I nodded that it was all right. Kuma accepted the offering and lay between us, happy and content. An hour passed. Kevin stood and walked off into the dark. One by one, the Ganado kids went to bed too, then Mary, the drivers, and finally, so did I.

Somewhere in the night, I heard the wolves. I lay awake in the tent listening to them calling from pen to pen, first from one side of the property, and then howls from the other. I heard Mary breathing beside me. I could feel the warmth of her body and where Kuma lay in the folds between us. His head rose up. He listened. He drew up onto his front feet as if ready to pounce. He lay his ears back a little in the dark; I could see his silhouette in the bright moonlight bathing us. Mary woke then as Kuma howled, his sharper, higher tone reverberating inside the tent. When he stopped, we heard silence. We heard the night air of the Sangre de Cristo in the silent moment as the wolves seemed to be listening. In resounding chorus, all of them, it seemed, answered the little dog. Kuma joined in again. I put my hand on his back, wanting to quiet him, and then withdrew it and let him howl. I listened with Mary as the wolves and the dog sang to each other and to the wild, wild night. We drifted off to sleep again after the wolves settled out and bedded down. And finally, Kuma too curled up and went to sleep.

On Monday in class, the girls glared at me. They were hostile, angry, ungrateful. Renee's words remained alive in my head: "I hate you," she had said, and when she looked at me that way in class, how she squinted up her eyes and her mouth turned hard and monstrous, now, only now did I believe her. She did hate me, and so did the rest of them. But why? Hadn't I gone to a great deal of effort and trouble to take them on a journey to Mission: Wolf? Did I not sacrifice my personal time away from the classroom to give them an experience of the wider world? Did I not introduce them to Navajo people they otherwise might never have met, and so offer them a glimpse of Navajo life in another part of Navajoland? I didn't deserve this kind of treatment, did I?

"Renee, Vanessa, Teresa," I said after class, "have you got a minute to talk?"

"Not for you," Vanessa said.

"Yeah, not for you," Renee said.

Teresa stuck out her tongue, which said it all.

"I don't need much time," I said. "I won't keep you long."

They stood there looking angry. I don't think their silence meant "Yes, let's talk," but I started in anyway.

"You see," I said. "I know the trip didn't go so well all the time, but you have to know that I put the trip together for you. I thought I was doing something good for you. I'm sorry you got cold, and that it wasn't much fun with those Ganado kids. I hoped it would be better."

They stood there motionless, angry, rigid as stone, but fragile-looking, like if I touched them, they'd shatter into a million pieces.

"So I hope you'll accept that those bad parts were not fun, but that other parts of the trip were fun. That you had an experience you learned from, if nothing else. I hope maybe you learned something."

Still silence. I wondered if they had agreed together to give me the silent treatment, and then walk away angry. Perhaps they wanted to hang on to that anger for something. Maybe it was useful to them.

"And Ms. Juzwik said too that she hoped you had at least a little fun, and that—"

"Why did you have to have sex like that with that other teacher, then?" Vanessa said.

"Yeah," Teresa said. "Why did you?" And she smirked a little, thinking of it.

"Wait, wait, wait," I said. "Ms. Juzwik? We weren't having sex. Why did you say that? We weren't having sex. Do you think on a school trip that I'd be in a tent next to yours doing that?" I was insulted, and little embarrassed.

"No," Vanessa said.

"Do you think so, Teresa?"

"No," she said.

"No," added Renee.

"Then why did you say that?"

"I don't know," Vanessa said. "But you didn't have to sleep in there."

"All right," I said. "I might have slept in another tent. You're right. I'm sorry I did that. I didn't know it would upset you."

"Well, it did," Vanessa said.

"And those Ganado kids," Renee said. "How come you went hiking with them? And how come you had to go around with them all the time?"

"Yeah," Teresa said. "You like them more than us, 'cause they're white like you."

"You like them better than us," said Renee, in case I didn't get it the first time.

"No I don't," I said.

"Yes you do," Vanessa said. "You didn't take care of us."

That hit home for me. That made sense. That seemed to explain why they were so angry. At the time, I didn't realize I wasn't taking care of them, but now that Vanessa said it, I realized she was right. I was angry at them, true enough. And I felt they were against me. And in feeling so, I positioned myself, if even in subtle ways, against them. They felt that, and responded to it.

"Besides," Vanessa said. "You're just here for the money anyways. You don't care about us."

I wanted to protest, to defend myself, to tell her she was wrong. But she wasn't all wrong, and she knew it. Offering a defense was just a form of denial anyway, a way of telling them that I didn't care about their feelings, which is what I was being accused of in the first place.

"Okay," I said. "I understand. I'm sorry I didn't take care of you. Thank you for staying to talk with me. See you next class, then?" What more was there to say?

They went out the door without another word.

I thought long about that night at Mission: Wolf, how the girls lay shivering in the dank green tent, and how small and helpless and scared they looked, but also how determined and forceful and resolute. I thought that despite their angry faces, their hands that threw the stones, their words that cut so deep, they were just children looking for guidance and support and love. To prosper, they needed a sense of safety and home. Maybe I hadn't been able to offer what they needed over the weekend because I was too preoccupied with my own fears, my own desire for that same sense of safety and home. I vowed to overcome my misgivings, the failures and mistakes I'd already made. I didn't really know how to get beyond the hostility I encountered every day in the classroom, sometimes in the cafeteria and on the playground, but I vowed to take care of my students, to care about them. For the next several weeks, though, I would continue to fail.

SEVEN

CARDINAL RULES

It was late, maybe ten o'clock, when someone knocked at my door. Kuma and Bud, my parents' Queensland heeler mix, went into a frothy attack, rushing the door, snapping and barking, and then snapping and barking at each other. My parents had arrived a few hours earlier for the Thanksgiving holiday. I had been talking non-stop since dinner about my life at Borrego, about my teaching, about the kids at school, while Kuma, still a wee pup, tested himself against Bud. He hid under the leather chair Juan Carlos had loaned me, and when Bud approached, he rushed out and snapped at him and then ducked under again for cover.

My mother kept saying, "I can't believe that pup! I just can't believe that pup!"

"He's really aggressive," I said. "He doesn't seem to back down to anything. Even me."

"Well, he should. He should just roll over on his back with Bud. I just can't believe him. You're really gonna have to work with him to train that out of him."

"Maybe," I said. "Maybe it serves him here. You gotta be tough to live here."

"Well, maybe so," my mother said, "but you're gonna have to be real careful with that dog. If he bites someone—"

That's when the knock came. The room went still a moment, then the two dogs went for the front door.

No one ever knocked at my door way out here, especially at night. And certainly never the front door. Even I rarely used the front door. I always used the back door. Beyond Gay DeLuz selling pies (and she came to the back door), the only other time someone knocked on my door was that night two drunk Navajos were fighting in the roadway in front of the school. I heard a commotion out there in the dark and looked out to see the shapes of two men faced off in the trough of light made by two idling cars headed in opposite directions. It was as if the two men happened to cross paths there, both remembered some unfinished business, and stopped to take care of it. I could see from my window that one of the men was much bigger than the other, taller, thicker, a huge dark shadow. I watched them rush each other and punch and swing and fall down dead drunk. It didn't seem they could do much damage to each other, as drunk as they were. They would probably do more injury to themselves just from falling down. Or more likely they would both be killed, eventually, and maybe take someone else with them, driving around drunk like that, especially at night.

Staring out the window like that, I heard a knock at my front door. I was immediately embarrassed to be caught gawking that way, for I hadn't seen anyone approaching through the dark. Whoever it was had seen me, a little goldfish staring through the glass of his reservation goldfish bowl. I answered it, opened the door right up to face my charge, and she stood there, her hand on the door now, already midsentence, talking so fast and panicked as she tried to catch her breath from running up the road and over to the light in my window.

"You got a phone?" she said. "You got a phone I can use? I haf-ta call the cops!"

She wore jeans and cowboy boots, a blouse cut low, long long black hair, and big glasses. Her nose was sortof flattened out, and she had beautiful hands—that most of all, her beautiful hands on my trailer door. I suddenly remembered I was lonely.

"I have a cell phone," I said. "It doesn't always work."

"I haf-ta call the cops!" she said again. "Can I use it? It's my uncle. He's fightin' again. And he's gonna lose. He always loses."

I understood her uncle to be the smaller man. Maybe. "Okay," I said. "Come in."

She called the Navajo police in Crownpoint, and they told her they wouldn't come out because she had called about her uncle too many times already. That made some sense to me, but not to her. She cursed and put the phone down hard and did not thank me and did not press "End," so the cops were still on the line burning my cell time. She rushed out the door without closing it, without saying "Thank you," without shaking my hand, at least, with her pretty fingers and knuckles and wrist. I saw her join the two men in the roadway in that beam of the headlights. She went from one to the other, the other to the one, and soon enough, the fight broke up, and the cars crawled off into the night.

"No one ever comes to the front door," I said to my parents. But before long there was another knock. I answered it.

"Mr. Cas-well," Virginia Puente said before I realized who she was. "We don't got no ride home." She stood at my door in the dark and the cold with three boys I did not know. She wore only a T-shirt and jeans, and she shivered as she spoke.

A student in my eighth-grade class, Virginia was quiet, kind of shy, but a little fierce in her eyes, angry-looking all the time. She had long lovely hair, and she stood only about four foot ten, not five feet tall, anyway. At sixteen, she was one of the older girls in her class, but she didn't have much pull among them. She seemed always on the outside of anything going on. She barely ever uttered a word in class, and here she was asking me for a ride home. Perhaps she had already exhausted all her other options. Perhaps this wasn't a matter of choice now, but of survival.

"You don't have a ride?" I said.

"No, we don't got no ride." she said again. "We were over there at the dance, ya know? And now we can't get home."

The seventh-grade class had hosted a dance in the gym that night. From where I stood, the parking lot looked empty. I couldn't see a car anywhere.

"Don't you have a coat? It's cold out," I said.

"No, we don't got no ride, and no coats neither. And it's too cold out here too."

"You mean everyone just left you?" I asked.

"Well, yeah," Virginia said. "There wasn't no room in no one's car. So of course they left us. So will you take us?"

"Of course," I said. "I'll take you home. Let me get my coat."

As the seventh-grade class adviser, I was in charge of raising money for the class and planning a spring field trip. While making plans to hold the dance, one of our big fund-raisers for the year, I told the class that Thanksgiving break was not a good time for me. My parents would be coming from Idaho for the holiday. We could put on a dance the weekend before the break, or the weekend after, or any other time. But not Thanksgiving weekend. And besides, the students would all be on vacation too. That seemed reasonable to me.

"Okay, you guys," I said. "What weekend do you want to hold the dance?"

"We wanna do it that weekend. Thanksgiving weekend," Jolanda said.

"I'm sorry, I can't do it that weekend," I told them again. "But I can do it almost any other weekend."

"No," Jolanda said. "It has to be Thanksgiving."

"Yeah," said Maria Young. "It has to be Thanksgiving."

"Why does it have to Thanksgiving?" I asked.

"Of course it just does," said Jolanda.

"Yeah," said Maria. "It just does."

"I can't do it," I said. "Let's choose another time."

"No," Jolanda said. "There isn't no other time."

Jolanda led this charge for the girls, and so I appealed to the boys. "Okay, you guys, speak up," I said. "Any other ideas? Caleb? Clemson?"

Caleb shrugged and didn't answer. The rest of the boys frowned and looked down, mostly apathetic. None of them would offer anything unless Caleb did. And it seemed Caleb had decided to follow Jolanda.

"Yeah," Jolanda said. "Let's have a dance over there. We wanna have a good time. That's all."

Two of the cardinal rules of teaching middle school, as I see it, are: (1) never get drawn into an argument with a student, because it is impossible to win. Offer a few choices, and let the student choose one. And (2) know when to bend (about 15 percent of the time) and when to stand firm (about 85 percent of the time). The second rule is the more difficult of the two because it is easy to bend or stand firm at the wrong times, even if you're getting the ratio right. So I talked about the dance with Lauren, who had been teaching far longer than I had, and then with Louise, who had been at Borrego for a hundred years and knew these kids. They both said that I should stand firm in this case and offer to hold the dance the weekend before the holiday, or the weekend after, which is what I had already done. Louise also suggested that maybe the kids could find someone else who was available that night, then they could have the dance without me. I think the idea just crossed her mind and she said it, but it violated the first rule, which encourages choices but does not open those choices to interpretation. When seventh graders interpret rules or choices, they forget all limits. It wasn't Louise's fault. She just offered her thoughts by way of consolation really and expected me to use good judgment. I did not.

"All right," I told my class later, "if you can find someone else to help you put on the dance, you can do it whenever you want to."

"We can do it on Thanksgiving, you mean?" Jolanda asked.

"Whenever you want to, provided you find someone who wants to help you," I said. "But I can't help you Thanksgiving weekend."

"All right!" Jolanda cheered.

Jolanda led the girls around the school courting teachers and staff to help them with the dance. No one was interested. Juan Carlos, who was usually into this kind of thing, said no. Like almost everyone who worked at the school, he was going to be somewhere else over the holiday.

The girls were desperate and they returned to me again and again. "You haf'ta help us," they said. "We're just trying to have a good time. We just wanna have a dance over there."

"Right," I told them. "I know. And you can have a dance. And I will help you, but on some other weekend. Let's set a new date. How about the weekend just after Thanksgiving?"

"No," Jolanda said. "It has to be on Thanksgiving."

"Why is that weekend so important?" I asked.

"Well, yeah," Jolanda said. "Why is it? Why can't you help us?"

"My family will be here."

"So."

"And I'll be busy taking them around and spending time with them."

"So."

"So. I can't do it that weekend. I don't see why it has to be that weekend."

"Oh, it just does, of course," Jolanda said. "Why can't you believe me?"

The frenzy seemed to die down and go away, and I didn't hear anything more about it. Perhaps Jolanda had given up, and after the break, I would meet with my class again and we would plan the event. But the first day of Thanksgiving break, the same day my parents were to arrive, Jolanda, Maria, and Clemson approached me as I was shoveling up the dog shit scattered behind my trailer.

"You have to help us, Mr. Caswell," Jolanda said.

"Yeah," said Clemson. "We're gonna have a dance over there tonight, and we need some help."

"Tonight?!" I said, baffled that they still would not accept my steady refusal.

"Yeah, don't you remember?" Clemson said.

"Well, of course I remember," I said. "But I can't help you tonight. Don't you remember?"

"You have to," Jolanda said.

"Don't you have someone else helping you?" I asked.

"Nobody," Clemson said. "We can't even get inside. So we need some help real bad."

"Well, how can you have a dance if you've not done anything yet to plan it?" I said.

"I don't know," said Clemson. "We just go in there and have one."

"Yeah," said Maria. "We just have one."

"You can't even get into the gym," I said.

"You can help us," Jolanda said.

"I don't have a key to those doors," I told them. "We can't do it tonight. I can't help you."

"Everyone's coming," Clemson said. "So many people are already coming. We have to get inside. You have to help us."

I couldn't believe it. They had gone this far with everyone around them saying no. Somehow they still trusted they could make this thing happen. And it sounded to me like they were going to do it. They were going to hold a dance. I should have given in then. I should have let go of my position and exercised my 15 percent flexibility quota, which to this point I had probably not even dipped into. I should have helped them because they were just kids trying to hold a dance, trying to have a good time, but I heard the warnings in my mind of seasoned teachers who had told me that to give in, especially at the last minute, was to lose face. "They will never respect you again," I remembered hearing, "because your word will mean nothing." My gut told me, however, that I should give in and help them, but then what grew out of control inside me was frustration and annoyance. How could they be so persistent? How could they be so insistent? How could they be so optimistic that they could pull this thing off? They were using me, and I wasn't going to let them.

"No," I said. "We've already been through all this. We can put a dance together next weekend. My parents are going to arrive soon."

"So?" said Clemson. "Oh, c'mon. You have to."

"No," I said finally. "I won't do it. I'll help you next weekend, but not tonight."

"Hey," said Clemson to Jolanda. "What about Alice?"

"Yeah," said Maria. "She'll help us."

"Of course Alice will help us," Jolanda said. "She likes us. Not like you."

Alice lived in the trailer a couple doors down. She was almost always home, keeping a weather eye on her supply trailer behind the school. She had everything in there for the classroom, and more. She ran her post with royal autonomy. She ordered and distributed supplies to teachers and staff, some days according to obsolete BIA guidelines, I guessed, and some days according to her mood. "Let's see," she might say, looking over her inventory list, "you can only have five sheets of black construction paper, but thirteen of red." On another day she might insist I take supplies I didn't need. "No, take 'em," she said to me one day, pushing two huge cotton canvas laundry bags into my arms when I came in for pencils. "Take 'em home.

For takin' laundry to Crownpoint. Take 'em. We don't use 'em. And here's some liquid hand soap, too. Kills germs."

"Okay," I said. "Go ask Alice, then. I hope she can help. I'm sorry I can't help you."

"You're not sorry," Jolanda said. "You're not sorry. You don't even like us."

"That's right," said Maria. "You don't even like us. And we don't like you."

"C'mon, you guys," Jolanda said, and she led them off.

Though I tried not to admit it to myself, I felt responsible for whatever was going to happen inside the gym that night.

I took up my coat and put on my shoes to take Virginia and her friends home.

"I'll go with you," my father said. "And we can take my truck."

"All right," I said. "See you in a bit, Mom."

"I'll just be here," she said. "I'll be here watching these dogs."

Outside, the three boys climbed into the back of my father's big Dodge under the camper shell and Virginia sat in the cab beside me to show us the way. We started down the bumpy dirt road toward the Trading Post.

"So who ran the dance?" I asked Virginia. "Juan Carlos?"

"No. Not him," she said. "He was there. But Alice did it. Alice let us into the gym."

"And she supervised all night?" I asked.

"Yeah," she said. "She stayed with us and helped us. Jolanda got a lot of money from there. You should have helped your class."

She was right, of course. A long silence went between us.

"Why was Juan Carlos there?" I asked, trying to find something to say. "I thought he wasn't going to be there."

"Oh yeah. He was there. He's always there," she said.

Juan Carlos hosted the prom each spring in the gym during the school day. He ran the event like a city dance club that allowed entry based on one's "look." All eighth graders were allowed in because it was their prom, but sixth and seventh graders, and anyone from the outside, was allowed entry by his evaluation only. It seemed to me that sixth graders were especially young to be worrying about meeting Juan Carlos's social standard.

"So did he help you guys?" I asked.

"Well, no. He was there not helping," she said. "Just hanging around, you know."

"Yeah, I should have been there to help," I said, agreeing with what she'd said earlier. I felt dumb about saying it. But saying it or not saying it, I felt callous and selfish.

"Right here," Virginia said then, pointing out the window. "Stop here."

My father pulled over where a driveway led away to a hogan and two trailers. One of the boys climbed out of the back, came around to say thank you through the open window on the passenger side, and then made his way home through the dark.

We dropped off the other two boys at their homes, and then Virginia was alone with two strange white men in a pickup truck at night. She grew quiet and pressed herself up against the passenger side door. I imagined that she felt both grateful for the ride and foolish for accepting it, that she felt both safe and in danger at the same time. The only other option she seemed to have had that night was to walk home, miles and miles down this long dirt road through the cold night with no coat. She would have had the company of the three boys, but that carried certain risks too.

We drove on in silence for a few more miles until Virginia pointed to a driveway.

"Here," she said. "This is my home."

We stopped in front of a small house with no lights on. In the darkness, I couldn't see much, couldn't see whether there were vehicles parked there to indicate that someone was home. The peak of the little roof looked sharp and unwelcoming where the landscape gave way to the night sky.

"Okay," I said. "I hope you have a good holiday."

"Yeah," she said. "Thanks a lot. See you laters."

She got out, crossed in front of the truck, and waved to us in the headlights before the place and the darkness swallowed her up.

We pulled away and the big truck followed the road back the way we had come. We bumped along through the little trough of light without saying anything, the truck carving out a safe path in the night, stars wheeling overhead, the high canyon walls up through the pass towering over us. Outside, the desert air was impossibly clear, while inside the cab we rode protected from any discomfort: the cold, the dust rising from the roadbed, the spiny, twisted desert vegetation, the hard, rocky country. And just as we were protected, we were also cut off from the landscape, cut off from what was happening out there in the desert. If coyotes were calling, we couldn't hear them over the thrumming of the truck's diesel engine. If a wind was scraping the roadbed or singing in the yucca and pinyon, we didn't know it. If a star went shooting across the night directly above our heads, we couldn't see it. All we knew was what came up in the narrow tunnel of the truck's lights.

We came alongside the deep plunge pool of the arroyo where I had watched that river of water in the storm, and in a blaze of white speed, a rabbit burst up out of the ditch.

"Goddamn it," my father said.

Hard to know, but maybe it was a black-tailed jackrabbit, the kind with ears almost as long as the rest of them. It laid itself out in front of us, and, unable to respond in time, we rolled over it, crushing it beneath the truck's big tires. All we felt was the slightest touch, a little tremor in the truck's frame. Before either of us recognized what was happening, it had already happened. The event was over. The rabbit was dead.

I turned back in my seat to look through the cab and the camper shell windows. I could see nothing but darkness and a weird reflection cast back through the layers of glass by the headlights in front of us. The dead rabbit had already vanished into the dark, and we weren't stopping to have a look.

"Damn things," my father said.

"Jesus," I said at the same time. "So impossible to stop for those things. They're like, suicidal."

"Yep," my father said. "You just gotta run 'em over, or you end up in the ditch yourself."

"I guess so," I said.

"But I sure wish they wouldn't do that," he said.

He was right. If he had swerved to miss that rabbit, we might have hit the cut bank on the right side, or we might have flown out over the edge into that great chasm. Neither option seemed worth a rabbit's life. But then, didn't you have to draw the line somewhere? What life was worth the ditch or the chasm? The life of a spouse or lover? A brother or sister? A parent? A child? An eighth grader at Borrego Pass School? Did ordinary people make such sacrifices, or was an act of selflessness solely the territory of fools and heroes?

I thought of Virginia vanishing up the driveway. How long would she have waited at the school had I not been home this night? Or if I had never come to Borrego in the first place? What would she have done? She would have figured out something, I imagined. She didn't really need my help, did she? That realization came to me just as I had begun to think well of myself for making this small sacrifice to take her home, that I was doing something generous and this gesture would somehow make a difference in her life. I had begun to think of myself as a kind of savior, her savior, at least for tonight. But then, sitting there in the dark inside the warm cab of the truck, I realized there would always be a Virginia at Borrego waiting outside in the cold with no coat looking for a way home. What could I do to help matters here? Nothing, it seemed. And maybe I was like the truck and Virginia was like the rabbit. Would I have to run her over to save myself? I wasn't going to fix Virginia's life. I wasn't going to fix the problems down here at Borrego. And what did I mean by "problems"? Did I mean alcoholism? That was everywhere off the rez, too. Did I mean domestic abuse? That was everywhere I had ever lived, hidden in my friends' and neighbors' homes. Did I mean poverty? I'd seen it next to the richest neighborhoods in the world's great cities: Paris, Rome, New York, Athens, Madrid, Tokyo, Beijing. I couldn't fix all that. All I was going to do by living on at Borrego was send myself into the ditch by striving and striving and striving without hope of success, and for every little gesture I might think would make a difference, there were ten or twenty or a thousand Navajo children waiting outside in the cold.

I wanted to believe—as the righteous do—that any gracious gesture would help change things. I wanted to believe that if one person, just one student at Borrego, found anything of value in my class, that that was enough. But I didn't believe this—not really. And this troubled me. Had my heart gone stone cold? Had it been so before I arrived, or could I blame it on the place? It wasn't the place, I knew, but I wondered what was going on inside me. It seemed that what at first shocked me about living at Borrego, startled me, troubled my dreams, now barely raised my temperature. I wondered if I'd ever get out alive. It occurred to me then that this was one of the fatal stages of giving a shit—you go from novelty and curiosity, to a weird unsettling indifference, to devoting your entire life to a cause. They would say about you after you died, "He made a difference," but of course no one knows what that means. Perhaps you did make a difference, but only for a few individuals. The rest of it was pretty much the same. Did I want this? Did I want to live my life out here making a difference? No. I wanted to go on wandering, traveling, learning, experiencing, getting in and getting out.

I had accepted this job at Borrego only to continue exploring; I never meant to care. And now that some measure of caring about what happened to these kids and this community had penetrated my defenses, I didn't quite know what to do. Caring just caused trouble for me. I could no longer live here without caring or leave here without regretting. Perhaps this had been my initial resistance to Borrego and to my students in the first place. Perhaps this kind of self-protection had been in my way all along. Now that I had broken through it and begun to feel this terrible desire to help, to save, I knew I had to get out. When I arrived I thought I would leave because that is what I did. That is what I had always done. I arrived in places and left them. Now I thought I would leave because I did not want to care about people whose lives seemed so battered and bruised as to be beyond healing. At least, I knew I didn't know how to heal them, and in striving to do so, I could only end up in the ditch. Was Virginia worth the cut bank or the chasm? Was Borrego Pass worth that? Probably. Certainly. But was I going to sacrifice myself for it? Thing was, no one was asking me to. The people who lived at Borrego were not looking for a savior, and even if they were, nothing about my time here so far told me it was me.

We drove on through the dark, and it wasn't long before we topped out and came by the Trading Post. The road led us along the fence and to the opening over the cattle guard. We parked and got out. In the quiet under the desert sky, I looked up into the countless stars that graced the night. It was beautiful.

On Monday, yet another Monday at Borrego, the seventh-grade class came in smirking and laughing after what they had talked about on the way out to the trailer. Were they laughing at me, mocking me because they were so angry about the dance? I took roll, found someone missing, who was it, let's see, and then the door opened as George George came in, a little late and alone, sour and a little downtrodden, but smiling weirdly. He sat down, and everyone laughed. I tried to get on with the lesson, pretend nothing unusual was happening, but something obviously was. It couldn't be about me, I thought, and was relieved. What, was I paranoid? I pressed on, had the class open their books to such and such a page, got nowhere, and finally said, "What? What is it?"

"It's George," Maria Young said. "He's doin' it again." And the class erupted into laughter.

To which George spouted, "I ain' no sheep fucker!"

And even I had to laugh at that.

After the class settled out, and surprisingly George George looked somehow at peace with the situation (perhaps this wasn't his first accusation), I expected to be harassed for not helping with the dance. Only Jolanda spoke a few sharp words.

"Here," she said, handing me a metal box full of money. "Even though you didn't help us. Alice helped us. And she kept the money for us. Maybe next time you'll help us."

"Yeah," said Maria. "Will you? Help us next time?"

"Yes," I said. "I will. I'm sorry I couldn't help with the dance. I hadn't seen my parents in some time, and so I had a nice visit with them."

"Did you cook a turkey?" asked George George.

"Yes," I said, unable not to think of sheep. "We did. I'm sorry, you guys," I pleaded. "I'm sorry I didn't help."

"And did you eat it real fast and make a pie?" asked Maria.

"We did make pies," I said. "Apple and pumpkin."

"What about those sour berries that look like Jello?" asked Jolanda.

"And did you go somewhere?" George George asked.

I didn't know why they were so interested. "Yes, cranberries. We had those. And we did go somewhere. We went out to Chaco to look around," I said. "I'm sorry I didn't help you all. I will next time."

"That's okay," said Samuel Smith. "Everything worked out okay. We made some money and everyone came and had a good time."

I felt relieved to hear Samuel's support. He had been the voice of reason from the first few meetings I had with my homeroom. He seemed always to be smiling, and he wasn't as wowed by Caleb Benally as the other boys, maybe because he outweighed Caleb by at least twenty pounds, and his good nature allowed him to laugh off petty challenges and potential conflicts. One day on the playground, I watched Samuel break up an argument between Caleb and Tom when they collided in midair trying to catch a football. "C'mon, you guys, let's play," Samuel said. "This isn't any fun." He reached in and took the football out of Caleb's hands, and the game resumed.

"Yeah, that's okay," said George George, picking up Samuel's enthusiasm. "We had a good time. And, oh, that road to Chaco is real bumpy, you know."

"As long as you help us next time," Jolanda said. "But only if."

It sounded like she was offering me some grace, that she was going to forgive me on the condition that I didn't cross her or the class again. I vowed not to.

"I will," I said. "I will help you next time. In fact, let's talk about next time. Let's make a plan for our next event. I think we need a little more money for our field trip."

"We do," Jolanda said.

"Yeah," said Samuel Smith. "We do. If we want to have a real good trip."

We went to work. We settled on running a cakewalk at the Christmas Bazaar and organizing a car wash in Crownpoint sometime in the spring.

"That might do it," Jolanda said.

"Good," I said. "And now it's time for breakfast." Everyone lined up at the door. "When it's quiet, you can go," I said. Remarkably, no one said a word. "Okay," I said promptly, and the group filed out to the cafeteria.

"Sit with us today, Mr. Caswell," Samuel said as he walked by me.

"All right," I said. "I will."

I didn't regret not helping with the dance that night, not completely. I didn't feel good about disappointing the class, but I had stood my ground, and it seemed that something had shifted in our relationship. Did they respect me now, more than before? Everything seemed to be working out. But perhaps it wasn't that at all. Perhaps Virginia had told the story of how she got home that night, and a few of the kids decided that I wasn't so bad. Looking back, I realized that trusting too deeply in the two cardinal rules was as dangerous as not trusting them at all. I had found their limitations. I came to believe that it wasn't the rules that helped me save face that night, but adapting to a fluid and unpredictable set of circumstances, which translates into acting like a human being instead of a teacher.

I had yet to resolve my conflict with Caleb Benally, and I hoped that I could use this little bit of positive momentum with my home-room to do that. I tried as well as I could not to antagonize him, but it was very difficult when he, by his very presence, held much of the classroom hostage. For all my lesson planning, little could happen in the way of learning unless Caleb somehow approved. The other kids, even the girls, responded to his choice. And his choice was always unspoken.

In class one day the week of the Christmas Bazaar, Caleb said something to George George in Navajo when he came into the classroom. George walked by Caleb on his way to a seat and hit him in the shoulder. Then Caleb stood up and George sat down. It didn't matter that we were in classroom. Caleb was ready to fight.

"Caleb, sit down," I said.

Caleb pushed his chair back and started around the table toward George.

"Caleb! Sit down," I said.

He stopped, but he didn't sit down.

"Now," I said. "Sit down." I spoke the words slowly without raising my voice. I did not want to lose control again.

"I ain't afraid of you," Caleb said to me.

"Just sit down," I said. "That's all. I saw what happened. But you're in class."

"You can make me," Caleb said.

I had tried that with Tom Thompson, and it didn't turn out very well. The only weapon I had was my voice, and I wasn't sure what the limits were.

"You're a bully," I said calmly, pointing my finger at him. "And bullies are cowards."

That old musty truism—where had it come from? I didn't even know if I believed it, and I had just then issued a challenge, an insult, and escalated the situation. I wanted to achieve the opposite.

"I ain't afraid of you," he said again.

The class sat motionless, like statues. The heat was off Caleb now, and on me. It was like we were playing a tennis match, the ball going back and forth across the court. The whole class waited to see what I would do next. I didn't want to ruin any inroads I'd made since Thanksgiving break. I had to be careful.

"You *are* afraid," I said. "Not of me. I know you're not afraid of me. You're just afraid."

Caleb glared back at me. I didn't really believe this about him either. He wasn't afraid at all; in fact, he was recklessly unafraid. That was why people feared him. His instinct for fighting, the way he responded in his body to his opponent—athletes call this kinesthesia—was infallible. Did he have that knife in his pocket? Maybe in facing an opponent his mind disappeared and he became completely and wholly his body in motion, and his body then became a single purpose: to destroy the threat in front of him. If fear lived anywhere inside him, it fell away the moment he went into action, the way an actor loses all sense of stage fright the moment he becomes his character. I could see in Caleb's eyes then that he thought nothing of challenging me to blows, right here, right now, and that he believed in his heart that he could kick my ass.

"You're afraid," I said again.

I wondered if the idea of it might console some of the boys Caleb bullied. If they came to believe Caleb had a flaw, especially some of the stronger boys like Samuel, it might somehow weaken his grip on them, and so weaken his grip on the class. Weaken his grip on me.

Caleb made a clicking sound in the back of his mouth and jutted his chin at Clemson, who laughed in his nervousness. Clemson didn't seem to want to get involved.

"You have two choices," I said to Caleb. "You can sit down and we'll go on with class, or you can go see Frank. There won't be any fighting in my classroom."

Caleb stood there a moment trying to decide. If he went to Frank's office, he'd be confined to a desk in a tiny room for the rest of the day while Frank watched him do his schoolwork. If he sat down, everything would return to normal, he'd receive no reprimand or punishment, and instead of being forced to do his schoolwork, he'd exercise his near limitless opportunities to fuck off. He wanted that, as opposed to the other, I knew. Caleb had not yet let his anger take over completely, so perhaps he could still avoid doing anything stupid. Somehow, he also had to save face, to stand firm so as not to lose any ground with the other boys. He had to prove he wasn't afraid. I needed to give him an opportunity to do that, or there was no telling what he might do next.

"You can take care of your differences with George after school," I said, "but not here." I was not advocating fighting. I wanted to make a space in the moment for Caleb to cool down. He stood there, still as a post.

"I ain't afraid," he said calmly, and then he sat down.

Oddly, it was the best class I had yet had with my seventh graders, and Caleb led the way, raising his hand and answering questions, completing his writing assignments, reading aloud. Perhaps he felt he had improved his standing with the other boys, that he had proved only he was powerful enough to stand against his teacher, and now they would fear him even more. Or maybe it was the kind of happiness that comes with resolve, the way happiness comes just before the suicide.

That should have been the end of it with Caleb Benally, but it wasn't. Mary and I, along with Kuma and Ranger, made a long hike up the Ganado Wash that weekend. The cottonwood leaves were changing, and the cool, moist air of the wash reminded me of home. I also helped Mary and her friend Kris Chick, who worked with girls and family planning at Ganado High School, sell a few unwantables outside the Ganado post office. A bicycle. A few tables and a chair. Various items of clothing. We sold almost everything, and I came close to buying a beautiful handmade flute from a tall, cosmopolitan-looking Navajo from Santa Fe. We spent Saturday evening eating homemade pizza and drinking beer while watching taped episodes of the *X-Files*.

On Sunday morning I left early for Borrego because I had some planning to do before classes on Monday. Between Window Rock and Gallup, I passed all the hitchhikers lining the road, the usual scene, people on their way home or running from home after a weekend drunk in Gallup, some of them alone and ragged, some passed out in the ditch, some in small groups or coupled up, two thumbs hitching, and some holding dollar bills out, offerings to passing drivers or to the wind. I came to depend on these people for company each Sunday morning when I drove that lonely highway back from Mary's. I always felt a sense of loss leaving Ganado, as Mary's stability and optimism faded into the west behind me. I never picked anyone up along that road. I never did. Just that they were there, always there, told me that the world hadn't changed much over the weekend and that life at Borrego would be about the same too.

The dirt road north from Prewitt was quiet and empty that morning. I drove slowly, bumping along and looking at the country. Out ahead of me, I saw a long line of horses running fast across the desert. I saw two men on horseback among them, driving the horses into a little corral near the base of the sandstone bluffs. The figure on the roadside ahead of me had dismounted his horse. He stood there holding the reins in one hand, and a long rifle in the crook of his other arm. As I drove by, he raised the rifle and pointed it at me, the butt perched against his hip, tracking me with the barrel.

It was Caleb Benally.

The next day in class Caleb said, "Hey, did you see my gun? I was gonna shoot you."

He said it so that I knew he was joking and so that I knew he was not joking. I took Caleb's words to heart. I understood him to mean that we had come to a kind of impasse and our relationship could turn bloody if something did not change. He wasn't going to give up whatever power and position he had earned in this world, because it was all he had. If I was going to use force, then so was he. Now more than ever I felt like a trespasser at Borrego, and I had good reason to wonder about my safety. Not that Navajos are overly aggressive or violent (though this is the traditional view of the Hopi), but as a culture they had come face to face with their own annihilation and endured it, endured some of the most bloody, inhumane, stupid destruction imposed on another culture by any government in history. They had endured that. They were still here on their ancestral land. They still spoke their own language. They were still Navajos. And now their future, their identity as a people, hung in the balance: who were they now in this new world, and who would they become? No one was going to get in the way of these questions, even if blood had to be spilled. For Caleb's part, that was all there, buried somewhere in his mind, in his heart, in his belly, and on top of that he was defending something personal. Something intimate. Something only he could know. What I heard him saying with his rifle was that we needed to make some changes in our relationship, or he might feel forced to do something that would damage both of us forever.

Mary came to visit the night of the Christmas Bazaar. Always the inveterate teacher, Mary frequently asked me questions about working with kids who spoke fluent Navajo. What was it like? What were the differences? How did I plan my lessons to account for this? What kind of success was I having? The trip to Mission: Wolf did not answer these questions, so I suggested she come see for herself. The bazaar was not the classroom, but she would be able to meet my students, along with kids in the elementary grades, all the administrators, teachers, and staff, and the parents and local community members. Mary had also been studying the Navajo language and was eager to try out her skills with the people at Borrego.

I introduced Mary to Maria, Jolanda, and Samuel, who all showed up to run the seventh-grade cake walk. Jolanda knew Mary from our trip to Mission: Wolf, and she whispered something in Maria's ear. Samuel stuck his hand out and Mary shook it.

"Are you Mr. Caswell's girlfriend?" Samuel asked, smiling.

"No. His friend. I teach at a school over in Ganado," Mary said.

"Oh," Samuel said. "Okay. Why'd you come here then?"

"I'm just visiting," Mary said. "I came to help you tonight."

"Oh, okay," Samuel said. "Why don't you help us, then. Let's start it, Mr. Caswell."

We set to work. Samuel stood in front of the booth calling in contestants, while Jolanda and Maria arranged the cakes on a table. They arranged the numbered paper disks on the floor and set up the boom box for the music. When we had a full load of kids ready to walk, Maria played a rousing rendition of "O Come, All Ye Faithful" on cassette, and a little boy who did not go to school at Borrego won an angel food cake.

"Mr. Cas-well," I heard in a kind of loud whisper from somewhere behind me.

I turned around, but I couldn't see who had called me.

"Mr. Cas-well," I heard again.

I noticed that the side doors of the gym were open, slightly, and through it the voice came once more.

"Hey, Mr. Cas-well! I'm calling you."

I went to the double doors and peered out the crack into the night. Clemson and Caleb sat on their bikes in the dark. I pushed the door open wider.

"Mr. Cas-well. Who's that?" Clemson said, pointing with his lips at Mary.

"That's a friend of mine from Ganado," I said.

"What's she doing here?"

"She's visiting. Helping with the cakewalk. Why don't you guys come in and help us?"

"Uh-uh," Clemson said. "We got our bikes. They won't let us bring 'em in."

"You like low-rider bikes?" Caleb asked.

I was surprised that he spoke to me at all. "What's that, Caleb?" I said.

"You never seen one? I'll show you," Caleb said. He got off his bike and pushed it up close to the doors into the light. "Have a look," he said. "See, it's a low-rider bike. I built it myself."

The bike sat low to the ground, much too low for Caleb's long legs. The wheels seemed too small, like they wouldn't hold his weight, and the frame, all tricked out in chrome and painted in fiery symbols, looked more suited to training wheels.

"So what do you do with it?" I asked.

"So you know a low-rider car, right?" Caleb said. "Well, this is a low-rider bike. I'll show you."

He got on and rode out in a little circle into the parking lot, came back to the doors and went around again like he was winding up for something. When he had the speed he wanted, he hopped up off the pedals and landed on the seat with his feet, the pedals spinning empty now like ghosts were riding them, and rode the circle out and then back, and then dropped down now onto the seat again, popped the front wheel up, stood on the pins on the back of the frame, and hopped the bike like a pogo stick. Then, balanced on the rear wheel, he turned the whole bike around in a pirouette; then he dropped down and rode back.

"See," he said. "That's a low-rider bike."

"Jesus, that's good," I said. Caleb smiled. Maybe it was that simple. Maybe all I needed to do to communicate with Caleb was take an interest in his love for this bike, in his talent, in him. "That's really great, Caleb," I said. "How'd you learn to do all that?"

He beamed. "Just playin' around," he said. "Some tricks I learned from other people. People who're real good. Better than me. Some stuff just by playin' around."

"Well, it looks like it takes a lot of skill and practice," I said.

"It does," he said. "It's real hard to learn." He sat back on his bike, proud of himself.

It felt good to be talking with him instead of against him, and I wanted to press it further, but I didn't want Caleb to think I was baiting him, that I wasn't sincere. I was sincere.

I said, "Can you do that, Clemson?"

"Uh-uh," Clemson said. "I'm not very good. Not that good."

"Well, let's see it," I said.

"Uh-uh," Clemson said. "Not while she's watching." He motioned with his lips again.

Mary had come up behind us and was looking over my shoulder. I took her arm and pulled her outside and we let the gym doors close behind us. Now we had the light of the moon and the lights in the parking lot.

"Watch this," I said to Mary. "Clemson, do it."

"Uh-uh," he said.

"C'mon, man," Caleb said. "Do it."

"Uh-uh," Clemson said.

So Caleb pushed off then and went through the same routine as before, out into his circle, popping up on the seat, then down, then into a wheelie, then the pogo thing and the pirouette.

"Wow," Mary said, clapping her hands. Then she looked at Clemson. "Now you."

"Really?" he said. "I'm not very good."

"Doesn't matter," Mary said. "Do something easy."

"Okay," he said. He got on, pushed off, and started out into a circle as Caleb had, rounded it a couple of times, said "Wait," and then stood on the seat, turned the circle, came down, jackknifed his handlebars, and stalled and fell off.

"Oh," Mary said. "You okay?"

"Yeah," he said. "I'm okay. My bike's all somehow though. Hey, watch this."

Clemson turned around backward on his seat and started pushing with his feet on the ground. He made the circle around holding onto the handlebars behind him, craning his neck back so he could see forward as Caleb joined him, popping up into a wheelie, and they went around the circle in opposite directions, around and around, giggling and laughing. Mary and I started clapping and cheering as they circled, shouting cheers of their own now, and we forgot about the Christmas Bazaar inside, forgot about the Christmas carols, the people inside winning cakes and buying cookies and fry bread, buying little dangling Santas for Christmas trees, and pledging their love to Jesus Christ and the American economic holiday revival because in front of us Clemson and Caleb rode low-rider bikes like they were things made for wheels, like they were a circus act of unicycles on a high wire, like they were birds tucking and pulling together on the wind.

"Woo-hooo!" Mary shouted, and we both cheered for them.

Watching those boys ride around together, I felt something shift between me and them. I didn't expect Caleb and Clemson to be my pals, or expect them to become stars in the classroom, but I thought that maybe after this night we wouldn't weigh on each other so heavily. I would let Caleb be, not corner him again so that he had to defend himself before his peers. I would expect him to offer me that same freedom, somewhat, expect him to perhaps mind himself more and seek to rule the class less. I let the tension we had built between us dissolve as Mary and I clapped and cheered for Caleb and Clemson in their grace on their low-rider bikes.

"We're riding off now, Mr. Caswell," Clemson said. "C'mon, Caleb."

Clemson straightened his wheel and headed out across the parking lot as Caleb waved and pulled up on his handlebars to hop a Coke can lying there, charged up his legs and zipped by Clemson, and they both disappeared into the night.

EIGHT

THE HOGAN

Sand borne aloft on the wind came into the trailer through the walls. It would thread its way through the corners of the place so that every closet shelf was paved with it, swirled and patterned like a sand painting in the strange currents caught in there. In the bedroom where I slept, the back wall bowed and shivered with the strong arm of the wind, rattling the mirror on the wall in the bathroom and covering the linoleum floor in fine dust. The roof rattled too, shivering in waves as the wind coursed over it, drawing my attention upward: I fully expected the whole thing to go flying off. I tried to go walking, but out beyond the berm along my usual route, blowing sand stung my face and eyes and caught in my hair, settling down at the roots in the sweat breaking over my skull. Truly there was no place to go, but it was almost more unpleasant to stay inside on a windy day because the wind seeped in and swirled around me like a gnat, or a headache from too little coffee.

If I did stay indoors, I found myself moving from room to room, window to window, book to book, slightly agitated, always yearning. I watched through the window how the sad branches of the little trees along the fence bowed down to the wind and scraped at the hard earth. Then the wind gusted and pushed the branches back into themselves, turning them wrong side out. I couldn't escape the wind.

It was like a bully, always waiting for me in the gaps, pressing at me, pushing me around.

Pretty much every derelict tire in Navajoland ended up on somebody's trailer roof to keep it steady in the wind. But not my roof. Dean West, the maintenance supervisor, thought them unsightly and would not allow anyone on campus to place tires on roofs against the weather. I drove out the long desert dirt roads passing trailer after trailer, the roofs dotted with black tires like chocolate donuts, and I was envious. Not because of the rattling so much—I thought I was getting used to it—but because those roofs looked more concrete, more stable, more at home in the wind. If only it were that easy—if only placing a few old tires on my roof would bring me a sense of home, a fitting into the land—but I suffered from a far deeper malaise under that roof. I was in love with living at Borrego, with working out here on the edge of the world and wandering the empty trails through the broken rock, and at the same time I detested it. Every time the wind blew, it threatened to peel away the already thin membrane of my patience, my tolerance, my sanity, and blow me to the moon.

I made morning phone calls to Sakura in Hokkaido from the pay phone inside the school. I loved her, I thought, or was she just a distraction, a beautiful imagining to keep my loneliness at bay? I wanted to marry her, I told myself, but I wasn't sure. I feared that I would only be asking her to come and live with me to comfort me, for around her she made an atmosphere of life, and I feared that my desire for her company wasn't love, but merely an antidote to loneliness. I resisted asking her—for her sake, I told myself—but I had grown too close to the idea to keep it from her. She could sense it with a woman's sensing, through our conversations and in my letters that forever worked the edges of the question (could we be married?), and she began to hang on the idea of it, to hang on my every word in expectation of a proposal that would never come. Inside the gaps, the long silences over the telephone across the thousands of miles of ocean, the ocean that was water and the ocean that was land, she would wait for me to ask her. I knew she was waiting; my senses went that far, at least. To divert this awkward instance, I might interject some petty detail about my day, or about the Navajos and life on the rez, or about a memory I had from Hokkaido. She was in love with me, she said, or maybe with the idea of me, the idea of marrying a foreigner, and yet I believed her, that it was love. I knew she wouldn't confront me about what we were together, about what we were both thinking, about what we wouldn't say. She regarded herself as meek: "It's hard to speak up for a person like me," she had said. But she was not meek. She held tight to her vision of a beautiful courtship and a marriage proposal that would sweep her away from her native land. She would then find herself in a foreign landscape—the Navajo reservation—and she would yearn for home, for the green trees and blue rivers of Hokkaido, while simultaneously in love with the notion that my love completed her. A Japanese woman suffers quietly for love, for longing, without complaint, and she is rewarded by the great beauty of her own tragic endurance. Such grace is exemplified in the image of spring cherry blossoms, their brilliant and full life met by a sudden, beautiful death, a wind that takes them from tree to earth. I knew that Sakura would wait for me as long as I asked her to, as long as I hedged and drew near her from so far away. If I asked her to wait, and she believed that the waiting would end, we would remain caught in a timeless sorrow: safe from commitment to a real life, and victims of a desire for it. How could I be so cruel?

> Will you turn towards me?
> I am lonely too,
> this Autumn evening.
> —Bashō

Out wandering one winter day, I came upon an abandoned hogan east of the Trading Post. It was set back a little distance from the road.

The area surrounding it was scattered with household goods and tools and tires rotting in the sun and car bodies and the crystal glint of glass broken on the rock. It didn't look like anyone had been here in years. The hogan was built of timbers stacked up log cabin style, with six sides that formed a rough circle. The roof was also constructed of heavy timbers that rose up to the center and were covered over with thick tarry shingles that softened and crippled in the sun. Something was piled up inside in front of one of the windows, and the others were so dirty I could hardly see through. The door of the hogan had been chained shut, and a great padlock held it. Standing by the door, I was mostly hidden from the road. Anyone driving that road couldn't see me until they had already passed by. I stood there in secret and pushed the door open an inch or two, to the length of the chain, to peer inside. Dust rose up where the bottom of the door disturbed the dirt floor. I could see a table where someone had left it, and a broken chair, a few pots and pans scattered about, and several garments slumped against the wall like people without bones. And directly facing me were two framed photographs, pictures of young girls in Borrego Pass School graduation gowns. The photos looked new, like someone had recently framed them. Along the edges of the walls were years of mouse droppings pushed into the shape of waves by slivers of the wind. I thought of hantavirus and pulled the door shut.

The shape of a hogan, the circle, symbolizes the sun, and the Sun god is one of the most honored gods of the Navajos. In fact, the hogan is considered a gift from the gods, not just a shelter or a place to live. The Navajos believe that the first hogans were built by the Holy People from white shell, jet, and abalone shell. Traditionally, the door faces east, the direction of birth and spring and the rising sun, so that the first thing a Navajo sees in the morning is the new day breaking over the world. The old-style hogans didn't have windows. Inside, it was dark and cool in the summer, and in the winter a little cook fire kept the whole room warm as the smoke drew up through a hole in the roof.

Everything inside a traditional hogan is placed according to a prescription of the gods, so that housekeeping becomes a sacred occupation. Some accounts have the south side of the hogan belonging to the women, and the north side to the men. Others say just the opposite: that the women sit on the north side, and the men on the south. I imagine families worked those details out for themselves. By most accounts, the west side of the hogan is reserved for the male head of household and for distinguished guests, who, when seated there, face east toward the door. While a man might be the head of his family, in the old days, Navajo society was generally matriarchal. The wife owned and controlled the hogan and the land it was built on. She owned her children who dwelled inside, and they were considered part of her clan. The hogan itself is said to be female, so it is also a symbol of the womb, the mother who gave birth to the family, and the womb of the earth, big reed, through which the Navajo people were born into this world in the myth-time. And there are male hogans too.

Most hogans are relatively small, perhaps twenty-five feet in diameter, but a family can get on well if they keep everything in its place. Seldom-used items are stored up in the rafters, like guns and winter clothes and dried spices and herbs used in cooking. Everyday clothes and food are stored in trunks that are either hung from or stacked up against the walls. The cooking pots and utensils are kept near the central fire pit. If it's kept tidy, a hogan has plenty of space for a family to cook and eat and sleep and make love. What else is there? Out around the main hogan, Navajo people often build smaller hogans if they need additional storage, and sometimes even a studio hogan for the women to weave in. If a family owns sheep, it might maintain seasonal hogans in the mountains or in a valley where the sheep can graze and find water. In summer, people mostly live outside around their complex of hogans and build brush shelters for shade.

Traditionally, a hogan is abandoned if someone dies inside. The body is removed through a hole broken out in the north wall, the direction of evil and death. Then the place is boarded up and no one ever goes there again. A hogan might also be abandoned if struck by lightning because it is then said to be *chindi*, bewitched.

Things are quite different now, but traditional Navajos are notoriously fearful of the dead. They are not so afraid of dying, but of dead bodies. This fear rises out of the story of the first person who died. She was a hermaphrodite, but the story refers to her as "she." When she died, the people searched everywhere for her breath. They did not know what had become of it. The inanimate body lay there, and the people decided that her breath had been lost somewhere and they needed to find it. Some people went out to look for it. After the people looked everywhere, far and wide, finally two men came to the Place of Emergence, where the Navajos came into this world. They looked back down through the hole, back into the former world, and they saw the dead woman sitting down there combing her hair. The men returned home and reported that the woman was not really dead, but that the place she was in was static. In that place, nothing ever changed, they said. They concluded that to die is to live on without change. After awhile, both of those men who looked on the woman, died. And since that time, so the story goes, Navajo people have feared looking at dead bodies. And they are terrified of ghosts.

I knew I was guessing, but I came to think of the abandoned hogan as a place where an old Navajo man had died.

That winter, I walked with Kuma among the derelict things, and out to the far reaches around the hogan, where under a collection of juniper trees was a great mound of rusted steel cans, not one of them with a label. I inspected an outdoor charcoal grill, a doll's head half buried in the earth, the seat and handlebars of a bicycle. A kitchen stove with an oven still clean and a refrigerator with the doors torn off and lying over there. Empty gas cans, and brittle plastic bottles that once stored motor oil. Out at the edge of the mesa top, where I could see north into the wide world, I found tires stacked in some places and scattered in others, heavy spikes driven into trees on which things had once been hung, coils of brittle wire and rusted chain, and a red flannel shirt tangled in a juniper, flying like a war-wounded flag in the breeze.

I did not know if everything in the junkyard around the hogan belonged to the man I had conjured in my mind, or if over the years people had come by and dumped their garbage here. Either way, I felt sad wandering about the place. I felt that something had been lost here, some issue of respect or reverence for the dead. Not that any Navajo would come by and feel this way. Not that the old man's spirit felt this way. But I did. Standing here in the presence of the hogan, I felt a deep emptiness haunting the place. I heard the wind in the pinyon like a voice that was weeping. I was sharply aware of some great gap in myself that rose up from I did not know where. Walking here near the hogan, where the memory of this dead man was interred forever, the thought struck me without warning: what if I died in a place that was not my own? It seemed that I had to make a choice. I had to choose a life and a place, or to go the way of smoke, which is whatever way the wind blows it, as the poet William Stafford said. Although I felt grateful for the experiences I'd had out there in the world, the many places I'd lived, the wild lands over which I had roamed, I also felt that choices were making me, that I was who I was by accident, and that I had no control over it. Was I ever going to stop wandering and choose a home? Did I even want to?

I wandered without direction or purpose through the maze of the remnants of this old man's life as if they were my own, as if I was looking back at the broken history of myself through someone else's eyes. Was this a life lived well? Was this a life worth remembering? Would mine be? I returned to these questions and to this loneliness each time I went to the hogan. And though I feared and hated them, I kept coming back.

A grass hut less than five by five—I regret living
even in it: if only there were no rainfalls.
        —Bashō

That winter I read Bashō and *The Tale of Genji* by Lady Murasaki
Shikibu. Entering those pages returned me to Hokkaido, the deep
green trees and dwarf bamboo on Chitose River, and the evenings in
the quiet dark of my apartment with Sakura. She was living at home
at that time, and we hid our love from her parents. She worked in
graphic design for an advertising agency in Sapporo, around which
we easily constructed stories of her staying in the city with a coworker
so that we could spend some nights together. Her father was a colonel
in the Japanese Self-Defense Force and highly respected in Chitose.
He had spent several years stationed in the U.S., in Georgia, on a dip-
lomatic visa. Sakura finished high school there, then earned a bache-
lor's degree at the Savannah College of Art and Design. In Hokkaido,
I once introduced Sakura to Saito, the man I worked for at the school,
and later he said to me, accusingly, "She is daughter of Colonel Haga.
How did you manage to meet such person of good family?"
    Sakura would park her car up a side street some blocks from my
apartment and arrive at my door, her hair wet and glistening black
from the rain and sometimes from white snow, which settled on it
and melted as she stepped out of her shoes in the doorway. She hung
her coat on the peg over mine, leaned into the room and giggled a
little before entering. Her shoes were so small, and she was beautiful in my hands. I would turn up the heater to temper the damp air,
and soon we would be naked and fully involved like a house on fire,
pressing into each other on the cool tatami mat. She told me that it
didn't matter to her if we lasted, that she wanted this one chance,
that maybe I would go home to America and leave her behind, that
she was of very little consequence—what was she but a Japanese girl

who spoke a little English?—and so if we could be this way for now, that was enough, she said, for her. She told me that it was a common thing for a Japanese to have a "sex friend," not someone to marry, but someone to laugh with, cook with, make love with, and find a simple freedom that could exist nowhere else, because marriage was often an arrangement made on other principles. Often marriage had nothing to do with love, and we were too in love for marriage. Maybe that is what we are, she said, lovers only. And lovers find an end, while marriages stagnate and go on forever. I told her no, that we were not just lovers, that we were more than that, though I questioned the merit of what that "more" would mean. Lying entwined on the floor in the warm room, she would look up at me through the darkness of her oriental eye and nod her head sharply, and close her eyes and soften her mouth to say that she was ready, that it would hurt what we were doing, this kind of love, but that she was ready, as small and fragile as she was, because "the day was a woman who loved you. Open."

Afterward she would cook for me. She would tell me to sit and talk to her while she cooked. She would take care of it all, she said, but I always wanted to help, to attend her like a chef's apprentice and learn from her how to cook so many Japanese dishes. I would play the music of the Pat Metheny band, and she would dance in place at the counter cutting vegetables. She had a little niece, Satomi, whom she adored and often talked about. I knew that when she had a baby of her own, her quality would make it a girl. Sometimes she wanted to smoke cigarettes, but she knew that I did not smoke and thought I would not approve. She would say that she had to get something in her car. She would walk outside and hide around the end of the building and smoke a cigarette, or half of one. I could smell it on her, of course, when she came back in, and she would smile and giggle and act a little drunk. We would eat together sitting on the floor at the table and drink beer, sometimes wine, and go to bed together again and then sleep in the soft folds of the futon with the window partly open to the night sounds, the songs of crickets and the stray cat that walked the concrete wall in the spring with its kittens. I would wake in the morning to find her there beside me, and I would lie there and watch her in her beauty, and I thought I would die if I left her to go to my desk.

> Look, so holy: green leaves young leaves in the light of the sun.
> —Bashō

Sakura and I made plans for her to visit during the winter holiday. When school let out, I would drive north to Oregon to spend Christmas with my family. Sakura would fly into Eugene on December 26, meet my parents and sisters, my two brothers-in-law, my grandmother and uncles, and the next day we would drive the long road back to Borrego. During the weeks before her arrival, I so looked forward to seeing her that I felt a greater sense of purpose, perhaps an edge of that balance I so wished for. I found myself looking longingly at furniture and dishes, towels and bedding, and voluptuous foods like ice cream and feta cheese, red wine and a four-dollar loaf of bread, whatever exotics I could find at Smith's in Gallup. Perhaps it was time to stop living like a monk on pilgrimage, I thought, and make as much of a home for myself at Borrego as I could. And then later, if it came time to leave that place, make a home somewhere else with Sakura. Still, I was reserved and thrifty, and couldn't bring myself to invest in anything I would later feel obligated to take with me. I'd brought all my possessions down in the back of my truck, and I wanted to take all my possessions back in the back of my truck. I thought a lot about making such a home for myself, but never truly believed I would ever have one.

For the Navajos, a good life embodies *hózhó*, that proper balance between what happens to you and what you make happen. It is peace, beauty, good health and fortune, and harmony in your own life, as well as the lives of your relatives and friends. One must seek *hózhó* at all times, especially during periods of great chaos and misfortune. Sakura brought into relief how much I desired this kind of balance, and how much, however oddly, I feared it.

It was about this time that I noticed a silver bracelet Jane Wiseman wore. She showed it to me when I asked about it. A story bracelet, she said, depicting the major icons of Navajo life. From left to right, in relief, a horse, a mesa, a stack of firewood, a dog, a hogan in the center, and then a wool rug on a loom, a pinyon tree, and a wagon. Marvin Tsosie, the husband of one of the teachers at Borrego, had made it. I asked Mrs. Tsosie that very day if Marvin had time to make two before Christmas—one that fit me, and one a bit smaller for Sakura. I felt on the edge of asking her to marry me and thought of the bracelet as an engagement gift. I never much cared for rings. I didn't know whether I would do it, whether I wanted to get married at all, but I could decide in the moment, I thought. If by December I had made up my mind to ask her, I would ask her. If not, I knew Sakura loved silver. We had been together about a year. I would give her the bracelet to mark that length of time, or for Christmas, or for no reason at all. I thought ill of myself for wavering, and for imagining the way I might propose, for backing out on myself in my mind, for being uncertain about marriage and children, about her, about the source of my own loneliness. I couldn't let her in on this unsteadiness, I thought; I couldn't bear to hurt her by letting her know I was so unsure.

On the southwest side of the school, up against the rock, I found a small pile of four-by-six timbers. The surface of the wood was deeply grooved and weathered and scattered with bent and rusting nails. I bought a handsaw and a hammer in Crownpoint and decided I would use the timbers to build a little table, Japanese style, like the table I had in my apartment in Hokkaido. Out on my walks I would come home this way and hoist one or two of the big beams onto my shoulder and bring them along to the trailer. When four or five days had gone by, I had enough material to work with. I pulled the nails and straightened them. I sized the beams with the saw. I set five side by side and joined them with two beams across the underbelly, then hammered on the legs. The table was just under two feet off the ground. I would set it in the corner of the trailer and kneel at it like a Japanese to take my meals and sometimes read there or correct student papers, and sometimes write. The table was so heavy I couldn't manage it by myself through the door. I removed the legs and carried it in in pieces, then nailed it together once more.

The table reminded me that I could have anything I needed for my place for free, if only I was patient enough and let the desert decide. Then when I moved on from the place, I would abandon these found objects to the next traveler who passed this way. This was a familiar rhythm, a knowledge of the wandering life that I had grown used to in Hokkaido. In most Japanese towns, one day each week is designated "big garbage day," the day when people discard all manner of useful things by the side of the road to be picked up by a truck. Most Japanese people would never be caught rummaging through one another's garbage, and this made the pickings safe for foreigners alone. On that good day, I would make sure to go out for a run or a walk before sunrise, and in that way I furnished my apartment. I had heard that in larger cities, big garbage day became a kind of social scene for young Westerners working in Japan. An honor system based on need was at work: people came together to agree on who got what. At Borrego, I competed only with the desert and the slow decay of time.

Out wandering with Mary one weekend near the head of Canyon del Muerto near Tsaile, we came upon a little treasure among the low trees, a weathered hutch good for storing books and things (just what

I needed in the trailer), and a wooden crate full of tools and cooking utensils: a hammer with a broken handle; a few crescent wrenches of different sizes; screwdrivers; a wood plane with no guts and no blade. Maybe someone had stored these things here and would be coming back for them later. Or was this someone's summer sheep camp? The tools were rusted, some of them beyond use, and the crate choked with sand. They had been here a long time, we figured, and if we left them they would remain even longer. The desert seemed to be offering them freely, so what harm would packing them off do? Besides, we reasoned, these things would not leave the desert. We would commit all that we gathered to the places we lived, leave them in my Borrego trailer and Mary's Ganado apartment to the next fresh white teacher from suburbia. Of course, this was mere justification for the joys of treasure hunting, because the next tenant might as easily chuck everything back out into the desert as take it all home.

We hefted the raggedy hutch into the back of my truck and placed the crate in there too. Mary would use the crate as a coffee table. She kept most of the tools. I would place the hutch in my trailer under the window looking southeast. As we drove out the bumpy reservation road, I felt like I was stealing.

That first December night with Sakura at Borrego, she stood at the stove cooking the evening meal when Everett knocked at the door to repair the heater. It had coughed and died before I left Borrego for the holidays in Oregon. Although Everett planned to fix it while I was away, he hadn't. I held Kuma back—he welcomed almost no one into his space—and Sakura went on with her work in the kitchen. I introduced her to Everett. He looked awkwardly at his feet and mumbled something that I couldn't make out. As he worked, he kept peering around the heater to have a look at her. She looked very industrious at that moment, very good with her hands in the kitchen. Her tiny nose, rounded against her face and a bit flared, looked something like his. I could see that he wanted badly to ask about her. She wasn't Navajo, or Hopi, or Zuni, was she—but he couldn't place her. When he finished his work, he explained that the heater would run for awhile, he thought, but needed to be replaced. He would have to order one and come back to install it. Maybe it would take about two weeks.

"The less you use it," Everett said, "the longer it will last. It's gonna get real cold soon, and if this thing breaks down, so will you." As he talked, he stared past me at Sakura stirring something on the stove.

After supper, Sakura and I sat together at the little table I had made drinking hot sake, a bottle she brought from Hokkaido, while Kuma lay asleep on his bed. I had turned the heater down so as to extend its life a little, and the cold drove us into the bedroom and under the covers. We lay in bed together in each other's arms, wearing only our T-shirts for warmth, a little drunk and whispering in the dark, and listening to Kuma breathing beside us in the quiet spaces. Sakura began to cry a little, and I asked her what was wrong.

"Nothing," she said. "Just this feels like a home to me. That's it."

I held her closer then, and we made love in the cold dark and slept away the desert night.

In the morning, I found Sakura already up, drinking Earl Grey with cream and sugar, sketching the view from the window in her notebook. She wore her jeans, heavy socks, and a warm wool sweater of mine she'd pulled from the closet shelf. She had the sleeves rolled up by a third, and her hair tied up in the back so that little black wisps of it flowed down around her ears, her face, and the back of her neck. I watched her work with the pencil, making long smooth motions with her hand and the big mesa behind my trailer came up off the page like a miracle.

"Ohayo gozaimasu," she said.

"Ohayo," I said.

"Are you *genki*?" she said. "Did you sleep good?"

"Of course," I said. "You?"

"Of course, yo." She smiled. "I wanna make you a breakfast," she said.

"You don't have to." I said. "I'll do it."

"I want to. That will be nice for me. Maybe nice for you?"

"Of course. But don't hurry. Finish that. What you're doing."

"I'm done," she said. "I'm done with this one. I'll paint something again later."

"Before we have breakfast," I said, "I have something for you." I handed her an envelope with the silver bracelet inside. "It's a Christmas present, I guess."

She took it out and held it up. "It's beautiful," she said. "It's so beautiful for you to give me it."

I put my arm out and jacked up my sleeve to show her mine. She drew in her breath a little and smiled and grinned and pursed her brow. "You have one," she said.

"We both have one," I said.

"That's-a-beautiful for us," she said.

I took it from her and she held out her arm. I slipped it on her wrist and pushed the opening together a little to make it fit.

I could see that she knew I meant to ask her to marry me, but that I hadn't done it yet was a puzzle to her. She waited for it. She didn't seem to know whether she should trust her intuition, whether she was making up in her heart what she thought she wanted and it wasn't really there. She didn't know. I felt awkward, strange, unsure about what to do next. I was possessed by the fear that she would find me out, that she would ask me, that she would take the opportunity from me before I could act, even as I was letting it slip by, and though I still had time to do it, I secretly wished she would rescue both of us from this terrible inertia, as we sat looking at each other and the bracelets as if we were watching a movie about us and we both knew what would happen; I was paralyzed by wonder. Silence went between us as we sized each other up. She looked a little downcast, waiting for something. I still couldn't bring myself to do it. I thought I was in love with her, but I was also lonely living at Borrego and I wasn't sure about the difference. I doubted whether I could live the life she wanted—a place, a home, a job, and beautiful children. I wanted to want it, but it existed as a fantasy for me, the way journeys to exotic lands are fantasies for others. I didn't think I could stop roaming, I didn't know why, as lonely as it was most of the time, as empty and desolate. Did I love loneliness and emptiness and desolation? I told myself that I loved Hokkaido but didn't love her. I think it was the other way around. I felt tormented by my desire to marry her and my fear of it, by my desire to be with her and my fear of being alone. I did not know which way to turn.

> "Answer me, answer me!" Genji says to Fujitsubo: "I cannot live without you. And yet, what use to die? For I know that in every life to come I am doomed to suffer the torment of this same heinous passion."

"What shall we cook?" I asked, pushing the moment away.

"I'll do it," she said. "I'll do it." And she did.

And that was all. That moment faded away from us like it hadn't ever been. I didn't know how it was for her, but I felt foolish and weak, ugly and cowardly. I wondered why what some people did so recklessly tormented me. Was I shallow and selfish? Was I broken? Was I mad?

She wanted to visit one of my classes, the "littler ones," she said. "I want to meet some of the little children."

So it was that I brought her along to the portable that day to talk to my sixth-grade class, to tell them about the world she lived in, about Hokkaido, and Japan, about how far she had traveled to be here, about her impressions of this place called Borrego. I wondered if her visit wouldn't open the door a bit wider, if my students wouldn't begin to wonder about other places and other cultures, if they wouldn't come to wonder about anything at all.

The class was utterly silent as I showed Sakura into the room. She was dressed in a grey wool skirt and a black blouse with a lacy collar, her hair pulled back and up and held in place by a silver hairpin from Tiffany. She wore black tights and black shoes, shiny, with low, squared-off heels. She looked lovely and happy and a little formal, as a guest might look, but also approachable and open, and she was smiling. I wondered why in the previous few days I couldn't tell her that I loved her.

My class sat upright and still, like they were about to meet the Queen, and Sakura went to the front of the room with me and I introduced her. "Maybe you can say 'hello' in Japanese," I said.

"All right," she said. "Konichiwa," she said.

No one moved. No one said a word. I had never seen them like this before.

"*Konichiwa* means 'hello,' in Japanese," Sakura said. "Maybe you can say it. 'Ko-ni-chi-wa,' " she said again, her voice trailing up on the end of it.

"Ko-ni-chi-wa," the class said together.

"That's good," she said. "One more time. 'Konichiwa!' "

"Koni-chiwa," the class said again.

"Now your turn," she said. "In your language."

"Oh, I know," said Joseph Jones. "Yá'át'ééh!" he said.

"Yá'át'ééh," Sakura said. And everyone cheered.

"Koni-chiwa," Shane said. "Koni-chiwa, yeah."

"Oh," Sakura said. "Good. Konichiwa. O genki desuka?"

The class went silent again.

"That means, 'Hello, are you doing fine? Are you doing okay?' " Sakura told them.

"Oh, I get it," said Kyle Bigfoot. "Genki desk-o," and he patted the table with his hand.

Sakura laughed then, and the whole class laughed too, and then went stone silent again, as if to study Sakura laughing.

"Hey, hey, hey," said Shane. "Can you tell us about China? What do they eat over there anyways?"

"Shane," I said. "I keep telling you. Not China. Japan."

"Yeah," he said. "I know. But can you tell us about it anyways?"

"Don't you have Chinese restaurants here?" Sakura said.

"I don't know," Shane said. "We only eat Indian food."

"Japan is one of a different country," Sakura said. "It's so small island near China. Well, not so small, but China is very big."

"And do they use soap way over there?" asked Kyle. "Do they wash with soap?"

"Yeah, hey, do they have alligators over there?" asked Charlie Hunter.

"No, stupit," said Valeria. "That's way down in Texas."

"They could have alligators," said Charlie. "You don't know."

"No," Sakura said. "No alligators. But soap, for sure."

"See," said Valeria. "Told you."

"Told you," Charlie said to Valeria. Then he said, "Hey, you ever eat fry bread? It's real good."

"No. Never tried it. Maybe before I go back," Sakura said.

"Yeah, you have to," said Shane. " 'Cause it's real good. I eat it every day too."

"Can you eat lunch with us?" asked Leanne Yazzie. "Just us girls, I mean. Not those boys. Can she, Mr. Caswell?"

"Yeah, can you?" asked Valeria.

Sakura looked at me.

"That's up to her," I said. "Don't ask me. But we should include the boys too, don't you think?"

"Yeah," said Michael. "Include the boys."

"No way," said Valeria. "Boys just mess everything up."

"No, we don't," said Shane.

"Okay, okay," I said. "Sakura is going to show you something."

"Yes," she said. "I brought some papers." She took out a package of origami papers, small squares about six by six inches, of various patterns and colors.

"Wow," said Leanne. "So beautiful."

"They are," said Sakura.

"So beautiful like you," said Shane.

All the girls laughed, and Shane blushed like he hadn't meant to say it.

"So beautiful like you," Valeria said, laughing again.

"Oh, I don't know," Shane said. "I didn't mean nothing, for reals," he said. "For really reals, Mr. Caswell, oh, wait, I gotta go to the bathroom," and hurried away.

"So we're making crane," said Sakura. "It's simple one. And for good luck."

"What's that?" Michael said.

"Of course it's a bird, anyway," Leanne said.

"Yeah, it's a bird," Valeria said.

"Oh, you mean like an eagle," Kyle said.

"No, well, a little, but a crane is more longer, and tall," Sakura said. "In Japan a crane is for long life and good luck."

"Like a horny toad," Shane said, returning from the bathroom. He seemed to have recovered himself, and was happy and confident.

"What's that?" Sakura asked.

"It's a horny toad," Valeria said. "It's a horny toad for good luck."

"I'll make you one," Shane said, and he drew one out on the back of an origami paper. "Like this, see."

"Oh, I see," Sakura said. "Those live here?"

"Of course they do," Valeria said, looking a little disgusted.

"How do you make a crane, anyways?" Michael said.

"OK, right. Let's try. First you choose a paper you like," Sakura said, and we started in.

Step after step, Sakura taught them how to make an origami crane. They were focused and attentive, asking a few questions here and there about Japan, about her life there, about food and cars and Wal-Mart, and about China. Somehow, they couldn't get China off their minds.

"I should have brought a map," I said.

"You can show it next time," Sakura said.

"Yes, I will show them next time."

I was surprised how the feeling in the classroom shifted, how Sakura seemed to soften the class, bring it together. For that day at least, we did away with taking sides—me versus you, us versus them—and we were all one people working toward a common goal. I had to ask, then, was the aggression I usually felt in the classroom really coming from them? I always thought it was. I always blamed them for it. Perhaps it wasn't them at all. Perhaps it was me. Or at least, I was so much a part of it that its presence, how it continued from this day forward, was at least partly in my hands. If I could learn from Sakura today, perhaps I'd have a much better spring semester. I didn't know what I was learning, what I needed to learn, but I realized then that these kids were not defined by their bad behavior and that I needed to find a way to access this other side of them, to keep us all moving together in the same direction. I felt hopeful, even eager to come to class the next time.

I took Sakura to see the abandoned hogan at the end of a day when snow came out of the north in short bursts and flurried around us like moths in pursuit of the moon. We drove my truck the little way beyond the Trading Post to the V in the road, bumping along over the frozen ground. I parked aslant in the ditch. I asked Sakura if she really wanted to see this place, explaining that the Navajos believe a place like this is bad luck, that for us to go here was to disturb the dead. She said yes, she wanted to see it, and if the dead man's spirit was here, maybe she would be able to see that too.

Sakura came from a devoted Shinto family. Her mother prayed to Shinto gods and paid close attention to her dreams. Sakura once told me that her mother could see ghosts and spirits, especially those that stayed close to people. Sakura said she could sometimes see ghosts and spirits too. When I was still in Hokkaido, Sakura's mother had a dream about me. She dreamed that I would betray her daughter one day by choosing another woman, a woman who would appear before me wearing a red dress. The story angered me. I passed it off as superstition.

A few weeks before I left Hokkaido, I traveled to China with a small group of friends. We traveled in Shanghai, then to Guilin, and finally to Beijing. I was making my way from the Earthly Tranquility Palace to the Imperial Garden in the Forbidden City when I met Sheryl. I had caught her eye several times that morning among the crowds. Finally I approached her and asked for her name. Her Chinese name was Shi Rong. She was an architectural student at China People's University working on a thesis comparing ancient and contemporary architecture as a way of understanding political shifts in China. "Everywhere you look," she said, "you see the new on top of the old." She was not wearing a red dress, but the Forbidden City, the sanctuary of all the emperors of China, from Yong Le in 1420 to the last emperor, Puyi, who was crowned the Son of Heaven at age two in 1908, was now draped in the deep red of communism, and I had passed through the front gate beneath a great red banner with the image of Mao Tse Tung.

It was spring in Beijing, and everything was green where we stood. The flowers were brilliant and innumerable, tiny white and purple displays against the hardened brown of the stones of so many years. The structures around us were very old, the roofs low and red and soft to our eyes. For that moment, at least, I was in love with Sheryl. She was seductive, the way old memories are, and I wanted to consume her. I met her later that night in the lobby of the Hotel Xin Da Du. She came dressed all in black. She was thin and tall and graceful. Her hair was long and black, and it hung straight down her back reflecting light as she moved. She took my hand and led me out through the city into a series of dark, empty streets that were closed to traffic on either end for construction. At one point I stopped.

"You know," I said. "I have no idea where I am. You have the advantage, if you want it."

She turned toward me then, fixing me in her eyes, only I couldn't see them, just the presence of them, in the dark. She didn't understand.

"I mean, I'm a foreigner here," I said. "If you wanted to take advantage of that, take my money or my credit cards or something . . . I'm a little vulnerable right now."

She held my hand tighter. "That's not the advantage I want," she said, and led me on.

We turned into a little bar owned by people she knew. There was no one else inside. We sat down next to each other in a booth in the back corner. She ordered drinks for us, I don't know what, and she pulled her long hair forward over her right shoulder. She put her mouth on mine and I moved into her then. We did not stop when the drinks came. She pulled away, a little breathless, and said, "It's so much how I want you," and then we made love in the booth in the darkened corner with most of our clothes on.

When I returned to Hokkaido, I told Sakura about Sheryl. I told her that as her mother had warned, I had betrayed her, and I could not be the lifelong partner she was looking for. She cried then, but she said she didn't care, that it didn't matter to her, and that we should forget about it and go on. "This is our one chance," she said. "Maybe we won't know each other ever again."

Of course it did matter to her, I knew. And it mattered to me that faced with this moment in which I might have accepted a life with a beautiful and intelligent woman, I denied it, denied Sakura and a future with her. Was I mad? What was I doing? How could I be so cruel? Yet what she said to me—"it didn't matter"—made me feel uncomfortably powerful. I accepted it, and we spent the night together inside our folded lies.

> If only you allow me,
> I will willingly wipe
> Salt tears from your eyes
> With these fresh leaves
> —Bashō

At the abandoned hogan, I wandered with Sakura for an hour or more through the field of derelict things. It was quiet and cold, and our footsteps broke the brittle branches of desert shrubs. I showed her to the hogan, and we circled the outside until we arrived at the door. She stood in front of it, beautiful and frightened.

"You can push it open," I said. "It opens a little way to see inside."

"What will I see inside?" she asked.

"Just have a look."

She turned away from me then, pressed the door open with both her hands. It went in to the length of the chain, and Sakura bent to peer inside. The wind swirled in behind us, kicked up some dust and then cleared it.

"It's okay," Sakura said, looking back at me. "He's not in here. There's nothing left here but his memories."

A few days later, Sakura returned to Hokkaido. We were at a kind of stalemate, or an impasse, or, more honestly, we avoided, here at the end, talking about a future. I drove her to Albuquerque, where she boarded a plane for home. She cried in my arms there in the empty, hollow-sounding space that makes airport partings almost unbearable. I wanted to feel it with her, the deep grief and joy that wracked her so, but nothing lived inside me then but emptiness. Was something wrong with me? Had my heart died since last we parted? I held her close as her tears splashed against my shirt. Then she straightened and stood tall to bear it, kissed me, and turned to make her way through the gate where only travelers could go.

NINE

THE EASTERN NAVAJO AGENCY
SPELLING BEE

In February, Bob King asked me to work with students who wanted to compete in the local spelling bee at Mariano Lake. I agreed, and Lauren agreed to go with me to the Eastern Agency Bee if any of our Borrego kids qualified. And qualify they did—two girls and two boys. For the boys' team it was Miles Wiseman, the white boy (who had an obvious advantage in that he was one of the few students at Borrego who spoke better English than Navajo), and his best friend, Tom Charlie, both of them in the fifth grade; and for the girls' team, Vanessa Angel, in the eighth grade, and Valeria Benally, in the seventh. A few more kids came along as support. They had practiced hard all spring but were easily eliminated at Mariano Lake. They were Renee Benally, my star eighth-grade English student, whose defeat surprised me; Linda Yazzie, a very bright sixth grader who also surprisingly did not qualify; then Carmen Yazzie, Linda's sister; and Marcella Brown.

Marcella, the sixth-grade girl whose mother I had met at Bashas' in Crownpoint, once told me that she had been stopped by the Navajo police while driving the family car, a thirty-year old Chrysler almost as big inside as a hogan. She was en route to Bashas' to steal food, she said. Of course she didn't want to do it, because, for one thing, it was too hard to drive. She could hardly see over the dashboard. And besides that, her mother worked at Bashas'. They knew her in there and trusted her. She didn't want to steal, she said, but she had to, she explained, because her parents had been away for four days, she didn't have any money, and her little brothers and sisters and cousin-brothers and cousin-sisters said they were starving to death. So she was going to have to steal. It wasn't her driving that gave her away to the police, she said. She had done it before, so she knew how to use the signal on the car, and she knew that she shouldn't go too slow or too fast so as not to draw attention to herself, and she knew she had to be real careful and go straight down the road like an arrow, not swerve back and forth and be all crazy. She knew all that. But what attracted the police that day was that here went this big car down Highway 371 and there didn't seem to be anybody at the wheel.

It wasn't uncommon on this part of the reservation to hear stories like Marcella's. Lots of children got left at home, way out beyond the borders of the world, especially around the first of the month, when government checks came in and people again had money for travel-ing and shopping and liquor. It wasn't that the parents were cruel or crazed by addiction (although in some cases they were) but that, like everyone else, they were just trying to survive. Everyone had to do their part, even the young children. They learned to be resourceful, these Navajo children left at home, so that for someone as young as eleven or twelve, being stranded in a little hogan with nothing to eat in the cupboards, a huge stack of firewood, and a few brothers and sister to care for became little more than routine.

As I saw it, none of these children were going to the spelling bee to win a championship or to prove that they had mastered the English language and would prosper in a white, literate society. They just wanted to go somewhere, anywhere really, and do something differ-ent from what they had always done. Anywhere outside Borrego Pass was a good place to go, because for most of them the world beyond Borrego was a dark mystery. Who could say what it was like out there? Who could say what other Navajos did in this world, how they lived, what they ate, how they talked? And who could say what white people did out beyond the borders of Borrego, what they looked like, what they wore, how they smelled? This alien world frightened many of these children who lived so isolated and so simply. Time to face it, perhaps, time to get out and have a look around and live some stories that would sound good now, and years later, when told back home.

Renee, Vanessa, and Linda had all traveled with me to Mission: Wolf. I was a little surprised and also honored that they trusted me enough to try it again. Maybe they had forgiven me for all the misadventures of that last trip, or perhaps they had decided those misadventures were just the sort of adventures they were looking for. If so, I had something to learn from the way they let those feelings go, or transformed them, or whatever. I still packed around a load of guilt and sense of failure about that trip.

I worked with the children on their spelling words while the front office staff arranged for three rooms at the Thunderbird Inn at the mouth of Canyon de Chelly, secured a bus driver and some cash, and registered the spellers in the bee; and soon we were off.

The sun rose up into the morning behind us, a clear New Mexican spring morning, as we motored down the bumpy dirt road. It smoothed out as we crossed the cattle guard and hit the pavement, then merged onto Interstate 40 headed east to Gallup.

Judy Yazzie sat across the aisle from me, three rows from the front of the school bus, perched at the outside of her seat looking onto the New Mexican landscape unfolding in front of her. She wore round glasses that looked like big balloons resting on her cheeks. She was in the third grade at Borrego Pass and had never traveled very far from home. She had never been anywhere, really, except to school and to the Gallup Wal-Mart. Her parents had been away for a week now, and her big sister, Carmen, was in charge of the house. Since Carmen was going to the Eastern Navajo Agency Spelling Bee in Chinle, Judy was going too.

Betty, our driver, had requested the trip because she loved to travel, she said, not unlike Redd, who had driven to Mission: Wolf.

"But I don't go for no camping out," Betty had said. "I want a nice room and a nice restaurant."

Betty was popular among the students because she was light-hearted, patient, and kind. She always carried in her coat pocket a can of chew that she might at any moment pass around the bus. Do I hear repeat performance? She did her hair up high above her head, and she was thin and frail-looking from smoking too much. If ever she raised her voice at the children while driving, they would watch her reflection in the big rear-view mirror, because the more excited she became, the more forceful her voice got, until a vaporous fume of residual smoke steamed out of her mouth against the glass. They quieted down real quick, not because they were afraid of her but because they wanted to see that smoke come out. I'd heard them call her the Dragon Lady.

Somehow it happened that the only bus available for our trip was the four-wheel-drive monster that sat so high above the ground. The extra clearance made it a dream in winter, in heavy mud or when it snowed, but on the open highway, it was a slow, jumpy ride, the bus bumping up and back over the smallest imperfections in the asphalt. The children sat as close to the back as they could (except little Judy, who sat near the front), and when the bus went over a bump in the road, it catapulted them up off their seats. If it was a particularly good bump, they might even be so lucky as to knock their heads on the ceiling.

We shot down the interstate at a wild fifty miles per hour, everyone in the back waiting, waiting, waiting, and then the nose of the bus sank into a sharp trough in the freeway, and the tail end of it came up. "Whooooaaa," we heard as they came back down, their eyes big and round. And then another, and then bump, we heard as the suspension stiffened and press down against the axles and the earth like we were flying out on a Borrego dirt road, and then *thunk!* we heard as a cluster of little heads smacked the roof. I looked back to see them all rubbing the sore spots with their hands and laughing. We hit maximum speed, maybe 55, and I watched as cars, pickups, tractor-trailers, and even old ranch trucks hauling mile-high loads of hay driven by old ladies with glasses so thick they were legally blind, all of them moved out into the passing lane to steam by us, a stream of bright yellow New Mexico license plates lining out into the distance.

"Did you hear about Marcella?" Lauren asked. "Since she's on the trip."

"No," I said.

"You know how she always carries that bag around school? Even out at recess?" Lauren said.

"Yes," I said. "I've noticed that."

"Well, Bob King asked her if he could see it on Tuesday. And she didn't want to show it to him. He insisted, of course, and she still refused. So he asked her to come into his office. She went along, and Louise and a couple other teachers were in there to help. Marcella let them open the bag, of course. And it was filled with stuff she was selling at school. All stolen stuff. Candy, sodas, little portable CD players, music CDs, hairspray and cologne, cigarettes, Copenhagen, makeup, lots of stuff."

"For reals?" I said.

"For reals," Lauren said. "I just thought you should know."

"So what happened to her? No suspension or anything?"

"I don't know. I think she went home for the day. Louise talked to her mother, I think. What can you do?"

Betty pulled off the interstate at Thoreau. We drove along a fence line crowded with trash and tumbleweeds collected against it by the wind. On the edge of the reservation boundary we passed a store where, if you knew which door to knock on, you could enter and buy alcohol. The big cottonwood across the road was the only shade nearby, except for the freeway overpass. There were always a few Navajo men lying or sitting or standing around it. We stopped at the gas station, and Betty ordered everyone off the bus. "No one on the bus while gassing up!" she said. "Regulations."

Everyone filed down the steps and outside. The children raced into the store, digging into their pockets for hidden money. Despite the poverty on this part of the reservation, every time I traveled on a school outing, the kids had money for candy and sodas. Plenty of it. Lauren and I discussed setting a candy limit, but we knew we couldn't enforce it. We decided that the faster their money was gone, the better. Soon we were back on the bus and rolling down the freeway to the spelling bee.

When we arrived in Chinle, we drove east on Highway 7 to the mouth of Canyon de Chelly. The Thunderbird Inn was usually crawling with tourists, but it was early in the season and we had the place largely to ourselves. We checked in at the front desk. Betty took us around the building and parked the bus. When the room doors opened, the kids rushed inside in a wave, the boys into one room, the girls into the other two. They inspected everything: the beds, the telephone, the TV, the running water, the free shampoo and soap, the clear plastic drinking cups. They looked at themselves in the mirrors, bounced a little on the beds, turned on the bathtub spigot until the water was too hot to hold their hands there. They pressed their faces into the fresh white towels. They pulled open all the drawers in all the dressers. In the boys' room, Tom Charlie discovered the Holy Bible, placed by the Gideons. The telephone rang.

Tom, who was leafing through the pages of Exodus, looked at the phone as it rang. He had probably used a telephone only a few times in his life, and he certainly did not have one at home. It rang again. And then again.

"Well, pick it up," I said.

He did, and pressed it to his ear. He waited. Nothing happened. We waited with him, and still nothing happened.

"Say hello," Miles told him.

"Hello?" Tom said.

"Hello?" said Valeria Benally, calling from the girls' room. I could hear her voice coming from the phone and also from the open door.

They both sat there.

"Hello," Tom said again.

"Ask her what she wants," Miles said.

"What do you want?" Tom said.

In the other room, Valeria turned to Lauren and said, "What do we want?"

Lauren told her to ask if we were ready to eat dinner.

Valeria asked us. "Are you guys ready to eat dinner?"

Tom looked at me. "She wants to know if we are ready to eat dinner."

"Are we?" I asked.

"Yeaaaah!" everyone said.

Tom sat there.

"Tell her yes," Miles said.

"Yes," Tom said.

"Wait," I said. "Tom, ask Valeria if they want to go up to Spider Rock before dinner."

"What rock?" Tom said.

"I know," Miles said. "The one up there in the canyon."

"Go ahead, ask her," I said.

"Do you want to go up to Spider Rock before dinner?" Tom said. Nothing happened.

"She didn't say nothing," Tom said. But he had let the receiver drop under his chin, and Valeria probably couldn't hear him.

Renee poked her head into the room from the open door. "Talk into the phone," she said. "We can't hear you."

Miles raised the phone up for Tom and said, "Ask it again."

"Do you want to go up to Spider Rock before dinner?" Tom asked.

Valeria turned to Lauren in the other room. "He says do we want to go to Spider Rock before dinner?"

Lauren and I had already talked about driving up to the canyon overlook, so she told Valeria to say yes.

"Yes," Valeria said, and hung up the phone.

Then Tom hung up the phone. He went back to looking at the Bible.

Everyone waited, staring at him.

"What did she say?" Miles asked.

"She said yes," Tom said, turning pages and not looking up.

"Then let's go," I said. Tom dropped the Bible on the bed, and we filed out the door to the bus.

None of the kids except Miles, the white boy, had ever been to Canyon de Chelly, even though it is one of the most important historical and spiritual centers of Navajo culture. It was first occupied by the Anasazi some two thousand years ago, then by the Hopi people, sporadically, from about AD 1300. The Navajo displaced the Hopi about AD 1700. Until the early 1800s, the canyon was a Navajo stronghold; its sheer walls and a winding system of spur canyons offered good protection and defense. It was a place of dependable water where the people grazed sheep and goats and grew melons, corn, squash, and peaches. The Navajos looked after some five thousand producing peach trees in Canyon de Chelly until 1864, when Colonel Kit Carson and his soldiers burned them all.

Today Canyon de Chelly is a National Monument of about 83,000 acres under the joint management of the National Park Service and the Navajo Nation. Except for the trail to White House Ruin, to enter the canyon one must hire a Navajo guide. The canyon floor is still private property. Navajo families live and work down there, as they have for the past three hundred years.

The kids clustered in the back of the bus waiting for the bumps, and sometimes stuck their arms and heads out the open windows as Lauren and I sang in unison, "Don't put your arms or heads out the window!" while the bus chugged and strained along the steep grade and we rose up and out and above the town. The air cooled and patches of snow dotted the landscape. We wound along, curve after curve, and we could see into the canyon now, see how high above we were, then again how much higher.

At the top, where the road changed from National Monument pavement to reservation dirt, we angled north along the drive and into the parking lot. The kids filed off the bus and into the evening air.

"Take your coats," I called to them, but most of them didn't bring a coat, or didn't have one.

Valeria turned to face me at the bus door and said, "We don't need no coats. We're Nava-joes," and she laughed and leaped down into the world.

By the time Lauren and I got off the bus, the patches of snow had already become a thousand snowballs launched among the short, twisted pines, helter-skelter. The parking lot was empty except for an older couple who hurried into their Lincoln Town Car and shut the doors. We watched as the red taillights faded into the dust kicked up from the road.

Now we were alone.

At the overlook, we stood before the canyon, which is shaped like the footprint of a great dinosaur. The toes are the north and south canyons, and the heel is the mouth of the canyon, spilling west into Chinle Wash. The sun was dropping fast into the western lands, and the light on Spider Rock was muted a soft red. The kids stood together along the railing, looking over into that huge open chasm, all the way to the bottom. A hawk sifted in and out and along the cliff face. We watched the soft movements of the wings in shadow for as long as we could see them, out over the empty space and across our dreams, all of us. It drifted beyond where we could see now, away and beyond somewhere inside the belly of Canyon de Chelly.

As we stood there together looking out on Spider Rock, the wind came up and blew through us. The air was sharp and cold. I was ready to go, ready for supper. Then Valeria called everyone over to the plaque on the sandstone retaining wall that told the story of Spider Woman in both Navajo and English.

"All right, everybody, listen up," Valeria said as we gathered around her. "I'm going to read this story."

Valeria had never been a strong reader in class. Most days she was reluctant, even frightened to read aloud in class, especially in English. That she was volunteering now to read to us was surprising. Perhaps something about this moment had taken hold of her, something about this place; perhaps, seeing her own language on the plaque next to the English, she felt a sense of ownership, even kinship with that language, with the canyon, and with Spider Rock. She read the story aloud, first in Navajo, then in English. The story she read goes something like this:

It was Spider Woman who gave the Hero Twins power to find the path to the Sun's house. They claimed the Sun was their father, and after passing a series of tests, the Sun agreed. He gave them magical weapons, and taught them how to slay the monsters of this world. And so Spider Woman is revered by the Navajo for helping make the world safe. After her great deed, she chose this rock spire, now known as Spider Rock, to make her home.

Spider Woman is regarded as both generous and potentially dangerous. Navajo children know that if they misbehave, Spider Woman will descend on a silken thread and take them to her home on top of the great sandstone spire. There, she will devour them as punishment for their crimes. The top of Spider Rock is white because it is blanketed with the bones of bad Navajo children.

But Spider Woman also taught the Navajos how to weave. Spider Man, her husband, constructed the loom. He made the cross poles of sky, and the chords of earth. The warp sticks he made of sun rays. He made the healds of crystals and lightning. The batten he made of a sun halo, and the comb of white shell. It is because of Spider Woman that the Navajos know how to weave, a skill that has sustained them for generations.

After the story, we lingered for a few minutes as the mood of the place and the moment transformed into memory. The children became children again, and a few snowballs went sailing. We walked back on the paved path, got on the bus, and drove back down into Chinle to find a place to eat.

We stopped at a diner with all the usuals: burgers and fries; chicken-fried steak; soups and salads; Navajo tacos. What I didn't realize as we waited for a table was that these Navajo kids had never been to a restaurant with a waiter. On most school trips, the driver stopped at Furr's Cafeteria in Gallup, an assembly-line style of dining that offered large portions for little money, and a comfortable degree of self-service. And of course, at school too, they ate this way in the cafeteria. What they were about to experience, they didn't know existed.

The hostess led us to a table, and everyone sat down. Judy sat next to me at the end of the table, and across from Lauren. She noticed a big, barrel-chested Navajo man with a broad, flat nose walk by with his wife or girlfriend. They laughed together, holding hands, and he repositioned his black felt hat on his head.

Little Judy Yazzie tugged on my shirtsleeve. "Navajo people come in here?" she whispered. "They eat in here?"

I nodded. "Yes. They do."

Our waiter appeared and handed around menus. Judy opened hers. It was big and colorful, almost as big as she was. She looked at me, then back at the menu. What did it all mean? She had never seen a menu before, never been asked to read the options and make a choice. She could read all right, as well as any third grader in America reading English as her second language, but she didn't know what she was reading. A description of a mushroom burger made little sense to her. I tried to give her some options. Navajo taco? (She had never heard of such a thing.) Patty melt? Roast beef and mashed potatoes? Double burger?

"Double burger!" she said. "And hot chocolate."

"That's a pretty big dinner," I said. "That's two burgers on one plate."

"Yeah," she said.

The news that Judy had ordered a double burger spilled around the circle, and because everyone was equally befuddled by the menu, they all decided to have double burgers and hot chocolate.

"Can I have dessert?" Judy asked.

"Sure," I said. "But let's wait until after we eat. Then you can order again."

"I want the double burger," she said. "Can I have it?"

"Yes," I said. "But you have to wait a moment. When the waiter comes over, he'll ask you what you want, and you tell him the double burger."

"Okay," she said.

The waiter came over.

"Double burger!" Judy said.

He wrote it down. As he went around the table, each of the children ordered a double burger. Miles joined in. Lauren and I ordered Navajo tacos.

When the waiter returned with a round of hot chocolates, Judy smiled. She picked up her cup. She looked inside at the dollop of whipped cream. She stuck her tongue into it, and set the cup back down.

"Can I have this?" she asked.

"It's yours, yes," I said.

"This?" she said, holding up the cup.

"The cup?" I said.

"Yeah," she said.

"No," I said. "That cup belongs to the restaurant."

"Oh," she said.

"What about dessert?" she asked again. "I want apple pie."

"You have to wait until after you get your supper," I said.

"Okay," she said, and went back to licking the whipped cream.

Each of the meals came with a salad, and the waiter brought them out, along with a tray of dressings and a basket of crackers.

Judy looked at me. "What's this?"

"A salad," I said.

"Don't you get one?"

"No. The Navajo taco is like a salad. So I don't get one."

She reached for the crackers. "Can I have this?"

"Yes," I said.

"Can I take this?"

She meant the basket. "No," I said. "It belongs to the restaurant. If you take that home, they have to buy more baskets next time. And if everyone took them home, they would have to buy so many baskets the price of the food would be very high."

She paused and considered. "This costs money?" she asked.

The waiter brought the food out on a big tray and set it down on the stand next to the table. Everyone's eyes got very big. Double burgers all around. The waiter dealt them out like aces, and the kids went to work.

Everyone was eating happily until Lauren asked for the salt and pepper. They looked at each other. They waited. "Tom," Lauren said. "Could you pass the salt and pepper?"

Tom looked at her. Then he looked behind him. Then he looked at Miles.

"Pass the salt and pepper," Miles told him.

Tom didn't move. Miles pointed out the two little shakers on the table. Tom picked them up and handed them to Lauren. Everyone started eating again. I don't know how these children used salt and pepper at home—maybe they didn't at all—but at school, it came only in little paper packages, and there weren't any little paper packages on the table, except for the crackers.

"Can I have dessert?" Judy asked again.

"In a little bit," I said. "First the waiter will come back and ask if everything is okay. You say yes. Then he'll come back again when you are finished to take your plate. That's when you ask for dessert."

"Okay," she said.

And it happened just like that. The waiter came back. "Is everything all right here?" he asked.

Judy looked at me. I nodded to her. "Yes," Judy said.

The waiter went away.

"Now he'll come back one more time when you are finished eating," I said. "And he'll ask if you are finished so he can take your plate. If you are, you say yes. If you aren't, tell him no."

And it happened just like that. The waiter came back. "Are you all finished here?" he asked.

"No," Judy said. "Can I take this?" She looked at me, a little sad this time, because every time she had asked so far, the answer had been no. The double burger was so big that Judy only ate half of one.

Most of the kids were able to eat one burger, and still had one whole burger on their plate.

"Yes," I told her. "This you can take."

"For reals?" she said, and smiled big.

"Me too," everyone said.

"I'll bring some boxes," the waiter said. He went away.

"Can I have dessert?" Judy said.

"He's coming back," I said. "He'll give you a box to take home your double burger. And then he'll ask if you want dessert. That's when you tell him apple pie."

"Okay," she said.

He came back. The waiter set a stack of Styrofoam boxes down on the table. "All right," he said. "Will anyone have dessert tonight?"

Judy looked at me. Her moment had finally arrived. I nodded to her.

"I want apple pie," Judy said. Then everyone ordered apple pie.

"Thank you," the waiter said, and went away.

Then Judy, who had been holding it back for far too long now, leaned across the table to Lauren and whispered, "Mrs. Sittnick, how does Mr. Caswell know what's going to happen?"

After supper, we loaded onto the bus and went back to our rooms. Valeria had brought a Nintendo video game console. She didn't have a TV at home, so she rarely played. Like the cash that miraculously appeared every time we stopped for gas, the Nintendo seemed to me a mysterious possession. Why own one without a TV to hook it up to? I wondered where and how she got it? But no matter. We plugged it in and all the children sat on the bed around the TV in the girls' room. They played until about ten, then Lauren and I sent them all to bed.

Saturday. Spelling bee day. Everyone woke early to get ready for the big competition. In the boy's room, Tom and Miles showered and dressed and sat on the bed watching TV. We waited on the girls for a long time. When they finally came out, primped and ready, we walked to the restaurant at the Thunderbird Inn for breakfast. That's when Lauren told me the story about the showers.

She was sitting on one of the beds waiting for the girls as they got ready for the day. She has roused them early so that they would have plenty of time to shower and get dressed. Two of the girls had showered and now stood at the sink outside the bathroom drying their hair with the blow-dryer built into the wall. The others were in the bathroom together, still using the shower. Sitting there, Lauren noticed a wide, dark stain on the carpet near the bathroom door. It was water. She knocked on the door.

"Yeah?" the girls called from inside.

"Are you okay in there?" Lauren asked.

"Yeah," they answered.

"Can I come in? There's water all over out here."

"Yeah," they answered.

Lauren went in. The shower was on, and steaming water poured from the showerhead as the girls took turns under it. They had pulled the shower curtain back and left it hanging outside the tub. Rotating in and out of the shower, one of them lathered up her hair with shampoo, and then stepped out for someone else to take a turn. Water and soap were everywhere, dripping off them onto the floor and splashing out of the shower. The carpet was soaked. The wallpaper was wet up the side of the walls. Even the framed picture on the wall was soaking wet.

"Oh my gosh," Lauren said. "You have to put this inside the bathtub," she told them, pulling the shower curtain closed.

"Okay," they said, unmoved by Lauren's panic.

"Oh my gosh. All this water," Lauren said.

You see, this is the way they had always done it, when they showered at school. They did not have plumbing at home. They did not have running water. They did not take showers except at school, and those showers, sometimes called "gang showers," did not require shower curtains. The water fell all around them in a tiled room with a central drain. So here at the Thunderbird Inn, how were they to know?

"Hurry up now and come on out when you're finished," Lauren said. "I'll have to try to mop this up."

"Okay," they said.

The girls took turns, standing in the shower for a very long time, with the curtain pulled closed now. Finally, after each of them had taken a shower, they came out, dried their hair, primped at the mirror, and announced that they were ready.

Now they had some free time before breakfast. Despite the mishap, they had been fairly efficient. They sat in the room for awhile watching TV. Then Valeria got up and went into the bathroom. She closed the door. The other girls heard the shower come on, but Lauren wasn't paying attention.

"Can I take a shower too?" Carmen asked.

"No," Lauren said. "You just did. We're almost ready to go."

"But she's doing it in there," Carmen said.

"Yeah, me too," Judy said. "Can I again?"

"Yeah," said Carmen. "Can we? It's so nice for us."

"No," Lauren said. "We have to go soon."

But it was too late for her to change their course, and soon most of the girls were in the shower going through the whole drama all over again.

After breakfast, we loaded onto the bus and drove out to the Chinle High School gym for the Eastern Navajo Agency Spelling Bee. Tom, Valeria, Vanessa, and Miles were all very nervous. Vanessa decided she really didn't want to compete after all.

"But we drove all the way here just so you could," Lauren told her.

"Is it?" she said. "But that's okay," she said. "I don't mind."

She did compete, though. When her name was called, she stepped up to the microphone. She looked out at the crowd of a hundred people from all over the Eastern Agency, foreigners to her, all of them, except the little island that was us in the back of the room. A man at a table called out a word. He wore thick glasses and an unkempt beard. He pronounced the word clearly, almost too clearly. It was a word Vanessa knew, or at least a word I had known her to spell correctly in practice. Maybe it sounded funny to her, or maybe standing in front of the crowd like that was too much. She didn't need to get this word right only to have to stand up there again in the second round. She missed it and sat down, her lip jutting out like she wanted to cry.

Everyone consoled her, put their hands on her shoulders and said, "That's all right. You did great," and other kind things. Her lip returned to its usual position and she was okay again. It was all okay. In fact, she smiled. She was finished. Her long trial was over.

Valeria made it into the third round, and so did Miles. Tom made it all the way to the finals, but didn't place. And that was it. The Eastern Navajo Agency Spelling Bee was over. There were a few panicked moments when the judges didn't seem to know what they were doing, and spelling coaches from various schools raced around in the hallways of the high school looking for a higher power. But things settled out, maybe because the teachers and parents put things in perspective and realized that these were just kids playing a game, trying to spell English words in a little town in Arizona on the Navajo reservation.

We thanked our hosts and loaded the bus for home.

In Gallup, we stopped at Furr's Cafeteria for lunch. The children could see what they were getting and heaped their plates full and ate in peace, no nosy waiter to bug them. Then we loaded the bus again and roared off down Interstate 40 headed east.

Somewhere between Gallup and Church Rock, we stopped for fuel one more time. Betty ordered everyone off the bus.

"No one on board while gassing up," she said. "That's regulations."

The children hurried into the store to look at things and use the restrooms. I didn't think they had any money left, but a few dollar bills came out of pockets as they entered the door. When they returned, everyone had something sugary to eat or suck on or chew. Judy had a pocketful of candies of all kinds, which she showed off as she sat down in the seat next to me near the front of the bus. She had something else in her hand too. I asked her what it was. She held it up. It was a little plastic doll with blue eyes and yellow hair tied in pigtails and dressed in a pink lacy dress like gossamer with ruffled sleeves.

"Did you get that inside?" I asked.

She nodded yes and busied herself straightening the doll's clothes. The bus pulled out and headed down the road striking a rough rhythm that put Judy quickly to sleep. She fell into an awkward position against the window.

A few minutes later, Linda, who had been so quiet for most of the trip, came forward from the back of the bus. She sat in the seat behind me. "Mr. Cas-well," she said. "Judy took it from the store."

I turned to her. "The doll?" I asked.

"Yeah, she took it from the store. And some other stuff."

"The candy too?" I asked.

Linda nodded.

"I see. Thank you."

"I didn't wanna tell you, but she took it," Linda said.

Of course Lauren overheard us talking. We looked at each other helplessly because it had suddenly become obvious that Judy was not the only one on the bus with stolen goods. For the rest of them I wasn't so surprised, especially Marcella, but little Judy? How could she? How could she shatter my image of her as a pure, uncorrupted innocent? I looked over at her asleep there in the seat. She breathed peacefully and happily, propped up against the window, the stolen goods held loosely in her hands. She looked like an angel. Perhaps stealing was innocent, to her. She was just doing what everyone else did who needed something they could not buy. It did not excuse her, but it was the way of things here.

I scanned the back of the bus. All I could see was a busload of thieves. Every one of them looked guilty, even Linda. We had just knocked off a convenience store, and Lauren and I had provided the getaway car.

An hour later, the bus slowed into the off-ramp at Prewitt, and we were as good as home. And just in time, too. I was ready to be home. I had had a good time, mostly, and I didn't want the heist to sour my attitude. We paused at the stop sign to make our turn, and the change in speed woke Judy up. She rubbed her eyes and looked around. She saw a sign at the freeway on-ramp headed the other way, a green road sign that read "Gallup," with a white arrow pointing straight up into the sky. Judy turned and looked at me. Her eyes were wide and white. She couldn't believe it.

"Mr. Cas-well," Judy whispered, "Gallup's in heaven."

TEN

THE LAST BEST WALK

I watched the New Mexican new moon over the rough-edged mesa from my desk, heard coyote calls, and stared out through my reflection in the window. It was Sunday, and spring, and everywhere on campus, no one stirred. I was alone, and alone with my thoughts, and my thoughts turned to Sakura, her visit to Borrego, and our walk out to the hogan. Images of that day flashed in my mind, and I was so absorbed that it was some time before I heard Kuma mewling at the threshold. He had been out romping in the early day, because on days like this, he could run free. No one bothered him. No one bothered me. But he had returned now, and he begged me to join him, to venture out.

In good weather, I often left my trailer door open. I'd set a stone down in the sun to keep the wind from bringing it closed, while Kuma visited the old dog tied to a dilapidated wood box next door, and then the puppy tied to a little cottonwood in front of the cinder block duplex across the way. Once the Tsosies, who lived in that duplex, spent the weekend away. They left that pup tied there to the tree with no water and no food. I went out looking for Kuma—he'd been gone for at least an hour—and I found him there lying in the shade patch with the pup. He lay there like the pup's guardian, as if he knew it was defenseless and so thirsty that it had grown lethargic and wagless.

The pup looked a bit like a heeler, at least a heeler mix, a rez dog to be sure, but in its stillness it also looked old and sad, faceless and without a country. Kuma had decided, so it seemed to me, that if danger came along, he would rouse himself to that pup's defense, that poor spent pup, that creature of the brotherhood. I knew I too had to do something. If I did not, I was certain the pup would die, waste away in the desert like the old horse fallen dead among the stones. I brought it water, and it drank and drank, swelling its belly round like a melon. As Kuma and I looked on, it choked and coughed and puked the water back up, then drank some more. I kept the pup hydrated for two more days, gave it a little food, and even moved it from spot of shade to spot of shade. When the family returned, I saw the old man outside inspecting the pup, as if surprised to see it still alive. Had he decided he didn't want to care for it and left it there to die? Or perhaps in his mind the pup's fate wasn't tied to his, and the desert would decide.

To many Navajo people, dogs are among the lowest of creatures. They carry ticks and fleas and other unsavory bugs. They're scavengers, like their cousin the coyote. And they get mange. They're not good for much more than barking the alarm when a skinwalker comes around, or, in the old days, for working. Of course some Navajo sheepherders still use dogs, but those dogs are not pets. They work or they don't eat. They are never allowed into the home. Every small rez town I drove through supported packs of free-roaming dogs, thin and grizzled, shy and beaten down, starving for food and love. Some of them were so sick with mange they hardly looked like dogs at all. Some of them made a meager living hanging out with drunks and addicts. I learned from the boys in my classes that the way they took care of their dogs was to throw them a few dead rabbits that they had killed for sport with a .22. And one day in class, when the subject of dogs came up, Shane Yazzie said, "I like it when they fight."

I, however, did not like it when they fought, and the shrieking cut-sounds of Mary's dog, Ranger, attacking the poor beast in Ganado we'd come to call Sidecar persisted in my memory as the most horrifying of experiences. Sidecar, a German shepherd mix, had adopted Mary and Ranger, as much as they had adopted him. Mary named him after his lame rear leg and the kind of life that that leg encouraged. The leg had likely been broken in multiple places, and, uncared for, it healed into a withered burden. It looked like maybe he had been hit by a car, accidentally or purposely, it didn't matter. I envisioned him getting slammed one morning while crossing a Ganado road and then dragging his mangled back end behind him into a secret place to lie down, go to sleep, and die. But he didn't die, and it wasn't his fault. He didn't mean to be alive. It just happened. And, being alive, now he had to do something about it.

He appeared one spring morning at Mary's door in Ganado, standing on his three good legs, looking for a handout. His powerful head and wide shoulders told the story of the dog he once was, and beyond those features his body skinnied into his ravaged rear hips and leg. Ranger didn't have the physique or the fighting talent to best Sidecar, but Sidecar had lost all confidence because of the way the world had brutalized him. Sensing this weakness, Ranger charged Sidecar that first day when they met, and Sidecar cowered and whimpered and gave Ranger the captain's chair. Thus acquainted, the two dogs became good friends, and almost every morning Sidecar appeared at Mary's door. He accompanied her, with and without Ranger, followed her to school on workdays, and followed her with Ranger on morning runs into the red rocks country, and up onto the mesa tops, and down, hobbling alongside or trailing far behind, as best he could. When I visited, he followed us out on long wanderings up the Ganado Wash, or down to the Hubbell Trading Post, sometimes to the post office. He was always there, getting along quite well despite his leg, and he was as much Ranger's sidecar as Mary's. Kuma had met him too, and they seemed to get along all right. Mary spoke fondly of Sidecar, like he was her dog, and he would gladly have moved in, but she also thought of him as a creature of Ganado, a resident of that place and that time, and so never dared to let him sleep in the house, or load him into her truck to take him with her farther afield.

So it was that lazy afternoon with Mary in Ganado, after a long walk up and over the red mesas, that the fight broke out. Mary and I had gone inside her place with Kuma for something cold to drink, while Ranger and Sidecar found shady places to rest against the brick wall in the shade, happily tired from the day's action. All was well, and nothing portended of any ill will between them.

From the kitchen, Mary and I heard the rattle of the low chain-link fence as Ranger charged and slammed Sidecar against it. Then the howling screeches brought us outside fast. Ranger had Sidecar down on his side, and his jaws clamped around his bull-like neck. Sidecar howled in fear and amazement, his grotesque leg wildly kicking. What had he done, a poor, wretched three-legged thing, to shatter their friendship? I held Kuma back and then shut him inside, knowing how he loved to fight. Mary ran up on the tangle of dogs, shouting and cursing and kicking up dirt with her boot, as I picked up a handful of gravel and hurled it into them, into both of them, pelting them with little pricks, which amounted to nothing. Realizing that her efforts and mine were futile, Mary ran back inside. I had thrown another handful of gravel by the time she returned with a pitcher of cold water. She cast it over them, a violent baptism, and that broke it up, for a moment, while Ranger prepared to charge again. But Mary had him now by the collar, giving Sidecar a chance to retreat around to the back of the building.

What a pitiful sight. Nothing wounds my heart more than an injured dog in sad retreat.

Mary led Ranger into her apartment and closed the door, and then together we went to check on Sidecar. He stood off at the edge of the brush, and slunk away as we came. We called for him, but he loped out and away as if he was never coming back.

He did come back however, later that evening, when Mary and I were cooking supper and drinking beer. We heard his whines at the door, and Kuma rushed over to lick at him through the metal screen. We went out to welcome him. He lay down in submission on the concrete walk, turning over to expose his soft belly, and we knelt and checked him over with our hands, finding the places where Ranger's teeth had broken the skin. Puncture wounds only. Nothing too serious. We slathered the places with Bag Balm against infection, then let Kuma out to say hello. And then a bit later, Ranger, and the three joined together again like a happy pack, romping in the cool spring night. It was as if nothing at all had happened between them, or, better, as if the anger or insult had been released and no remnant, no guilt or grudge at all remained. I thought then: if only people could behave like that.

Kuma standing in the doorway looking at me, whining, then barking a little, then barking a lot, brought me back from my meditation, from that distant land I'd gone to in my mind with Sakura, to the dreams and fantasies we had yet to fulfill. All right, I thought, indeed, time for a walk.

I sat down on the kitchen floor to lace up my boots. Kuma circled me and pressed his nose up under my arm. He knew we were headed out, and he never tired of roaming. Indeed, his enthusiasm always roused me from dark thoughts, and for that I was grateful. But there was nothing exceptional about this preparation. We performed the ritual almost every day. Despite the many walks that merged into one long memory of walking, despite the long monotony of the unchanging land, each time I put on my boots and took up my walking stick, I felt the promise of something new. How often I shrugged off loneliness by walking. How often I sorted out every kind of question by

walking. I held on to this ritual, this monkish routine, as I held on to
memories and old guilt:

> From this day forth
> I shall be called a wanderer,
> Leaving on a journey
> Thus among the early showers
> —Bashō

I led Kuma out through the school parking lot and through the
big gate, down to the baseball field below the sandstone cliffs. Kuma
was at home walking the open country around Borrego, ranging out
in front of me as fast and far as he could go, me trailing behind, walking a slow and steady rhythm out through the rolling desert. From
where we were now, I could see the Christian revival cemetery, doing
its revival work so well that no one had been buried there for a very
long time. The cemetery was without an entrance or a perimeter, a
collection of gravestones near a little tree, only some still standing. I
intended to wander straight through, but I lingered a few moments,
walking among the markers, the plots that rounded each little life,
passing over the bones laid to rest so close to the soles of my feet. I
moved in and out, back and forth, reading a few names and dates.
And so they went, dry and forgotten, these stones and the bones buried under them.

Against the little pine tree on the southern edge of the cemetery,
I discovered a rusted shovel. I hadn't seen it here before on any of
my wanderings, but perhaps I hadn't looked closely enough. The
handle, too, was steel, the end of it split, with a handhold welded in
crosswise. It looked like it had been here a long time, a forgotten relic
free for the taking. I wanted to keep it. Since the shovel I bought at
Bashas' I used mostly for cleaning up poop, I thought this one might
be handy for storing in my truck to dig myself out when it rained. I
shouldered it and carried it off, worrying that it may have been used

to bury—or unbury—the dead. I wondered if, driving around with that shovel in my truck, my dreams might not be visited by ghosts. But no matter. If a ghost was to visit me, so be it. I wasn't through with my walk yet and didn't have time for that kind of worry. I unburdened myself, leaving the shovel propped in the crook of another tree closer to the sandstone cliff. In moving it, I thought, I had claimed it as my own. I would come back for it later.

I continued on around the edge of the bluff to a draw where water ran when it rained. The ground was littered with pottery shards, large pieces ornamented with black lines, and pieces with patterns in relief. To my untrained eye the pot looked to be pinched together from a continuous coil of clay. Anasazi pottery, I knew, perhaps eight hundred to two thousand years old. It was everywhere, lying derelict like the hogan and its detritus out the Borrego Pass Road, like the trash collected along fences near the freeway in Thoreau. I crouched and examined piece after piece, noticing how some were still emerging from the powdery soil. An edge leaking out of the ground would burst forth on the occasion of the next good rain. Some I left as they lay—I would not touch them; they seemed too bright, too buried, too beautiful. Others I picked up, cleaning the dust from the pattern to eye them better, then I returned them to the small outline in the soil marking their former position. And still others I selected—knowing I should not, knowing I had no right to commandeer the past—and placed in my pocket. Later I would lay them out on the little hutch in my trailer; even the hutch I had stolen out of the desert.

I heard Kuma whining somewhere out beyond the low pine trees. I made my way across the flatlands under the shadow of a redtailed hawk that seemed to follow me but soon disappeared against the cirrus clouds. I found him stranded in the middle of a wide patch of cactus, where any direction he went was a painful teacher. I picked him up and carried him out. I turned him over on my legs in the shade of a little tree to pull the spines from his tender puppy feet. He whelped and whimpered against the barbs. As he struggled against me, something caught my eye. Just beside me, partially buried in the sandy soil, was the bottom of an Anasazi pot, the biggest piece of ancient pottery I had ever found.

I kept on doing what I was doing, watching the potsherd out of the corner of my eye as if it were a rabbit and was bound to get away. When I had removed the harm from my dog's feet, he righted himself and ran off, wiser, perhaps, about cactus, or more worldly, or more wary of the world, which can bite.

I leaned over onto my elbow near the potsherd and brushed the sandy soil back. The piece kept going, deeper and deeper into the ground. Traditional Navajos do not generally disturb Anasazi relicts. Not out of respect for ancient people or wisdom so much, but because they fear retribution by the Anasazi dead. Later I would learn that many Navajos don't believe in this anymore. For what that's worth, I wasn't really afraid of ghosts, at least that's what I told myself, but perhaps to dig deeper was to violate the spirit of the place? Or was this just some old chip of fired clay, a broken vessel cast aside in a forgotten corner of the desert that every day risked returning to dust beneath the hoof action of Merle's cows? I brushed back more sand. Where the deeper ground was harder, I used my fingers pressed together like a spade to get down to the rooted edge. It came free. I brushed the dirt from my hands and paused to admire the beauty of the piece. It was as big as both my hands set side by side with my fingers spread wide, and roughly shaped like Australia. I inspected it closely for fractures. None. The piece was solid, the outside decorated with that intricate houndstooth pattern. The inside was smooth, curved, a little moist from the deeper sand.

I wanted to keep it.

I knew I should leave it.

But there were thousands and thousands of potsherds like this one scattered all over Navajoland, all over Borrego. And what would any archaeologist desire to know from this barren spot of cow pasture?

Kuma was gone again. Likely he had grown bored and followed his nose to some sun-mutilated skeleton on the desert. I called for him. I stood and walked a little way away, still calling. I was alone, and yet wandering off in search of the dog with the potsherd in my hand, I felt like someone was watching me. I kept walking, looking around me in all directions and then up at the blue, blue sky. I called for Kuma and kept walking, the hard flat shape of the clay cupped in my hand. When I had gone some distance, maybe I had been walking for five minutes, maybe ten, Kuma came up out of the shimmering distance. He met me there and we started on together. I slipped the potsherd into my wide vest pocket.

I walked along the northwest side of the sandstone bluff, past the half-buried timbers of an old hogan and up the bouldered canyon beyond the dead horse, pausing only for a moment to inspect it once again. I stared into its empty eye sockets, its hollow belly, its fierce grimace. If I was to fear a visit from any ghost at all, perhaps it should be this horse. Kuma hardly noticed it now. We climbed up on top, up and up to the tableland on the great mesa. I looked down over the edge into a village of ponderosa. Having been down in those trees before, I knew a wealth of pottery shards lay scattered there as well, especially the rarer pieces burnished red, and a number of arrow points, some perfect and gleaming in the sun like gemstones.

Everywhere I roamed I found the remnants of forgotten lives, forgotten families, forgotten peoples, mostly Anasazi and Navajo who roamed before me. Why forgotten? A trace of them is here—the timbers of an abandoned hogan alongside ancient and scattered potsherds and arrow points—but what could I know about them, really, but that they *were* here? Their individual stories are gone forever. And so would mine be, the traces of my passing through this country, over this land. My footprints. The ground that I disturbed. The conversation I was having with my dog, which, when released to the air, flew away from me like birds. Yet I could imagine much because at all times walking in the desert, I felt the presence of these peoples, these histories, these stories waiting to be picked up along the roads they traveled. They passed through this place, and now I was passing through it too.

The Navajos of old rode sturdy ponies and sometimes walked, following their sheep herds and sheepherding dogs. Though they were good farmers, much of Navajo life was about movement. It is still about movement. Indeed, their identity is bound to the way and the places through which they travel. Such a life of movement is not random or unstable; it is movement itself that creates stability, defines the Navajos' place and affirms their identity. "The deep impulse to run and rove upon the wild earth cannot be given up easily," writes N. Scott Momaday. "Perhaps it cannot be given up at all."

The thought of that comforted me, that perhaps my identity too arose from movement, and that my struggle with staying put, my reluctance to choose a life with Sakura, the place and home and job and children, was wrapped up not in some aberrant flaw in me, some undeveloped or atrophied part of my psyche, but from the indomitable truth of who I was and where I came from. Perhaps, as Momaday claimed, I was born with this deep impulse to range and rove upon the wild earth, and that impulse was not going to go away, even if I wanted it to. I didn't want an excuse, but I did want to understand.

Up around the mesa top, I followed Kuma into a field of stones along an edge I had not seen before. I took the lead now, showed him the way, dropping through a slot to a hidden pathway opening to us. It led around the side of the mesa as I walked it, like walking a window ledge around a tall building. Out before me I could see the campus and my trailer and the greening desert floor in the new spring. The air cooled me, and I felt the warm rock radiating the yellow sun.

Kuma seemed unaffected by the closeness of the edge, but I pressed up against the cliffside, the long way down spinning out beyond me. We came around a curve in the shape of the mesa, and going back in, it opened into a kind of room with a few juniper and yucca, and scattered cacti near the walls. I thought I had gone as far as I could go.

Kuma growled low in his throat, his head down, eyes directed up to the rim of the mesa encircling us. Something was up there. I thought of mountain lions. The sun was behind me now. I could see clearly back against the rock, but rock was all I could see. The heat of the day had passed on. The sharpness of the air and the shape of the rock inlet amplified Kuma's growling. I thought I heard voices. Was it god talking to me, or just the wind? Kuma growled again. I could see nothing. Hear nothing. Maybe it *was* just the wind.

"Hel-loo," said a voice from above.

The shape of a man appeared, bent over and looking in. In all my months of walking at Borrego, I had never seen another human soul, nor even a sign that anyone had passed my way, except me. The man's face was sharp and clean, his black hair professionally cut. He wore blue jeans and a white T-shirt. He looked about my age.

"What are you doin' here?" he asked down at me.

"Hello," I called back, waving.

"You the teacher here?" he said.

"Yes," I said. "I teach down at the school."

"Yeah, I know you," he said. "I've seen you walking out here a lot."

"I've never seen you," I said.

"That's right," he said.

"You live here?" I asked him.

"Back from college," he said. "In Durango. You know Alice? She's my aunt."

"Yes, I know Alice."

"What're you doin' up here?"

"Just walkin' around."

"All right, then. Try going that way," he said, pointing where I thought the pathway ended. I could see only the edge of the alcove and the long drop down.

"Go right on around past that little tree," he said, noticing my skepticism. "There's some ol' ruins in there."

"Really?" I said. Maybe he could see them from up where he was. He clearly had the advantage. We hadn't exchanged names, and something told me he didn't want to. Or maybe I didn't want to. At that height, talking the way we were, he was hardly a person at all, just a dark figure, a shadow talking down at me.

"Yeah. You wouldn't think there was anything back there, but there is."

"What kinda ruins?" I asked.

"It's an ol' corn cache. You know. They stored corn in there. There was a road between Chaco and Mexico in the old days. Those Chaco people ran back and forth, and they had to have food along the way. They probably camped here some nights."

"Is it all right to go back there?" I asked.

"Why not?"

"Just I thought . . ."

". . . that Navajos don't go near places like that?" he said. "That's just junk. Maybe it's true, but it's just junk. I go back there all the time."

"I'll check it out," I said.

"Where you come from?" he said.

"Idaho, but I grew up in Oregon," I said. "I haven't lived there in a long time, though. I was living in Japan last year, before I came here."

"Wow," he said. "Japan. Yeah." He paused, thinking a moment. "I wanna travel all around like that. That's what Alice told me. She told me to travel all around. See some places before I get married or something. Experience is better than any kind of money or big house or car or anything. You're lucky to be able to do that."

"Where do you want to go?" I asked.

"Oh, you know. Everywhere. Anywhere. All around," he said. "Doesn't matter so much about where, maybe. Just I want to go somewhere, make a journey somewhere."

"That sounds good to me."

"That's right," he said. "I don't know where. Maybe I have to go somewhere to know where I'm going."

That sounded kinda Zen, kinda New Age, kinda canned. But he said it and I couldn't help but agree.

"That's right," I said. "So what do you study in Durango?"

"I don't know. I'm a communications major. But I don't know. Maybe I'll change that next year."

"To what?" I asked. "What do you want to study?"

"I don't know. Whatever will take me all around."

"Sounds good. At least you're flexible. You don't have to decide just yet."

"That's right," he said. Then he looked behind him. It was getting darker. "I'm gettin' home now. Go on and look at that ruins."

"You going to be around for a few days?" I asked. I thought he was someone I might be able to get to know. He could be a friend, I thought.

"Yeah. A few days," he said. "I'll knock on your door, maybe. I know which one is yours."

"All right," I said.

He raised his hand and waved goodbye. Then he walked back away from the edge, a dark figure against the sky. I heard his footsteps trailing away. I never saw him again.

I pushed the branches of the little tree aside. Just as he had said, the pathway led on. I followed it and Kuma followed me. Brushing by the tree, and moving over and around a few big rocks, another little room opened up, a bit like the one I'd come out of. There on the southern-facing wall I found the corn cache tucked up under the protection of an overhang. Constructed of stone and mortar, it was about four feet high and three feet in diameter. Not a perfect circle, it bowed in on one side, pressing against the alcove wall that formed the backside of the cache. Looking down into it, I saw the remains of a roof structure, a number of small branches laid out in a crisscrossing pattern, perhaps cottonwood or willow, maybe juniper. Through the roof, scattered on the floor of the cache, I could see pieces of dry corncob, eight hundred years old, maybe older. I scanned the rock face for pictographs and found none. I searched the alcove for anything else I could find. Nothing. Just the corn cache, a simple stone storage bin constructed by a few travelers who had passed this way a long time ago.

I sat down near the cliff edge, the cache behind me now and the whole wide tableland sweeping out in front with the roads running through it. Kuma came nosing under my arm. I held onto his collar and sat him down beside me, fearful that he might approach the edge. I felt the warmth of him alongside my leg. I ruffed his neck and shoulders with my hand, looking out at the desert. It was good hanging out with my dog. Darkness was closing in. I heard the sounds of chirping insects and watched bats slipping and diving in the air against the sky. I felt a presence behind me, maybe the spirits of those ancient travelers who had camped here. Or was it him, the man I had just spoken with, watching me? Or perhaps I imagined something there, a presence that came from inside me, a presence that was my sudden contentment with who and where I was and what I was doing. Whatever, it filled the air around me like moisture, like smoke, like stars. I realized then that I had come to find the desert beautiful. I didn't know when this had happened. I didn't arrive here feeling that way. I had yearned daily for water and green trees. But something about this place had taken hold of me and would not let me go. I felt strangely unafraid, like I was in the company of a good friend. I felt like I was in the presence of the ancients themselves. I felt full and warm, alive and happy.

ELEVEN

ROMEO AND JULIET

In March, I had my seventh- and eighth-grade classes reading *The Tragedy of Romeo and Juliet*. I wanted to teach literature, and I wanted to tackle something my students would remember beyond Borrego. At first I thought it was selfish to attempt Shakespeare with kids who spoke Navajo as their first language, English as their second. They would struggle with Shakespeare's language, I knew, but certainly they could handle a story of misadventured love. In fact, I thought, they would thrive on it. Most of them lived far beyond their age, and some of them, boys and girls both, would have children of their own a year after graduating the eighth grade at Borrego Pass. Not because they were Navajos, but because they lived under conditions that made having children one of their better career options. Having children, they told me, meant they could collect a government assistance check. I imagined them in a few years waiting in line at Smith's or Wal-Mart in Gallup with a cart full of flour and sugar and babies. Even the sixth graders, as young as they were, enjoyed a daily relationship with the systems of government assistance and knew it would soon be an option for their own livelihood. There was so little time to be a kid in Navajoland.

For example: one day in my sixth-grade class, the boys were laughing and giggling uncontrollably. I didn't know what they were up to, but it was obvious they had something hidden that amused them. I tried to catch them with it, whatever it was, and then refocus them on our lesson. But in that covert way that kids always outsmart adults, they outsmarted me. I asked again and again to quiet down, quiet down, quiet down! They never did. At the end of class, I learned what had been so funny. They presented me with a stack of little papers, a stack of government assistance checks they had made for me during class. Each had been drawn a little different and issued in my name. One read: "General Assistance Check," issued to "Kirk Caswell; Age: 21; Height: 6.4; Weight: 64 pounds," who "works at chapter house," made out for "12,000" somethings, and stating that the check "goes to the first day of the month." Another read: "No job for peoples check" and, next to that, "SSI Check," written in the amount of "one hundred thousand" dollars from "Shane Y." They issued me an "EBT Card Foodstamp" reporting a purchase of "Cheese 1 pound; orange juice case; milk 2 gallon; candy 14 bars; beans 2 bag" under WIC, the federal supplemental food program for women, infants, and children. At the bottom, my name had been scratched out. Another name appeared there: "Marcella."

On several occasions, I asked these kids what they were going to do when they finished the eighth grade and graduated from Borrego Pass School. Except for a few, like Renee Benally, the answer I heard most often was "stay home." Staying home meant having babies and standing in line at the post office on the first day of every month to collect their government check. I had no moral position against staying home and having babies, raising a family, but most of the kids who opted for this life did so as a means of survival; they knew of few other choices. A few easy years might pass before the union of young father and mother grew stale, the family broke up, and the children were shipped off to school to be fed and cared for. Some of these young parents would end up moping around Borrego or Crownpoint or Prewitt for their whole lives, lost and destitute, empty and alone, feeding off the chaff from the Pink Tomahawk bar. Surely it didn't have to go that way—there had to be people out here who "stayed home" and lived prosperous, rich family lives, prosperous, rich Navajo lives. But I never saw it.

That world, those choices, however, were a few years away, and for now we'd read Shakespeare. I found the text of *Romeo and Juliet* on CD-ROM in the library, printed it off, copied it however many times, and bound a classroom set of little Shakespeare books.

We read Shakespeare aloud in class, every gorgeous word of *Romeo and Juliet*. I posted passages from the play on the wall under a banner that read: "Our Pal Mr. Shakespeare." We talked about tragedy, about romantic relationships, about the difference between young love and mature love; we talked about how choices you make now affect who you are and what happens to you later. We talked about how parents influence their children. How governments influence their people. We talked about making big mistakes that can never be undone. I prepared them for the end of the play, for the end of Juliet and her Romeo. I asked them to memorize lines. They memorized Juliet:

> O Romeo, Romeo! wherefore art thou Romeo?
> Deny thy father and refuse thy name!

And Romeo:

> Come, bitter conduct; come, unsavoury guide!
>
> . . . .
>
> Thy drugs are quick. Thus with a kiss I die.

And Juliet:

> O happy dagger!
> This is thy sheath;
> there rust, and let me die.

And the Prince, too:

> For never was a story of more woe
> Than this of Juliet and her Romeo.

As they worked on their lines, I heard Shakespeare reverberating through the hallways of Borrego Pass School, splintered and butchered, and spoken just right. I wondered if this wasn't the first time that Shakespeare had ever been spoken here.

On those perfect spring days, the clear sky and warm sun seemed to work the kids into a fever, especially the sixth graders, and I found no good reason to hold them indoors. We went out into the world and held classes near the shade tree next to the Special Ed trailer. The seventh and eighth grades could read their Shakespeare, and the sixth grade read aloud from their textbook and wrote in the journals we had made in class. We used blank white paper from the copy machine for the pages and colored construction paper for the covers. Some of the kids left the cover blank. Some of them took great care to decorate the cover by gluing shapes of flowers and butterflies and yellow circles that looked like the Navajo sun. Some days when we were outside I read picture books aloud to the sixth-grade class. After I finished one story, they would pause a little and look at me and someone would say, "One more," to which everyone would agree.

"Well, then, go pick one out," I would say.

Someone would run back to the classroom and bring out three more while we loafed in the warm sun. On a number of occasions, I read books like this for the entire class period. Maybe the kids thought they were tricking me, that they were stringing out the fun so they didn't have to spell any words or take any tests. But I didn't want to spell words or take tests either. It felt good to be outside in the desert listening to stories. Education, I decided, while I lived on the reservation, had to be defined as much by practice and experience as it was by memorization and exams.

So classes were going well for me that spring, and I thought it had something to do with the way I refocused my teaching. Perhaps, too, I had passed some kind of endurance test with the kids (most of them, anyway) and they came to accept that I was going to make it, at least until the end of the school year. Or maybe the fact that I had begun searching for a new teaching job for the fall allowed me the freedom and relief of knowing my time at Borrego was drawing to a close. Or perhaps something else had changed in me, shifted, so that I was less concerned when things didn't go as planned. Which was often. Which was almost every day. I felt lighter anyway, more at ease in and out of the classroom, able to take a joke, and sometimes to give one. I got on well with the kids.

I began to think more and more about my students. They would benefit from the stability of my staying another year. They didn't have to like me, or even like studying language arts. In the classroom they needed structure, consistency, and routine. They needed a predictable, safe environment to learn to read and write English. Borrego offered such a learning environment in the self-contained classrooms of the first through fifth grades. Many of those teachers were Navajo and intended to stay for a long time, for their entire career maybe, because Borrego was home. But in the three upper grades, where the kids moved from teacher to teacher, classroom to classroom, they encountered several white teachers like me and Lauren, youngish white teachers in the early stages of their careers who intended to stay one year, two at the most. Some didn't make it that long.

I felt like I had achieved a modest level of respect and order in my classroom that spring. For the most part, my students were coming in and doing their work. If I left now, they would start over with a new teacher in the fall, subjecting him or her to the same kinds of trials I had endured, which would once again result in a classroom focused on discipline rather than learning. It would be rough for the new teacher, to be sure, but the real tragedy was that these kids were getting half the education they needed and deserved. In a typical year, the kids devoted the first semester to frying the new teacher. If that teacher endured, they devoted the second semester to learning. I didn't think that Navajos should learn how to be little white kids in school—indeed, I believed they should guard against it—but education opened doors. The English language opened doors. I wanted to offer these kids a world of choices, so that they might be able to choose a suitable life and a life's work. Not for my sake. Not so that I could better the future of the Navajo Nation—I didn't believe I was saving the Indians from the white man, or from themselves—or for the advancement of society and culture, but just for them. Just for these individual kids. Just to offer the kids I had come to know a few more life options.

I also heard warnings about staying on another year. Mary was looking to move on. I wondered how I would do without her friendship and support. I lived alone at Borrego, but I always felt Mary's steadiness and experience backing me up. Lauren would still be living in Grants with Phil, but she wasn't planning to teach at Borrego that next fall either. She'd had enough, she said. Things were much rosier at Laguna Middle School, where Phil worked for a progressive, intelligent, fair principal and school board. Lauren thought she would soon have a job offer there. Mr. Wiseman and Jane talked about leaving, about returning to Indiana. They said that when Miles left the self-contained classroom and entered the sixth grade next year, he would have a rough time of it in the hallways and on the playground. Already the older boys threatened him whenever they could. Miles had taken up karate lessons in Gallup. Regardless, Mr. Wiseman said, it was simply a matter of time before Miles got the shit beat out of him, and maybe he shouldn't have to endure that just to go to school.

So. Most of my friends were leaving.

One day down at the Trading Post, Merle offered me this advice: "You should leave that school, you know. The politics are bad. Real bad. And you can't do nothing to fix it, or fix those kids. So think about what's best for you. That's what you should do."

"All right," I said, holding up my ice cream bar. "What's the biggest city in the United States?"

"Albuquerque!" said Joseph Jones.

"China!" said John George.

"No, wait. Texas!" said Charlie Hunter.

And then George George said, "Borrego Pass!" and everyone laughed.

I rolled my eyes, holding the ice cream aloft.

This lunch ritual started one day that spring when Shane Yazzie eyed my chocolate cupcake and said, "Hey, Mr. Caswell. Can I have your dessert?" Since he asked, I gave it to him. The next day someone else asked for whatever dessert I had, and again I said yes. It wasn't long before I was the most popular teacher at lunch, surrounded by kids, especially sixth-grade boys, who competed for the seats closest to me. Usually someone would pop the question just as I finished eating. As the competition stiffened, the question came earlier and earlier. It came just as I sat down, for example. Then as I waited in the lunch line. And one morning Shane accosted me in the hall as I made my way to my first class of the day.

"Can I have your dessert today, Mr. Caswell? I didn't get it now for a looong time."

Well, that got to be too much. I said, "How about we have a little contest at lunch. I'll ask a question, and the first one to answer correctly gets my dessert."

Shane thought about this a moment. "What kind of question?" he asked.

"Whatever question I think up," I said.

"Will I ever know the answer?" he asked.

"I think so," I said. "You go and tell everyone we're having a contest."

"Okay, I'll do it," Shane said, excited to be the bearer of the news. "Laters!"

That's how it got started. After about one week, the novelty had mostly gone out of it for me, but I didn't know how to stop it.

The ice cream bar was getting a little soft in my hand, but no one had the answer yet.

"Ah, c'mon, Mr. Cas-will," William Brown said. "Give it to me. It looks real good. It looks like mines!"

"For what?" I said. "You have to answer the question."

"Well, then, ask me one I know," he said.

"What's the biggest city in the United States?"

"Aw, shit," he said.

"William!" said Bernadette, the eighth-grade class sponsor, from the table behind us. "Clean up your mouth."

"Okay! Yes, ma'am, I will." And then under his breath he said again, "Aw, shit." And then to me, raising his voice now, "Now c'mon, give it to meee."

"Only if you answer the question," I said. "What's the biggest city in the United States?"

"You mean people or size, like bigness?" Gay DeLuz asked. " 'Cause it's different, isn't it?"

I hadn't been aware of her sitting there. She rarely spoke to me now after the pie incident. "You're right. It is different," I said. "I mean people. What city has the most people?"

"New York," she said.

"Bingo!" I said, and handed the ice cream to Gay.

She smiled big, not so much for the ice cream, I guessed, but because she had answered the question correctly and showed up all those boys.

"Ah, man!" William said, and the whole table cleared out, everyone running for the door to get outside into the sun.

To get a break from the contest now and again I sat with Vanessa Angel, Teresa Smith, and Renee Benally whenever they asked me to. And sometimes when they didn't. They were not so interested in my dessert, and especially not my game, but they had invented another game and they loved for me to play it. The three of them talked to me in Navajo to see how I might answer or to test my pronunciation of hard-to-say words. They would ask if I knew what certain words meant. Sometimes they would tell me, and sometimes they would not. Like *shash*, I learned, means "bear," and *nizhóní* means "good" or "beautiful," and *dibé* means "sheep," and *chon* means "shit." They also wanted me to repeat certain words that were difficult to pronounce, like "horse," which requires a force of air into the nose and so vibrates it and sounds funny, like you're talking with your nose plugged. I'd try. They'd laugh. "Do it again," they'd say, and so I would.

I came to realize the danger in this. When the girls asked me to repeat a word or a phrase, mostly I had no idea what I was saying. Of course, all the Navajo students, teachers, and staff did. Vanessa, Teresa, and Renee would ask me to say something. When I did, all the tables nearby went silent a moment to hear me. Then the three girls would laugh uncontrollably until they asked me to do it again. I didn't know whether the way I stumbled over the language was funny or whether there was some darker purpose in the words the girls had offered. The possibility remained that the word was unclean or the way I mispronounced an innocent word warped it into evil. What a great joke on me. Was I saying something offensive in Navajo? How could I know? No one interrupted to save me or asked the girls to stop. Perhaps they didn't wish to be impolite or make a scene. Perhaps what I said broke no boundaries in good taste. Still, I began to feel more and more uncomfortable in this shadow of language. To avoid it, I started asking Vanessa, Teresa, and Renee to talk to me in Navajo, and I would translate in English. This sounded like fun to them, since I knew only a dozen words or so in Navajo.

"But you don't talk Navajo," Teresa said. "You won't know what we're sayin'."

"Oh yes, I do," I said. "Try me."

"All right," said Teresa, and she spoke out an impossible string of words.

To which I responded with something random and silly, like, "Why don't you go up to the top of the mesa and eat some rocks!" and they laughed and laughed and laughed.

Somewhere in the middle of all that, I organized a car wash in Crownpoint to raise money for the seventh-grade class field trip. The gas station offered us free water and soap for as long as we wanted it. Redd agreed to take us into town on the bus one Friday after school. He dropped us off there and would pick us up when he finished his regular route. We set up our wash station, and Samuel Smith and Clemson Benally stood out on the street flagging down cars with the signs we had made at school.

Since that day at the Christmas Bazaar, Clemson had become more a member of the class than a member of Caleb's clan. And Caleb, though he still didn't seem to care much for me or for his studies, had mostly washed out as the classroom menace. I had to believe, though, that his muted presence was his choice, that he was still a menace, only somewhere else. My taking an interest in him and his low-rider bike gave me a credibility that raised our relationship from that of mortal enemies to some kind of neutrality. A cease-fire, perhaps. I wasn't sure why Clemson responded in this way and Caleb in another. I expected them to go the same direction, but they didn't. Regardless, I was happy to have Clemson's help. He led the car wash that day.

"Car wash! Two dollars!" Clemson yelled out, running along- side cars on the road. "Car wash! Two dollars. Come over to the caaaar waaaash!"

"Car wash!" Samuel Smith sang out. "Caaaaaarrrr waaaaaash!"

We waited with our buckets and hoses, but no one came.

"Hey, you guys!" Jolanda yelled to them. "Get some cars over here!"

Clemson ran up alongside a big car and leaped out in front of it. The car stopped and we heard the tires skreeking on the asphalt.

"Not like that!" Jolanda yelled back.

"Yeah," said Maria. "Not like that, you stupit boys!"

"Yeah," said Jolanda again. "You stupit Romeo!"

The man in the car rolled down his window. He wore a mustache and a besweated cowboy hat, darkened along the brim where he put his hand. "Hey, get outta the way," he said.

"Yeah, but we gotta car wash over there," Clemson said, hopping back onto the curb. "And your car's real dirty, too."

"All right," the man said, and he pulled into the gas station so we could wash his car. He gave us three dollars.

After that, the cars started rolling in, one after another. We were busy all afternoon. Jolanda collected the money in a paper sack. She handed it to me at the end of the day. "I counted almost a hun-dret dollars in there," she said.

Everyone cheered.

We cleaned up the buckets and put away the hoses.

Bob King had given me a little money from petty cash to get the kids something in the store when we were finished. I gave each of

them a few dollars. They filed in with the money and filed out with
ice cream and sodas and candy and chips, and other things tucked
away in their pockets. Most of it paid for, some of it not. We sat in a
line on the curb in the sun and waited for Redd with the bus.

A few weeks later we used our class money for a field trip to
Gallup. The kids couldn't settle on what they wanted to do. They
couldn't think of anything.

"We don't know," said Jolanda. "Let's just go over there to Wal-
Mart and buy stuff."

Well, that wouldn't do. Inspired by Miles Wiseman's karate
lessons, I arranged to view a demonstration at his teacher's dojo
in Gallup. After that we would go roller skating, and finally out for
pizza. We had done so well making money that we invited the sixth-
grade class to go with us. As sixth-grade class adviser, Lauren had
had a difficult time motivating the kids to help her with fund-raising
events. She was happy that we offered to use our extra money to help
her out. She told the seventh-grade class that they were very generous. They smiled and felt warm inside. That, more than anything
else, was the greatest success of all our fund-raising efforts.

One spring morning, the eighth-grade class pushed the desks back
so they could act out the parts as we read *Romeo and Juliet*, the scene
where Romeo meets Juliet for the first time. We were ready to go when
William Brown burst through the classroom door.

"See, Mr. Caz-will," he said. "I got thhhem! I got my new
teethhh."

He smiled wide so the whole class could see the bright white
teeth gleaming in his mouth. The wide gap I had come to know as
distinctly William Brown's was no longer gapping, the air through
the force of his breath no longer whistling. He had not yet grown accustomed to so much stuff in his mouth, however, and his tongue
stumbled and rammed into the back of the teeth. His words slurred

and slid around in his mouth like loose marbles. Spit gathered in the corners of his lips and foamed up. But he was proud. He looked happy to have his teeth back, the teeth that had been so unjustly removed by Tom Thompson's right jab.

"What do you thhhink of thhhem?" he said.

"Wow, William. That's great," I said.

And I meant it. It was great. The school nurse worked closely with Bob King and Louise to qualify William for some funding program that would pay for his teeth. They had been working on it all year. William had gone day after day in hope. Today, finally, hope had sprung. Going to school paid off for William. Of course, it was at school that William had lost his teeth in the first place. But no matter. The teeth were in his mouth now, and now he would protect them, not with his fists, not by learning to fight better, but by learning to make peace, by learning to use his voice to avoid fighting. And to prove it, he said so.

"I ain' gonna fight no more, Mr. Caz-will."

"That's good," I said. "That's real good, William."

"They are nice," said Renee Benally.

"Yeah. That's great, William," said Teresa. "Looks so nice."

"So handsome," said Vanessa Angel, and she giggled.

"Yes, and they're all mines!" William boasted.

"All right," I said. "Let's get to the play."

"I'll be Romeo!" shouted William, so happy to employ his good fortune.

"All right," I said. "You're Romeo, William. And who will take Juliet?"

No one moved a muscle. No one breathed.

"Give it to Leonard," said Vanessa Angel, and she smiled and laughed. "He likes dresses."

"No, I don't," Leonard said.

"How about you, Mr. Caswell?" said Teresa. And she thought that was hilarious.

No one volunteered. A long awkward silence spread out through the room.

"Renee," I said. "Will you read it?"

She rolled her eyes, but I knew I could count on her to do it. "Yeah, all right."

We started in.

William said:

> If I profane with my unworthiest hand
> Ttthhhis holy shrine, the gentle fine is ttthhhis:
> My lips—

And he paused to look at everyone, like he'd spoken a dirty word, and then proceeded on:

> My lips, two blushing pilgrims, ready stand
> To smoothhh that rough touch with a tender kiss.

"OOOOhhhh, yuck!" said Vanessa Angel. "A kiss!?"

"Now kiss her, William," Teresa said.

"Yeah, kiss Mary Jane.

"No!" said Renee. "Or I'm not doin' it."

"No one is kissing anyone," I said. "We're just reading the play."

"Okay," Renee said, much relieved.

"Awww," William said. "I want one, Mr. Caz-will. I want one real bad!"

"Kiss your dog, then," said Teresa.

"Or your grandma!" said Mary Jane. And everyone laughed.

"Anyway, your teeth are somehow," said Vanessa Angel, "and they look real nice too."

"Okay, okay," I said. "Renee, you're next."

And Renee said:

> Good pilgrim, you do wrong your hand too much—

"That's what he does, all right," Vanessa Angel said. "He likes his hand, Mr. Caswell."

Of course everyone laughed again. I laughed too. I couldn't help myself.

"No, I don't," grinned William, his white teeth sparkling. "I don' do it. For reals!"

"Yeah, you do," said Vanessa.

"No way!" William said.

"Yes, you do," said Vanessa.

"Nope," said William. "I don't like it."

"Yes, you do," said Vanessa.

William was silent. This didn't seem to be working in his favor anymore.

"All right. All right," I said. "Go on, Renee."

"Ahhh," William said. "So what!?"

"See," said Vanessa. "He does it for reals."

"All right," I said. "Enough. Renee. Read."

Renee continued:

Which mannerly devotion shows in this:
For saints have hands that pilgrims' hands do touch,
And palm to palm is holy palmers' kiss.

"He's gonna kiss her," Teresa said.

I gave her a sharp look, and she put her finger to her mouth to tell me she already knew to be quiet.

William said:

Have not saints lips, and holy palmers too?

Renee said:

Ay, pilgrim, lips that they must use in pray'r.

Renee put her hands together then as if in prayer, and Teresa, the born-again, put her hands together too.

William said:

Ohhhhhh then, dear saint, let lips do what hands do—

"Aaaahhhh yuck," said Teresa. "What hands do? What kinda story is this, anyway?"

"That's not what it means," I said. "Now, let's just let them finish the scene. We have a new rule: no one can talk unless they're reading from the play."

"Aahh," said Teresa. "Okay."

"Hey! Teresa's not reading from the play," Mary Jane said. "She's breaking the new rule already."

"So are you," Teresa said to Mary Jane.

"Now you are again," said Mary Jane.

They grinned at each other.

"You both are," I said.

"And now you are too, Mr. Caz-will," said William.

"Ooookay," I said. "William. Read."

He said:

They pray, grant thou, lest faithhh turn to despair.

Renee said:

Saints do not move, though grant for prayers' sake.

William said:

Then move not, while my prayer's effect I take.
Thus from my lips, by thine, my sin is purg'd.

And then William lunged at Renee, making a kissing sound and flashing his new teeth. Renee shrieked and shrank back. Everyone was laughing then, except Renee.

"Aaaahhhhh. No. No. No. No," Renee said fast and loud. And when she was a safe distance away, she said, "If you do it William, I'll punch out your teeth!"

He lunged at her again, laughing.

Renee doubled up her fists.

"William!" I said. "Be careful. She looks serious."

"I know," he said. "I ain't gonna do it."

"All right. Maybe we should have a little break," I said.

"Yeah, hey, let's go outside, Mr. Caz-will," William said.

"No," I said. "Let's take our seats and I'll give you all a couple questions to answer about *Romeo and Juliet*. You can turn in your written answers next class."

Everyone groaned, but they went right to their desks and sat down.

The weeks went on this way. Soon, instead of begging or assigning parts to read in class, most everyone volunteered at one time or another, and we read the play to the end. When we finished and I had explained everything, told them the whole story of *Romeo and Juliet* as we read along, and all their questions were answered, I bought a copy of the Franco Zeffirelli film in Gallup. What luck. Imagine, Shakespeare for sale in Gallup! I warned the class that I would speed through a little scene where Romeo and Juliet were in bed together and they would see Juliet's nipples and Romeo's butt. But, I told them, everyone had one, or two, and besides, they had seen much more graphic films in the library, films I couldn't fathom showing to seventh- and eighth-graders. They were babysitter films thrust in front of them when some teacher was gone, films with horrendous scenes of action and violence and scenes of death. And yet when they saw Romeo from the back getting out of bed naked, they gasped. I hit fast-forward and the flesh went speeding by, and the boys shrieked as they saw Juliet's flash of breasts. When we moved on into the next scene, the room relaxed. As the end drew near, their faces looked grave as Romeo approached the dark tomb that was like a hungry mouth. They felt the event to come. We had talked about foreshadowing, and now they knew foreshadowing in their bones and blood, they felt it there, the tragic scene about to unfold. The little trailer classroom in the middle of that vast desert went blank with silence as Romeo wept over Juliet's body and then tossed back the fatal poison and died. And then Juliet woke and wept and threw herself on Romeo's dagger and cried out and died. And the soft music moved into the room, and the mood shifted and released, and the Prince said his thing about sorrow and woe as the bodies were carried out, and Teresa Smith turned to me with big watery eyes and she said, "You never told us this was a sad story."

Well.

That was the end of *Romeo and Juliet*, for the most part, except for the papers I asked them to write. I don't know what I was thinking. Somehow it made sense to me then that they try to write little critical papers about themes we had discussed in class. About foreshadowing, for example. I was sure they could handle that. Or about the chance mistakes that lead to the death of our two heroes: the letter that doesn't get to Romeo, or the good Romeo gone bad when he murders Tybalt. Or about how Romeo's relationship with God changes, about how Romeo comes to feel that God betrays him. I made up an outline for the paper, a guide for the students to follow, and made a list of possible topics. We discussed the job ahead of us. Everyone in class proclaimed that they understood and were ready to begin.

I put on some music in the classroom, a little Mozart mix, and gave the two classes an entire period to write. Some of the kids sat in front of the blank page for awhile, then got up and wandered around, looked over a friend's shoulder at their paper, got bored, stared out the window for a bit, and then finally returned to their seats again to stare at the blank page again.

William Brown called out, "Ah, Mr. Caz-will. What is this stuff? This ugly music? I can't think right."

I turned it off.

I cruised the room helping a few students who would let me, trying to motivate them to get writing. I wasn't so concerned or hopeful that they would follow the outline to the letter. I expected them to finish about a page of writing about the play, type the paper in the computer lab, and we'd call it good.

Something about that last topic, the one about how Romeo's relationship to God changes, struck a chord in Renee. Before she started in, she discussed her ideas with me. We talked about how Romeo goes to Friar Lawrence to marry Juliet. That means that he loves God, at least trusts God. And at the end of the play, when he hears news that Juliet is dead (but of course she isn't), Romeo proclaims "then I defy you stars!" which she took to mean that he now hates God.

"Why do his feelings change?" I asked her.

"'Cause God took away his only lover," Renee said.

"Right," I said. "It doesn't matter if Romeo is right or wrong. Maybe it's not God's fault, but Romeo believes that it is God's fault. You know? You think you can write about that?"

"Yes, yes, yes," she said. "I got it. I can do it."

Renee sat down at the desk pushed up against the wall under the window and wrote feverishly through the entire period. She sat hunched over her paper. When I came by, she covered it over with her arms and body and looked back at me. "Not yet, Mr. Caswell," she said. "Don't look yet."

A few minutes before class ended, Renee showed me what she had written. It was every eighth-grade teacher's dream. The paper had an identifiable thesis, a body consisting of three paragraphs of about equal length, and a conclusion summing up the entire paper, just as I had outlined in my handout. Despite everyone in class beginning with that same handout and agreeing that they understood it, most of the other papers I looked at that day in class went every which way. I knew that I had asked for too much. What had I been thinking? I am still failing as a teacher, I thought, at least failing to properly gauge my student's competency level and shoot for something just above it, rather than shooting for the moon. When Renee showed me her paper, it delighted me.

"Renee," I said. "This is really excellent. It's very, very good."

"Really?" she said, beaming. "Oh, good. I worked real hard on it."

"I know. I saw you," I said. "Let me show you one more way to make it even better." Those words came too quickly. I wanted to take them back. Even as I considered how I had asked for too much from my class, I was now asking for more. I risked dashing Renee's confidence by sending her back to work on something already so good.

"All right," she said. "What?"

"No, no," I said. "This is already very good. Let's just keep it like it is."

"But you said I can make it better," she said.

"You can," I said.

"Then show me," she said.

"Really? You want me to show you?"

"Yes."

"All right," I said. "Here is your main point, right?" and I read her thesis back to her: "In *Romeo and Juliet*, Romeo's feelings about God change."

"That's right," she said. "They do, right? Romeo's feelings change?"

"Yes, right. So can you locate a place in the play where you know this is true?"

"Yes. We just talked about it, anyway."

"So show me."

Renee leafed through the pages and showed me the place where
Romeo curses the heavens in act 5 by saying: "then I defy you stars!"

"So," I said. "Where does that go in your paper? You can use
that as proof of what you say in your paper."

"Oh, okay," she said. "It goes here, in the last paragraph because
Romeo is mad at God now."

"Right," I said. "And what about the other paragraphs?"

"Oh, okay," she said again. "Now I have to find some proof for
every paragraph?"

"Yes," I said. "But that's a lot of work, isn't it?"

"But I can do it. I'll do it."

"Let's do it in our next class," I said.

"No," she said. "I'll do it at home tonight."

I wasn't sure I wanted her to bother with it at home. "Are you
sure? We'll have time next class."

"Yes, I'm sure. I'll do it at home tonight."

"Okay," I said. "Then let me show you how to record where
you found the lines in the play." I wrote down a sample quotation for
Renee, and wrote the act, scene, and line numbers in parentheses,
MLA style, but I didn't give her that term. For now, she needed only
to know how to do it.

Renee took a copy of the play home. The next time our class met,
she brought me her finished paper, written in very precise, beautiful
handwriting, with the drafts of her work attached to the back.

"This is excellent, Renee. Really fine work," I told her.

"No, wait. It's not done yet," she said. "I have to type it, right?"

"Right."

And she did that too.

What impressed me most about Renee was that she spent the year
reaching out for something beyond her, something that she could not
yet see. She was headed somewhere, and that somewhere was a place
she chose to go. I admired her will and energy and vision, and her

courage too. I think she inspired other students with her forward-looking hope, the kind of hope that prompted her to tell me one day, "I'm going to do something good for the Navajos."

Of course Renee earned the highest mark on her paper, and that meant something to her. The part that surprised me was that it meant something to *me*. I had not expected to be so happy about Renee's good work. I carried those feelings around for days. That, I surmised, was the heart of teaching. Perhaps I'd be a teacher after all.

TWELVE

GOODBYE, BORREGO

I woke that May morning to birdsong in the cottonwoods, a little bluebird I spotted haunting about my trailer. It went *zing-zang* from branch to fence to branch, and then off and away into the rock and cactus. It was spring. The mornings were still cool, and the sun heated the ground and the day. A breeze moved across me through the open window, and I felt content, alone and not yet lonely, happy and a little sad. I felt good about my future. I was sitting at my desk feeling good when I heard a knock at the door.

Kuma charged and barked and whined until I called, "Come in," still seated in my chair. He ran to me, and back to the door, making a ruckus I wished I could train out of him. "The door's open," I said, not wanting to get up but knowing I needed to, because no one would enter to challenge the dog. I got up, held Kuma back, and answered the door.

"Gay," I said. "Good morning." She surprised me standing there, and then again it also felt natural, like I had been expecting her.

She stood there as before, the basket in the crook of her arm, her long black hair shining in the sun. She looked down at the dog, then at me, wondering, maybe, if I meant to let him go. He would not stop barking and squirming against my grip.

"Just a moment," I said. I pushed Kuma back, asked him to

prove his great worth, to sit and stay just inside the door. Then I stepped outside, closing him in. "That's better," I said. Standing now on my little back step with Gay, "How are you?" I asked. Of course she was about to ask the question she came to ask. I felt happy and warm because I knew the question and I planned to say yes this time.

"I'm fine," she said. Then she paused, uncertain about how to bring our greeting around to the pies she had for sale.

"What's in the basket?" I asked.

"Apple pies," she said, smiling. "You wanna buy an apple pie? Only apple this time," she said. "I made them myself."

"Yes," I said. "I do. How much?"

I thought that might surprise her, but it didn't. I didn't find surprise in her face at all. Instead, she smiled easily, expectantly. It made sense to me then that she would not have come if she thought or knew I would reject her again. Something had changed between us, between Gay and me, because something had changed between me and all my students at Borrego. Something had changed between me and Borrego itself. She knew this somehow, and she knew I would say yes, that I would buy one pie. Maybe two.

"I'll take two," I said.

"One dollar for each," she said.

She opened the folded cloth over the basket. The freshness of the apple pie came fast to my nose. "Let me find you the best one," she said.

"Just a moment," I said and went inside for my wallet. I had three dollars in there. It was all the cash I had. I gave it to her. She handed me the pies.

"This is too much," she said.

"Take it as a tip," I said.

She nodded and smiled. "I hope you like them," she said. "I made them myself over at my grandma's. See you at school."

"Right. See you on Monday," I said.

She turned and walked back to the car waiting on the campus drive. Someone waved from the driver's seat. Gay got in, waved to me, and they drove away.

I went inside. I set the pies on the kitchen table. Kuma ran his nose along the edge, inspecting them. Perhaps if Gay came often now with pies, he would learn to like her, or to like anyone who knocked, but we had only a couple of weeks of school left. I made black coffee, another cup. I didn't need it, but it went well with the pies. I let the door swing open and the morning rushed in as Kuma ran out to reconnoiter, to learn with his nose what had happened on the porch. He inspected the place Gay had stood, maybe linking the pies on the table with the lingering scent on the porch, then down along the path she had walked until she disappeared into the car, and all that remained for Kuma was exhaust from the engine. Then he went to the fence under the cottonwoods to work the fence line for whatever had gone on there in the night, for whatever beasts had passed or lingered there in the dark. I sat down at the kitchen table, the hot coffee in my hand, the pies still warm and fresh and good. The day unfolded before me across the New Mexican spring like a bright dream. What would I do with it? What would I do with the day before me? Where might I go? What might I see? I sat inside this moment filled with promise: I had it all just then, the dog roaming free, the coffee, the pies, the good feelings, the door opening into the future, the questions.

The Santa Fe Flea Market, some market freaks will tell you, is the greatest show on earth. The greatest show in New Mexico, anyway. Vendors come from far off and nearby, from the pueblos and reservations, from every corner of the Four Corners, from Mexico, Bali, Turkey, Guatemala, India, Peru. Mary and I planned to go one Saturday in April. It was about time we made another journey together, perhaps the last time we would make such a journey together, as the school year was nearing its end, and we both had plans for moving on. We were not so much interested in the market, though Mary thought she would buy a Navajo rug; it was an excuse, a destination that gave us cause to venture forth, because our true joy when we got together was roaming the desert and mountain country and the countless reservation roads.

We loaded the dogs into the back of Mary's little red Toyota pickup and departed Borrego at dawn, following the back roads to far towns, out through the wide flats that rose into mesas around us, the shrubs and juniper and pinyon pine shortened and fuzzy against the dry and wild horizon, where the sun was rising. The ground sparkled as its rays glanced off scattered gypsum and broken glass from the myriad empty liquor and beer bottles cast out of passing cars. Sharp bayonets of yucca and twisted cactus marched up into the hills with coyote song. Headed east, we were on the hunt for a turn to take us out to highway 197, the road that would take us to Cuba. We drove and drove, watching the country pass, until something about the light and the time said we had gone too far, for far too long.

"I think we're lost," I said.

"Well, yes, but no, we're not lost," Mary said. "We're right here. We just don't know how to get to Cuba."

"Right," I said looking over the map. "What's that road there?"

"Just another dirt road," Mary said, as we passed it by.

"And that one? Maybe that one?" I said.

"Why that one?"

"I don't know," I said. "Let's go up it. We got all day, don't we? Maybe all night."

Mary turned the wheel hard and off we went, a tornado of dust spinning out behind us. We came to a crest in the road over which we could not see, and it narrowed into a cattle guard. We bumped along and up, and as we reached the top, a big truck going fast stopped suddenly just short of us, a big Chevy, and we stopped too. Three children rode in the back of the truck, two boys and one girl, and an old woman dressed in black and turquoise rode up front with the driver. Her face was creased and folded by the sun, and she looked stern and stereotypically wise. We could see now a complex of hogans and old cars and a long blue trailer, the roof covered with tires to keep it from rattling in the wind.

"Helloooo," the driver said.

"Hello," we both said too.

"We're sorry for driving into your place," Mary said, aware that we were trespassing now. "We didn't know there was a house back here. We're a little lost."

"Oh, don't worry," he said. "It's my place. You can go back there if you want to. I don' care. If you go back of the house," he said, "go way back in there, and go down into the canyon. It's real nice back there. You'll like it back in there. I don't even know if we'll be back tonight, so take your time." And then he revved up his truck and sped off, vanishing into the morning.

"Jeez," Mary said. "That was funny. I thought we'd get directions, anyways."

"Yeah, for reals," I said. "I thought so too."

On a map the roads are clear and go right where you want them to, but out on the ground the landscape is scarred with unmarked spur roads coming from all directions and leading nowhere. We noticed that somehow the sun had gotten onto the wrong side of us, but there was nothing to do about it now but follow the road out to wherever it went and hope we didn't run out of gas. Mary drove and I read the map, which told us nothing, since we didn't know where we were to begin with, but it was comforting to have a map spread out this way as we bumped along, even as it seemed to say: look at all this open country—you could die out here. We saw a little house in the distance and so turned up the driveway. Three tired dogs came loping out and barking, and then an old woman appeared in the doorway and walked halfway out to the truck.

"Excuse us, please," Mary called out. "Where are we? We're try-ing to get to Cuba."

With the weight of some ancient misery, the woman scowled and closed down her eyes at us. "This isn't Cuba!" she scolded. "This is Heart-butt!"

"You mean Heart Butte?" Mary said, a little hopefully.

The old Navajo scowled again. "Heart Butt!"

"How do we get over to Cuba?" Mary asked.

"It's over there," she said, pointing again with her lips. "Way over there." Then she turned and walked back inside.

"Thank you," Mary said, a little too late, and we drove away laughing.

From Heart Butte, we found the pavement to Whitehorse, and from there, finally, our road to Cuba. The day was getting longer than we meant it to, and so we hurried on across the desert. I had begun to think about the end, that Mary was leaving her school in Ganado. I knew that I would see her again, that we would keep in touch the way good friends do, but this was perhaps our last journey together in Navajoland.

"So," I said, as we made tracks across the land, "Boulder?"

"Yeah," Mary said. "Boulder."

"So why Boulder?" I asked.

"You ever been to Boulder?" Mary said. "It's pretty nice there. Plus I have this weird dream about living in Boulder and reading the *New York Times* on Sundays at a nice cafe. And you know I met this guy, don't you? He's going to Boulder. So we'll be going together."

"Yeah, I know. But you've not said much about him. That guy with cartoons painted on his car, right?"

"Yeah, him," she said. "It's not that I don't like being here. I love it, but it's hard here, ya know?"

"Yeah," I said. "I do know."

"Three years is enough, don't you think? Jeez. One year is

enough. There's other stuff I wanna do. Plus, I've told you already, I'd like to be closer to a doctor."

A guy, three years on the rez, and other stuff she wanted to do—these were certainly factors, but more urgently, Mary had developed a painful cyst on one of her ovaries, and she'd been making long, regular trips to Flagstaff to see a doctor. The doctor helped her clear up this problem, but why had it developed in the first place? Mary wondered if it wasn't loneliness, isolation, a deep need to move on. She came to crave the dynamism of a bigger town, the support and comfort of a community in which she felt completely at home. She wondered if she might find this in a place like Boulder, so she had to try. She had considered other places as well—southern Utah; a new teaching job in Kayenta, Arizona—but it was Boulder that drew her most strongly.

"Yeah. So how am I gonna survive here without you?" I said.

"I thought you were leaving too," she said.

"I am, maybe, but I gotta get a job first."

"Oh, yeah, that," she said. "Those pesky jobs. I don't have a job in Boulder."

"Yeah, but you have the cartoon guy."

"I do have that," she said. "So would you stay?"

"I don't know. When I think about spending another year up in that trailer? God. Plus, I just feel so antsy. I gotta move on."

"That's what you do. What you've been doing."

"I guess it is."

From Cuba we rode up into the high country, the cool, beautiful tall pines of the Santa Fe National Forest, passed Deer Lake, Seven Springs, and Fenton Lake. This wasn't the fastest route to anywhere, but we wanted to see this country and get a look at the 10,000-foot peaks of the Jemez and Bandelier. Who knows when we might come this way again? Maybe not ever. Looking over a map of the greater Southwest, you see such places that call to you, secret hidden places, you imagine, that few people have ever seen. And you want to come to know each of them, all of them—these mesas and peaks, ruins and canyons, rivers and springs—and claim them as your own. But really, you claim nothing—you're just passing through like a bird of migration.

This seemed to be my story with Borrego too. This was, as Mary said, what I had been doing. But something had happened between there and here, so that the place, Borrego Pass, in all its antagonisms, touched me, took hold of me, and wouldn't quite let me go. I couldn't bear to stay on another year, and I couldn't bear to leave either. This is the truth with all relationships, I think, relationships with places and with people. With your dog, your things, your habits. Maybe with your self too, or aspects of your self, the parts you move on from. All relationships end, and the greatest folly comes in not recognizing this end when it comes. So, then, how do you leave a place? How do you know when to leave? How do you know why? Or is it that the place leaves you, and when you come to recognize this truth, you pack up and take the road ahead into those long miles, waiting? When it's just you again, you are terribly lonely and lost. Time passes, miles go by, and then you see, again, out ahead of you, an endless possibility—and that, above all things, is what you live for.

The trouble with leaving a place like Borrego is that it comes with a great deal of guilt. People will say that you didn't stay long enough, that you were afraid, that you might have tried harder, sacrificed more. They will say that you could have "made a difference," whatever that means, but instead you bailed out, went home, went back out on the road. You chose the easy life. And what's more, even if other people don't say these things, you will say them to yourself. Before arriving here, I attached no weight or guilt to moving on. I just moved on. I expected this kind of freedom here too, to move in and out of this world in the high rocks without any kind of bothersome attachment. But the place and its people had gotten into me. I found myself caring more than I ever wanted to. And in caring, I had to face my feelings of failure with these kids. I don't know that I did fail, but when I reflected on the year, those feelings were the first to come up. What would happen to them, all the kids in my classes? Would they go on with their schooling after Borrego? Would they destroy themselves drinking cologne and huffing gasoline? Would they start a family too young, children raising children, and try to make a go of it in the world? Would they go out into the world, as Renee said she would do, and "do something good for the Navajos"?

And there was something else too, and it struck me very hard then, riding along in Mary's little truck, up the mountain track through the cloud-capped mountains, the gorgeous pines, the solemn alpine air, the great world open and opening before us. It came to me then that I had lost my belief in America.

Before Borrego, I could wander, travel, move, I believed, because I carried with me a sense of home, an idea of my home, of America as the purest, most noble, and even last good place on earth. This narrowed into the landscape of my native Pacific Northwest, and narrowed even more into Oregon and Idaho, and my family who are rooted there. It didn't matter where I traveled, what I saw, how desperate and lonely I might become out there passing through strange places, strange lands, because I could always return to the safety and sanctuary of home. "No man can wander without a base," wrote Bruce Chatwin, and I believed him. I had not seen it all, but I had seen enough to prove to me that America was the light. I had seen the dirty street poor in the Czech Republic; desperate-looking North Africans on the night train to Irún; Gypsy children in their tattered clothes haunting the markets and squares in anywhere-Europe, far too young to be panhandling, I thought, or manhandling fat tourists headed for yet another museum; the sleazy shysters who haunted the Moroccan border fleecing travelers who were into more than they could handle; the gaunt, rib-bare fishermen on the Li River in Guilin. I could see all that, experience all that, and still feel balanced because America was the counterweight. I thought it would always be there for me. It would always be the example of how to do it right. It would always be the best place to live, the only place to live—but now, after Borrego, I wasn't sure. Was the world really this harsh and dark and seemingly indifferent? Was there no place untouched by human suffering? Was there anyplace to go except on? I felt like I had just awakened to reality. At Borrego when I looked for the light, I always came up with more darkness. I felt the loss of this belief in America very powerfully, and I acknowledged that I had lived for all my years in the fog of an illusion.

Moving across the miles to the flea market with Mary, I already began to dread going back. I never wanted to see Borrego again, because to return was to crystallize the realization I had just come to. I would have to face it, and I didn't want to. The only way out was to never get off the road. When we arrived at the flea market, I knew, the only miles left to us were those of our return, and for me our day would fall into sadness. I wanted to keep going. I wanted the conversation never to end, my friendship with Mary to remain unchanged, my body never to age, the mountain country to transform into desert and back into mountains as I moved through them and finally to the sea, where I would not stop even then. I would board a ship and stand at the railing while the ocean, that pure and unlimited road, took me far and beyond, even to Timbuktu.

On the last day of school at Borrego, I met with my eighth-grade class in the morning. We had until lunchtime to clean up my classroom, pull down all the posters and student work on the bulletin board, return any unused supplies to Alice, inspect all the textbooks for tears and excessive scribbling, sort them into neat piles, and cart them off to Lauren's classroom for summer stowage. After lunch, everyone would assemble in the front parking lot for a field day, a melee of games and contests to celebrate the end of things. The school year was over. Just like that. Soon the buses would pull away, and the kids who had been so much a part of my everyday life these past months, those I had cursed, those I had praised, would be carried away with them. I knew I would never see them again.

But there was time yet before all that. In my classroom, we set to work. William Brown tackled the wall hangings. Renee and Mary Jane took the more challenging task of inspecting and sorting the textbooks. Juanita Hunter and Virginia Puente sorted and returned the unused supplies to Alice. Vanessa Angel and Teresa Smith sat outside on the front porch in the sun making jokes, maybe having a chew. Jerry Valdez didn't show up at all. The rest of the kids wandered around inside the trailer classroom or outside the building making long forays out into the playground or over to the Special Ed trailer to peer into the windows and make faces at whoever was in there. We finished in about an hour.

"What do we do now, Mr. Caswell?" said William Brown.

"I don't know," I said. "Any ideas? We can go for a walk," I offered. "We've got almost two hours until lunch."

"Naw," William said. "I'm too tired."

"Tired? You hardly did anything, and it's not even ten o'clock in the morning."

"Yep," he said. "Too tired. Maybe I wanna sleep now."

"Let's just hang around over here," said Teresa. "Let's don't do nothing."

"No," said Juanita. "Let's do something."

"Right," said Renee. "Let's do something."

"Let's go over there to the Trading Post," said Mary Jane. "Rosie maybe will give us some stuff over there."

"Yeah, okay," said William. "Let's go over there."

"I thought you were too tired," I said.

"Yeah, but she might give us some stuff," he said. "I'm not too tired now, Mr. Caswell."

"What if she doesn't?" I asked. "Then you'll have walked all that way for nothing. And you'll have to walk back too."

"No way. You can come get me in your truck," William said.

"I don't think so," I said.

"Sure you can," said William. "You got lots of money and a real nice truck too. You can give me a ride in it. I can't walk it back. My legs are all somehow."

"I got some money," Juanita said. "We can buy some stuff over there."

"Me too. I got a little money," Virginia Puente said. "We can buy something over there for everyone."

"Buy it for me," William said.

"All right, let's go," I said.

Everyone inside rushed out the door. Everyone outside, noticing the group of us headed toward the cattle guard, came following along.

"Hey, where you guys goin'?" Vanessa asked.

"Over there to the Trading Post," said Renee. "Maybe we can get some stuff over there."

"Is it?" Teresa said.

"My idea," said Mary Jane.

"Right," said Renee. "Her idea."

"Come with us," William said. "Mr. Caswell will come get us in his truck!" He grinned at me. "Let's not go out the road," he said then. "Let's go on the path back there. It's too dusty on the road."

Renee and Mary Jane turned and led the group back through campus. We passed my trailer, then Juan Carlos's trailer. We squeezed through the gap in the fence. We walked the pathway along the edge of the mesa in the cover of juniper trees. It wasn't too warm and it wasn't too cool. It was a great day for walking.

We climbed over the gate that kept Merle's cows in or out and went up the front steps of the Trading Post.

"Well, hello there," Merle said, as we came in. "Brought in some friends, I see."

"Yeah," I said. "Good morning. Last day of school, you know. We ran out of things to do."

"Well, bringing me a load of customers is as good a thing to do as any."

Rosie stepped out from behind the counter. "All right. All right. All right. You talked me into it," she said. "One ice cream and one soda for each of you."

Everyone cheered. Perhaps they had done this before? The kids went immediately to the ice cream freezer and stood with the door open, the cold air rushing over them.

"Ahhh," William said. "Feels good."

"C'mon, I can't see in there," Teresa said.

"Come over here," Renee said. "Get your soda first."

Teresa stuck her tongue out at the group crowded around the ice cream freezer and joined Renee to select a soda.

Moments later the kids rushed the front counter with their choices. Rosie rang them all up on the cash register. "The total is . . . nothing!" she said. "You kids have a great summer."

"Thanks, Rosie," Renee said.

"Yeah, thanks, Rosie," William said. "See my new teeth!" He grinned.

"Those are real fine," Merle said. "Now don't be gettin' into no more fights." he said.

"No way," said William Brown. "No more fights. I like my teeth just like this." He grinned big again.

Merle nodded his head. "Have a great summer, you kids."

"Thanks, Merle!" William said.

Then everyone else chimed in, "Thanks, Merle. Thanks, Rosie." They pushed and stumbled out the front door into the sun.

The kids sat on the front step of the Trading Post for awhile with their ice cream and sodas. After a bit, someone got up, and then someone else, and soon we were on our way back, this time walking along Borrego Pass Road. Teresa carried a little camera with her. As the group spread out, she stopped the few of us trailing in the back.

"Let's take a photo," she said.

"All right," Renee said. "Yeah. Let's take a photo."

"Hey, yeah. Let me do it," William said. Chocolate bits clung to his lips and hands.

"Not like that," Teresa said.

"William, clean up your face," Vanessa said. The girls giggled.

William wiped his hand across his mouth and rubbed it on his pants. "Okay now," he said.

Teresa handed him the camera.

We stood back off the road across the ditch and William snapped a photo.

"Here, now I'll get you guys together," I told them.

I traded places with William and snapped a photograph of the kids smiling in the sun. I snapped another photo and the film came to the end in the camera. I handed it to back to Teresa. She put the camera back in her little bag, her camera with those stills of their smiling faces, their ice cream and soda happiness, their last-day-of-school bliss. There was a little pause in the action, like we were not yet ready to move on, like we were waiting for a sign to urge us into the future. Then someone shifted a little, which was sign enough, and everyone got up and started walking again, walking together through the bright morning, as William talked and talked about nothing, Mary Jane scowled like she was already old enough for the rocking chair, Vanessa kinda plodded, plodded along, her shoes dragging too much like they didn't fit her, Teresa flittering about like a little bird either with too much energy or not enough, and Renee looking up at the cloudless New Mexican sky and south into that

distant vista as we traveled the long dirt road leaving a happy trail of
our own dust.

I came to leave. A new job came through for me, and I was on my way
to teach at a private boarding school in Arizona. I loaded my truck,
cleaned the kitchen and bathroom, left the keys on the counter near
the kitchen sink, and pulled the door of the trailer closed. I had put
all the pottery shards and the few arrow points I'd collected at Borrego into a small box and set them on the floor of my truck before the
passenger seat. I'd left everything else I stole out of the desert inside
the trailer—the hutch I'd found with Mary, the table I built from timbers rescued from the Borrego sands, the few enamelware cooking
utensils I borrowed from the derelict hogan on the hill. I thought it
best to leave as much of Borrego as I could behind. But the pottery
shards and the few arrow points?

I wanted to keep them.

I wanted to return them to the desert.

I took up the box of potsherds and with Kuma started out on one
last desert walk. We would do well to stretch our legs before the long
drive, and I also wanted to stop in at the school to call Sakura from
the pay phone.

"Hello?" I said over the telephone.

"Hello," Sakura said.

It was very early in the morning in Hokkaido, and I could hear in
Sakura's voice that she had awakened to answer the phone.

"How are you?" I said.

"Oh, I'm fine," she said. "You? This isn't your usual time to
call."

"No," I said. "I'm sorry to wake you. We finished school the
other day, you know. I just had to call you before I leave."

"Oh, good." she said. "And now you go to Arizona?"

"Yes."

"I'm wondering if you ever stay in one place?"

"Me too."

Then she said, "I need a someone to make a home for me."

"I know," I said. "I know."

"So maybe you can't stay in one place," she said.

"Well, it isn't that," I said. "I just don't want to live here anymore. I can stay in one place when I find the right place."

"You won't find it. You keep saying that. To yourself, anyway."

"I think I will. One day. But this isn't my home. How could it be? I can't stay here."

"Maybe. Maybe not," she said. "Anyway, I know you have to go do a something. Whatever you have to do. Without me, I mean."

A long silence went between us. Was this the end, then? I felt relieved and sad and a little desperate. Our fantasy of marriage had been a fantasy, and now this ending came simply, like rain from a soft cloud.

"Without you?"

"Yeah," she said. "You know it."

"Okay, but we don't have to lose touch," I said. "We can stay in touch."

"Maybe," she said. "Maybe we will."

"I think we will."

"Maybe," she said. "Do you want to?"

"I do," I said.

"Okay, me too," she said. "Let's keep in touch a little."

"I'd like that."

"Me too," she said. "I have one thing to tell you," she said. "I thought something. In December, that bracelet you gave me. I thought that was proposal. You know, for a marriage? You should know for your future case. My case doesn't matter anymore. But I want you to know about it, because maybe you can break someone's heart."

She waited for me to say something. I was sorry, so sorry for hurting her, and an overwhelming loneliness came into me then. I felt it rush up into my head and I was struck with the fear that I'd made a mistake. I knew, however, that this rush of fear and loneliness and loss would harden and dissipate when I got out on the road. And I'd feel different then, unable to be in touch with the same feelings that moved me now. What could I say to her except apologize? Over and over. Take it back. Ask to have her back again. I hated the hesitation in me, the fear that I'd fail at any choice I might make, or that it would be the wrong one, or that I would regret it later. I didn't know where that came from, if from some defect or deficiency in me, or from the place I was living. It wasn't the choice itself but the hesitation that felt so much like defeat.

"I hope you understand me," she said then.

"Okay, yes. I understand you," I said.

"I hope you do. At least, maybe you will sometime."

"I'll write to you," I said, trying to sound hopeful.

"Okay," she said. "Maybe I'll write back."

"Maybe?"

"Maybe," she said. "Goodbye, then."

"Goodbye," I said.

And she hung up the phone.

I stood there with the telephone in my hand. The light coming in at the entrance of the school was yellow and brilliant, so bright I closed my eyes against it as I looked up. For a moment then, blinded by the sun, I had no idea what I was going to do next. I did not think of Arizona and the new world that waited for me there. I did not think of the summer ahead at Bread Loaf in Vermont. I did not think of the long drive and the beautiful country that would unfold in front of me, the way the desert would rake me and cradle me and empty me out.

I wanted to dial Sakura's number again, take back the conversation we'd just had and try it again. What was it in her that convinced me we had no future together, and made me want, so desperately, a future with her? Or was it in me, rather, not anything about her at all? That was it, I knew, no matter how much I wanted to deny it. I knew it was in me, that had I been true and settled and rooted in place, had I not felt such desperate and terrible wanderlust, had I not, she would have embraced a life with me, wherever, even right here at Borrego. I could not hold that center together, I knew, and to call her again would have been the most cruel kind of lie, the most ugly and vicious selfishness. I backed away. I hung up the telephone and backed away, the sun coming in over my shoulders, turning me around, inviting me out, again, into the desert.

Through the gap in the fence behind the school, Kuma and I walked out into the desert flats at the foot of the mesa that we had come to know so well. We followed the edge of the sandstone walls around to the little arroyo where dozens of potsherds lay scattered and broken, where I had gathered up most of the pieces now in the box. The area around every juniper near this little wash was all cowed out, bespattered by countless cow pies spread and drying in the sun. The sandstone ledge there was as familiar and perfect to me as all my images of home. The way the wash drew down from it, the curve there and how my footprint remained week after week, week after week, and the bluebirds flittering about, the red-tailed hawks cruising the current there, the long desolate flats colored with spring desert flowers sweeping south into the Rio Puerco.

Why was I leaving such beauty? Did I really want to go? Was Arizona really going to be any better? At the risk of making too much of it, of being overly dramatic, perhaps I was leaving simply because I was born to travel, because I wanted to be born to travel anyway, because I was a romantic, because settling down makes you fat and dull and ugly, because the mind is made alive by seeing, observing, experiencing the new and unknown, because I feared seeing, observing, and experiencing the new and unknown and I couldn't allow that fear to rule me, because movement somehow cures sadness and loneliness, because the hardships of the road make you strong, because I couldn't sit still, because I was searching for home and I hadn't found it, because like Kuma, the blue heeler, I had to cover ground, because like the birds of migration I was compelled to go, because, as Robert Louis Stevenson put it, "The great affair is to move." I felt ready to settle my accounts with Borrego, to leave behind what was not mine, to leave the desert to itself.

I opened the little box. The potsherds lay nested inside each other like the petals of a flower. I selected a few from the top. In my hand, the smooth and shining pieces looked at once familiar and new. I saw markings on them I'd never seen before: chips in the surfaces, a roughness about their edges, shapes that reminded me of certain states (Nebraska, Oregon, New York), even the silhouette of a mountain. Which mountain, I did not know. I'd missed so much detail when I collected them. I wondered if I'd ever inspected these few. Had I ever really seen them?

I emptied the box of potsherds onto the dry ground. I sorted through them, making little piles of ones I liked, and ones I didn't like so much. I returned several of the pieces I didn't like so much to the wash. They seemed to go right in, like they wanted to be here. I returned several more, and a few more again, but the most beautiful ones, the ones I liked, and the big one I found that day with Kuma, could I really let those go? Maybe I would take them with me. After all, I wasn't going to keep them forever. I'd be here only a half dozen decades more, give or take a few years, and these chips of fired clay were going to last until the end. Or was this merely a trick to satisfy some other desire? I returned all the other potsherds to Borrego, and those few beauties I put back into the box to take with me.

Walking now with Kuma, we followed along the sandstone walls, golden in the sun, and made our way from the arroyo around the sandstone edge and into the shaded grotto among the junipers and the cactus. This is Borrego. A red-tailed hawk wheeled in the sky overhead. A few clouds sifted by on the wind. And this is Borrego. The light of the sun flashed at crystals in the rock as Kuma ran a pattern around the edge of the cliffs, weaving in and out of my view. And this is Borrego. I wanted to go on and follow the trail up to the mesa top again, to make that country clear and perfect in my mind and in my heart. I was also ready to go, ready to leave this place. I stopped and stood there in the sun, taking in its warmth, taking in the view, taking in the desert beautiful. Maybe for the last time.

I waited for Kuma to make his rounds. I waited, a little anxious, as if lingering too long would somehow be impolite. In the silence there among the rocks, I heard the wind. I heard Kuma's feet drumming the dry ground. In the distance, I thought I heard the sharpened barks of coyotes, those dream notes that first sang me into the desert at Borrego.

"Ku-ma," I called. "Ku-ma," I called again.

He appeared suddenly at my side, ready.

AFTERWORD

In your hand is the narrative of a difficult journey by a white teacher through Navajo Country. We have all taken this journey in our own ways. Sometimes we need to walk in worlds other than our own to learn more about ourselves.

Ultimately Kurt Caswell seeks *hózhó,* "a state of harmony, balance, and beauty between male and female, between the Self and community, between community and the universe," as he explores several landscapes while teaching at Borrego Pass School. His is the story of a human being journeying through a human country.

Mr. Caswell's experience is shaped by his worldview. After reading *In the Sun's House,* I thought about my own experience as a Navajo student learning from white teachers at the Rock Point Community School. I remember one male white teacher telling me that, with my attitude, I would end up sitting outside the local store asking for quarters. With degrees from prestigious universities, today I ask for hundreds of millions of dollars in Washington, D.C., which would make certain white teachers proud. Quarters or millions— that's the difference. How I dress when I ask, and whom I ask—that's the difference. The reason I ask would be similar. It's all a matter of perspective, rooted in our values.

At one point Mr. Caswell wonders why Navajos choose to stay

home instead of going on to higher learning or finding decent paying jobs, why they end up having babies and standing in the welfare line at the first of each month, why they do not live prosperous, rich family lives, prosperous, rich Navajo lives. He never sees it. That is so unfortunate. Indeed, Navajo life is a life of celebration. We celebrate when a child is born, when he or she first laughs and comes of age. We perform traditional and contemporary ceremonies and games year-round, singing, dancing, laughing, and eating. We honor national holidays, even Columbus Day, using it as an excuse to be with relatives. In fact, when I was in grade school, we all looked forward to the annual Song and Dance Festival at our school, where Borrego Pass students came and won. They still do so today. I hate to think that Mr. Caswell was never exposed to these talented and competent young people, and to the people who taught them, the families who offered such enriching and nourishing environments.

Borrego Pass is a community school where the locally elected school board works with parents to develop a culturally relevant curriculum, which consists of courses in the Navajo language, history, and culture. Again, it is unfortunate that Mr. Caswell was never exposed to the minds and lives of the people who developed and fought for such a curriculum. Taking on the federal government and the Navajo Nation to ensure that your children have access to a Navajo education is, after all, not an easy task.

Then again, any journey that is "for reals" is not an easy task. The twenty-six-year-old Caswell, with no real belief in education, would learn its true meaning, *educare*—in Latin, "to draw from within." His walks force him to dig deep within to respond to the demands of the external landscapes of the New Mexican desert, the Navajo students, and the stories of the Navajo, which ultimately become aspects of his own unexplored internal territory. He understands this in the context of literature, writing that when we read, "we discover that the foreign is not so foreign after all, that we are in fact reading a story about ourselves." This applies to Navajo stories, too: they open doors to the inner depth.

Walking the desert eventually teaches Mr. Caswell that he is wandering his internal landscape, one as harsh and honest as the desert he comes to regard as beautiful. Of one of his walks, he writes, "Standing between these sunburned walls, I listened to the greatest silence I had ever known." I, too, have walked in the silence of the desert. When you hear the greatest silence, you realize there is no such silence. For from within the depth of that silence, you hear your very own heart beat, your own breathing. Life! I am alive! And yet within seconds you realize that in this intense moment life is fragile and vulnerable. Death! You could die! Mr. Caswell expresses this in his own words: "I had that troubled, happy feeling that comes when you know the perfection of the moment cannot last, and what will come later is going to be hard, painful even, perhaps a kind of trial you might just fail." Yet he continues walking, feeling free and happy and complete. He paints the desert with words that give new forms of life to the landscape, stirring old and new emotions even for those of us who call this land home. I hope that as you walk with Mr. Caswell, you, too, will stop for those human moments where you realize that you are a spiritual being having a human experience. Treasure those moments.

Mr. Caswell came totally unprepared for wandering the landscape of Navajo students. But who is ever really prepared for encounters with people from very different cultures? This landscape is as challenging as and perhaps even more rewarding than the land itself. His first encounter with a student questions his very essence, as well as his presence at Borrego: "You wanna be an Indian?" His experiences of other people and other places didn't prepare him for kids who grew up in a harsh environment. His temper surfaces more quickly and more intensely than he has ever experienced. To survive and thrive in Navajo country, you must learn to laugh at yourself—and to laugh through your negative experiences. The clanship structure allows for a kinship with varying degrees of teasing. An individual may be my sister or brother because we belong to the same clan or because we are born for the same clan. How we become related determines how we can tease one another or play practical jokes on one another. These interactions play out in Mr. Caswell's classroom in ways that would have enlivened the classroom environment. But in looking through his own cultural lens, Mr. Caswell judges some students' comments and teasing critiques as rude and cruel, and his reaction makes engaging the young minds that much more difficult.

Laughing Woman, my paternal grandmother, never understood why contemporary homes had restrooms in the same building where people slept and ate—that's what animals did, not humans. The "dilapidated things" are homes where the people eat, sleep, tell stories, tease one another, laugh, and live. Most ceremonies, where the people communicate with the gods and the sick get well, take place in these homes. Laughing Woman informed us that we must always have a fire going in the *hooghan*, so we did; that we must always have water, so we did; that we must keep our home clean at all times, so we did; that we must have food in case someone showed up, so we did. But more importantly, she related to each of us as *shinálí*, as her paternal grandchildren. Along with it came the teasing and the funny stories she loved to tell. We ate, slept, loved, listened to stories, and laughed in these "sad dwellings" where the human spirit is alive and strong. And the Borrego Pass folks participate in these activities too.

After putting the book down, I invited several non-Navajo teachers from our school to cultural activities at my house. Several showed up, and a lot of learning took place. More Navajos need to open their homes to non-Navajo teachers who make sacrifices to help our children. Schools within the Navajo community also need to develop mentoring programs for new teachers and work with local people and colleges to offer courses and cultural activities. There always will be those few, of course, who come simply for personal gain. But more come sincere in their desire to help, and we need to welcome them as a people. With such programs in place, Mr. Caswell would not have to ask, "Why would a community like this one offer this dark part of itself to me, a stranger, and hide its best qualities?"

He writes: "The place, Borrego Pass, in all its antagonisms, touched me, took hold of me, and wouldn't let me go. I found myself caring more than I ever wanted. And in caring, I had to face my feelings of failure with these kids." And so, with all the dark antagonisms in this book—as the experiences of Mr. Caswell seem to be—the people cling to you until you learn to care about them and their land.

As much as I admire Mr. Caswell's ability to portray the desert landscape in vivid detail, he falters, like many before him, in his attempt to interpret Navajo stories and beliefs. His dependence on non-Navajo scholars, who themselves relied on translators with limited English and cultural proficiencies, for further interpretation resulted in similar conclusions that fit a Western scholar's paradigm. As a Blessing Way Singer, almost every weekend I sing the protection songs of the Bear and the Coyote and pray their protection prayers for Navajos of all ages. Coyote is alive and well during the winter season, constantly entertaining and teaching young listeners. Bear forever instructs and protects in the depth of the sweat lodge, where sacred stories, songs, and prayers are shared. The Monsters with Killer Eyes are everywhere, too; in fact, they shamed Mr. Caswell into putting down mirrors at his home in Borrego Pass.

And yet, although the stories are foreign, they helped shape the "Air-Spirit" Kurt Caswell into a better man. He awakens to a reality that only a deep commitment to self can allow: "At Borrego when I looked for the light, I always came up with more darkness. I felt the loss of this belief in America very powerfully, and I acknowledged that I had lived for all my years in the fog of an illusion." Earlier he informs us that he is rich because he has the power to choose to pursue wealth. We are fortunate that he chooses to pursue a wealth of stories and experiences, to sort them out and learn from them. We walk away from his narrative with a stronger sense of self, with a willingness to look deep within and search for the seed of greatness found in every adversity.

Before moving on, Mr. Caswell writes, "In the silence there among the rocks, I heard the wind." This is the wind of movement, the wind that moves within. This is breathing. This is the breath of Mr. Caswell's final encounter with the desert of Navajo country and people. This is an experience worth breathing and moving with.

Select Bibliography

Bashō, Matsuo. *Bashō's Narrow Road: Spring and Autumn Passages.* Trans. Hiroaki Sato. Berkeley: Stone Bridge Press, 1996.

——. *The Narrow Road to the Deep North: And Other Travel Sketches.* Trans. Nobuyuki Yuasa. New York: Penguin, 1966.

Bighorse, Tiana. *Bighorse the Warrior.* Ed. Noel Bennett. Tucson: University of Arizona Press, 1990.

Bowers, Faubion, ed. *The Classic Tradition of Haiku: An Anthology.* New York: Dover, 1996.

Brown, David E. *The Wolf in the Southwest: The Making of an Endangered Species.* Tucson: University of Arizona Press, 1992.

Brown, Dee. *Bury My Heart at Wounded Knee: An Indian History of the American West.* New York: Washington Square Press, 1981.

Camus, Albert. *Notebooks 1935–1942.* Trans. Philip Thody. New York: Modern Library, 1965.

Cassells, Steven E. *The Archaeology of Colorado.* Boulder, Colo.: Johnson Books, 1997.

Chatwin, Bruce. *Anatomy of Restlessness: Selected Writings 1969–1989.* New York: Viking, 1996.

——. *In Patagonia.* New York: Penguin, 1977.

——. *The Songlines.* New York: Penguin, 1987.

Chronic, Halka. *Roadside Geology of New Mexico.* Missoula, Mont.: Mountain Press, 1987.

Deloria, Vine, Jr. *Spirit and Reason: The Vine Deloria, Jr., Reader.* Golden, Colo.: Fulcrum, 1999.

Foster, Robert J. *General Geology.* 5th ed. Columbus, Ohio: Merrill, 1988.

Gabriel, Kathryn. *Roads to Center Place: A Cultural Atlas of Chaco Canyon and the Anasazi.* Boulder, Colo.: Johnson Books, 1991.

Gilpin, Laura. *The Enduring Navaho.* Austin: University of Texas Press, 1994.

Hugo, Richard. *Making Certain It Goes On: The Collected Poems of Richard Hugo.* New York: W. W. Norton, 1984.

Iverson, Peter. *Diné: A History of the Navajos.* Albuquerque: University of New Mexico Press, 2002.

Kierkegaard, Søren. *Letters and Documents.* Trans. Henrik Rosenmeier. Princeton, N.J.: Princeton University Press, 1978.

Kluckhohn, Clyde, and Dorothea Leighton. *The Navajo.* Cambridge: Harvard University Press, 1974.

Linford, Laurance D. *Navajo Places: History, Legend, Landscape.* Salt Lake City: University of Utah Press, 2000.

Locke, Raymond Friday. *The Book of the Navajo.* 5th ed. Los Angeles: Mankind, 1992.

Lopez, Barry Holstun. *Of Wolves and Men.* New York: Charles Scribner's Sons, 1978.

Matthiessen, Peter. *Indian Country.* New York: Penguin, 1984.

Momaday, N. Scott. *The Man Made of Words: Essays, Stories, Passages.* New York: St. Martin's, 1997.

———. *The Names: A Memoir.* Tucson: University of Arizona Press, 1976.

———. *The Way to Rainy Mountain.* Albuquerque: University of New Mexico Press, 1969.

Murray, John A., ed. *Out Among the Wolves: Contemporary Writings on the Wolf.* Anchorage: Alaska Northwest Books, 1993.

Newcomb, Franc Johnson. *Navaho Folk Tales.* 2d ed. Albuquerque: University of New Mexico Press, 1990.

Reichard, Gladys A. *Navaho Religion: A Study of Symbolism.* Princeton N.J.: Princeton University Press, 1963.

Shikibu, Murasaki. *The Tale of Genji.* Trans. Arthur Waley. New York: Modern Library, 1993.

Silko, Leslie Marmon. *Storyteller.* New York: Arcade, 1981.

Soshitsu Sen XV. *Tea Life, Tea Mind.* New York: Weatherhill, 1994.

Tapahonso, Luci. *Sáanii Dahataal: The Women Are Singing.* Tucson: University of Arizona Press, 1998.

Thompson, Hildegard. *The Navajos' Long Walk for Education: A History of Navajo Education.* Tsaile, Ariz.: Navajo Community College Press, 1975.

Wallace, Anthony F. C. *Jefferson and the Indians: The Tragic Fate of the First Americans.* Cambridge: Belknap Press of Harvard University Press, 1999.

Waters, Frank. *Book of the Hopi.* New York: Ballantine, 1963.

Wilson, Garth A. *Conversational Navajo Dictionary.* Blanding, Utah: Conversational Navajo Publications, 1989.

Wong, Hertha Dawn. *Sending My Heart Back Across the Years: Tradition and Innovation in Native American Biography.* Oxford: Oxford University Press, 1992.

Zolbrod, Paul G. *Diné Bahané: The Navajo Creation Story.* Albuquerque: University of New Mexico Press, 1995.

$40.00   12/17/09

LONGWOOD PUBLIC LIBRARY
800 Middle Country Road
Middle Island, NY 11953
(631) 924-6400
mylpl.net

LIBRARY HOURS

Monday-Friday	9:30 a.m. - 9:00 p.m.
Saturday	9:30 a.m. - 5:00 p.m.
Sunday (Sept-June)	1:00 p.m. - 5:00 p.m.